ELEMENTS OF POETRY IN THE MAHĀBHĀRATA

ELEMENTS OF POETRY IN THE MAHĀBHĀRATA

BY

RAM KARAN SHARMA

MOTILAL BANARSIDASS

Delhi Varanasi Patna

Bangalore Madras

First edition published in California, 1966
Second edition published in Delhi, 1988

MOTILAL BANARSIDASS
Bungalow Road, Jawahar Nagar, Delhi 110 007

Branches
Chowk, Varanasi 221 001
Ashok Rajpath, Patna 800 004
24 Race Course Road, Bangalore 560 001
120 Royapettah High Road, Mylapore, Madras 600 004

ISBN: 81-208-0544-5

PRINTED IN INDIA
BY JAINENDRA PRAKASH JAIN AT SHRI JAINENDRA PRESS, A-45 NARAINA INDUSTRIAL AREA, PHASE I, NEW DELHI 110 028 AND PUBLISHED BY NARENDRA PRAKASH JAIN FOR MOTILAL BANARSIDASS, DELHI 110 007.

To My Learned Guru

MURRAY BARNSON EMENEAU

In Token of Gratitude and Esteem

To My Learned Guru

MURRAY BARNSON EMENEAU

In Token of Gratitude and Esteem

PREFACE TO THE SECOND EDITION

I am glad that the book is reappearing in India for the second time. The first edition was brought out by my Alma Mater, University of California in 1964. I am grateful to my esteemed friends and colleagues all over the world for their kind encouraging remarks about the work. The journal of the American Oriental Society, The Purāṇa Bulletin (All India Kashiraj Trust) and *ZDMG* may specially be mentioned in this connection as repositories of representative scholarly opinions on this humble exposition of the poetic tools of the Great Epic.

The second edition is just a reprint of the first edition except that the indices have been appended in order to facilitate its referential readability.

Being first published in the U.S.A., the book was not easily accessible to Indian libraries. Thanks to M/s Motilal Banarsidass, this second edition will now be available for the use of scholars in India and elsewhere.

Only about one-sixth of the *Mahābhārata* is covered in the present study. Through the blessings of my Guru Prof. M.B. Emeneau and encouraging guidance and help from my esteemed friends and colleagues, I have been able to complete this work in a form acceptable to scholars.

May 6, 1988 R. K. SHARMA

PREFACE TO THE FIRST EDITION

THIS WORK IS BASICALLY THE SAME as that submitted in partial satisfaction of the requirements for the degree of Doctor of Philosophy at the University of California in June, 1959. It owes its present shape to the esteemed guidance of my learned guru, Murray Barnson Emeneau, Professor of Sanskrit and General Linguistics of the departments of Classics and Linguistics at the University of California, Berkeley. I cannot express in words my sense of indebtedness to his intellectual gifts in connection with the work. All that is good in it is his; the rest is mine: punaś ca bhūyo 'pi namo namas te.

I must record my grateful thanks to Professors Madison S. Beeler, Joseph E. Fontenrose, John J. Gumperz, Arthur E. Hutson, S. M. Katre, V. Raghavan, and the late Professor Ferdinand D. Lessing for their kind suggestions and generous help with the work.

My visit to the University of California was made possible by a grant of leave from the University of Bihar and by financial grants from the State Department of the United States under the Fulbright and Smith-Mundt acts through the United States Educational Foundation in India and the Institute of International Education. To add to this, the Committee on South Asian Languages of the Association for Asian Studies granted me a fellowship for the year 1958–59. My special obligation is due to all of them.

I wish also to offer my sincere thanks to the Editorial Committee of the University of California, which has so kindly agreed to undertake the publication of the work.

RAM KARAN SHARMA

CONTENTS

ABBREVIATIONS

ABHS	Abhijñānaśākuntalam
Adhy. Ram.	Adhyātmarāmāyaṇa
Br. sam.	Bṛhat saṃhitā
C	consonant
Epic Myth.	E. W. Hopkins, *Epic Mythology*
JAOS	*Journal of the American Oriental Society*
Kavy. Pr.	Mammaṭa's Kāvya Prakāśa
Megha.	Meghadūta
MW	Monier-Williams, *A Sanskrit-English Dictionary*
PW	Böhtlingk and Roth, *Sanskrit-Wörterbuch*
Ragh.	Raghuvaṃśa
Rām.	Rāmāyana
RV	Ṛgveda
SD	Viśvanātha's Sāhityadarpaṇa
V	vowel

INTRODUCTION

THE PRESENT STUDY IS BASED ON MATERIALS from the Mahābhārata (Critical Edition, Bhandarkar Oriental Research Institute, Poona), Books 1 (Ādi, 1933) and 3 (Vana, 1941) edited by Vishnu Sītārām Sukthankar, and Book 6 (Bhīṣma, 1947), edited by Shripad Krishna Belvalkar. An attempt is made here to present a detailed account of what we may call poetic expressions of the corpus. It is not a rhetorical discussion of the soul of the poetry of the Mahābhārata. It rather aims at enumerating the symbolic, alliterative, paronomastic, or repetitive linguistic features that beautify the body of the Mahābhārata.

Chapter 1 deals with the similes (upamā) of the corpus; the arrangement of the sections is based on the fields from which the objects of comparison (upamāna) are collected. Chapters 2 through 8 deal with the metaphors and other figures of meaning (arthālaṃkāras) that are found. Chapter 9 presents some specimens of popular idioms found in the corpus arranged again according to the fields from which they are collected. Chapter 10 is the compilation of the passages representing typical figures of sound (śabdālaṃkāras). To complete the study, chapter 11 analyzes passages representing the techniques of oral poetry.

As J. Gonda informs us, Arnold Hirzel in his *Gleichnisse und Metaphern im Ṛgveda* tried to collect as completely as possible the similes in the Ṛgveda; he arranged the materials "nach sachlichen Gruppen." Mrs. Rhys Davids took practically the same point of view in her "Similes in the Nikāyas."[1] No such study seems yet to have been made of the Mahābhārata. E. W. Hopkins in his *The Great Epic of India* merely suggests that "on epic similes and metaphors an interesting essay remains to be written."[2] Of course, he lists many examples of epic similes and metaphors (pp. 403–444); but the purpose there is to show the parallelism in the two epics rather than to present a study of the epic figures.

Emeneau in his paper "The Sinduvāra Tree in Sanskrit Literature" suggests that the compilation of an encyclopedia of traditional Sanskrit stock-in-trade comparisons "would be an aid to the scholar who occupies himself with the interpretation of Sanskrit literature."[3] The present

[1] J. Gonda, *Remarks on Similes in Sanskrit Literature* (Leiden, 1949), pp. 4–5; Arnold Hirzel, *Gleichnisse und Metaphern im Ṛgveda* (dissertation, Leipzig, 1890), 107 pp.; Caroline Rhys Davids, "Similes in the Nikāyas: A Classified Index," *Journal of the Pāli Text Society* (1906–1907), pp. 52 ff., and "Some Additions . . .," *ibid.* (1908), pp. 180 ff.

[2] E. W. Hopkins, *The Great Epic of India: Its Character and Origin* (New York, 1901), p. 205.

[3] M. B. Emeneau, "The Sinduvāra Tree in Sanskrit Literature," *University of California Publications in Classical Philology*, XII (1944), 333.

study of the Mahābhārata may be said to be an attempt in that direction, viz., a study of the figures in Sanskrit literature.

As Hopkins rightly points out, "the presence in the epic of rūpakas, metaphors, of this or that form, no more implies acquaintance with a studied ars poetica than do such phenomena in other early epic poetry."[4] What Patañjali says about language in general:

ye punaḥ kāryā bhāvā nirvṛttau tāvat teṣām yatnaḥ kriyate/ tad yathā ghaṭena kāryaṃ kariṣyan kumbhakārakulaṃ gatvā 'ha kuru ghaṭaṃ kāryam anena kariṣyāmī 'ti/ na tadvac chabdān prayokṣyamāṇo vaiyākaraṇakulaṃ gatvā 'ha kuru śabdān prayokṣya iti/

An effort has to be made for the accomplishment of things that are to be made; for example, one who needs a pot goes to the family of a potter and says, "Make me a pot; I will use it." But nobody who wants to use words goes to the family of grammarians and says, "Make me words; I will use them."[5]

applies to the figurative language of epic poetry as well. It does not follow, however, as stated for epic grammar by Kulkarni and Yarrow, that many 'aberrant' poetic usages exist in the Mahābhārata.[6]

Any discussion of aberrancy implies a previous canonical formulation of some rigid norm. Such a canon did exist in the field of grammar, in the prescriptions of the great grammarians (munitraya). But the tradition of rhetoric has been somewhat different. The definition and concept of poetry have always been changing and growing, from the time of Bharata (first century A.D.) to the time of Paṇḍitarāja Jagannātha (seventeenth century A.D.). What is still more significant from our point of view is the fact that the poetic techniques as evolving in the works of rhetoricians through the ages and those successively adopted by the poets concerned have not been synchronous. We cannot say, for example, that as Śrīharṣa belonged to the twelfth century when the *dhvani* school was at its highest peak, his poetry would be necessarily based on the principles of *dhvani*.

Poets have been traditionally regarded as unrestrained persons (niraṅkuśāḥ kavayaḥ). Their poetry is free from the restrictions of nature (niyatikṛtaniyamarahitām, Kavy. Pr. 1.1). As a seed is to the growth of a creeper, the earth and irrigation being just accessories, so is the poetic intuition (imagination) to the growth of poetry; study and practice are accessories thereof (pratibhai 'va śrutābhyāsasahitā kavitāṃ prati/hetur mṛdambusambaddhabījamālā latām iva, Candrāloka

[4] Hopkins, *The Great Epic* . . ., p. 205.

[5] Patañjali, Vyākaraṇa Mahābhāṣya, ed. by F. Kielhorn (2d ed. rev., Bombay, 1892), pp. 7–8.

[6] E. D. Kulkarni, "Unpaninian Forms and Usages in the Critical Edition of the Mahābhārata," *Annals of the Bhandarkar Oriental Research Institute*, XXIV (1943), 83–97; Andrew Henry Yarrow, *Aberrant Forms in the Mahābhārata* (dissertation, Yale University, 1950).

1.6). The poetic defect arising from a poet's lack of learning can be hidden by the excellence of his poetic intuition; but failure in imagination is too apparent to be hidden (avyutpattikṛto doṣaḥ śaktyā saṃvriyate kaveḥ/yas tv aśaktikṛtas tasya jhag ity evā 'vabhāsate, Locana on Dhvanyāloka 3.6).

In every community, poetry appears first. Rhetoric may follow. If a community's language of poetry is rhythmical, allegorical, or alliterative, it is not because of a rhetorician's prescription. By nature, a community's emotional language of lamentation, honor, anger, wonder, etc., is what we call poetic in the real sense of the term. We can always hear, for example, the so-called elements of alliteration, repetition, introduction, refrain, rhythm, rhyme, and allegory, even in the language of lamentation of an illiterate village woman. Thus Viśvanātha's definition of poetry (vākyaṃ rasātmakaṃ kāvyam SD 1.3, poetry is a language of emotion) seems to be a universally recognized fact.

The result of the above discussion may be summarized thus: Firstly, if the language of the Mahābhārata is poetic, it does not follow that there is some influence of the science of rhetoric in it. Secondly, even if we do not get evidence of a well-developed science of rhetoric prior to the composition of the Mahābhārata, we should not deny the poetry of the Mahābhārata the place it deserves, in the light of what has been said about its poetical virtues by later rhetoricians, poets, critics, or other writers.

Raghavan[7] presents the views of Ānandavardhana, Abhinavagupta, Kṣemendra, and the author of the Bhāgavata that the Mahābhārata is essentially and primarily a work (prabandhakāvya) of the sentiment of tranquillity (śānta rasa). As these critics have shown, all the struggles of the Pāṇḍavas, their wars, victories, and sufferings, lead to one central theme, that peace, quietude, and tranquillity are the *summa bona* of human life.[8]

Viśvanātha Kavirāja classes the Mahābhārata as an ārṣa mahākāvya (SD VI 561–562), and quite in agreement with Ānandavardhana and Mammaṭa, quotes the following passages from it as examples of *arthaśaktyudbhava dhvani.*[9]

alaṃ sthitvā śmaśāne 'smin
gṛdhragomāyusaṃkule /
kaṅkālabahale ghore
sarvaprāṇibhayaṃkare // 12.149.8

---

[7] V. Raghavan, *The Number of Rasas* (Adyar, 1940), pp. 31–33.

[8] *Vide* Dhvanyāloka 4.109 (vṛtti); Kṣemendra, Bhāratamañjarī, concluding verse 3; Bhāgavatapurāṇa 1.5.15.

[9] Dhvanyāloka 3.71; Kavy. Pr. 4.42.

na ce 'ha jīvitaḥ kaś cit
kāladharmam upāgataḥ /
priyo vā yadi vā dveṣyaḥ
prāṇinām gatir īdṛśī // 12.149.9

ādityo 'yaṃ sthito mūḍhāḥ
snehaṃ kuruta sāṃpratam /
bahuvighno muhūrto 'yaṃ
jīved api kadācana // 12.149.15

amuṃ kanakavarṇābhaṃ
bālam aprāptayauvanam /
gṛdhravākyāt kathaṃ bālās
tyajadhvam aviśaṅkitāḥ // 12.149.60[10]

This is a description of a scene in the cemetery where the affectionate kin have brought the dead body of a child for burial. The two claimants of the flesh of the dead body, the vulture and the jackal, are already present there. The vulture's interest is that the kinsmen should leave the place while it is daytime. The jackal, on the other hand, who can eat the flesh only in the night, wants the kin to wait until sunset. Both these selfish creatures, however, appear in the garb of 'friends, philosophers, and guides.'

The vulture says: "Do not stay (any further) in this cemetery surrounded by vultures and jackals, full of skeletons, terrible, frightful to all creatures. None, whether friend or foe, having come under the rule of time has ever revived here; such is the fate of all creatures."

The jackal says: "This sun is still present, O fools! Indulge your affection (for the child) now. This time is full of many obstacles. Maybe the child would revive (after some time). Why should you fools unhesitatingly leave this child, which appears like the color of gold, not yet having attained youth, just because of the word of a vulture?" (Cf. chapter 1, XXXII,1.)

(It may be noted here that the passages as appearing in the critical text present some variation, viz., 12.149.9a *na punar* for *na ce 'ha*, 15b *mā bhayam* for *sāmpratam*, c *bahurūpo* for *bahuvighno*, d *jīvetā 'pi* for *jīved api*; 60a *imam* for *amum*, b *bhūṣaṇaiḥ samalaṃkṛtam* for *bālam aprāptayauvanam*, c *putram* for *bālās*, d *pitṛpiṇḍadam* for *aviśaṃkitāḥ*. I have quoted the Sāhityadarpaṇa version (which tallies sound for sound with that in Kavy. Pr.) for convenience. The long gap in the Sāhityadarpaṇa example between 12.149.15 and 60 is not well accounted for. It is strange that except for *jīved api* in vs. 15, which appears in MSS V_1 $B_{1.2}$ Da $D_{1.7}$ S, none of Viśvanātha's variants occurs in any of the

[10] SD 4.262.

MSS listed in the footnotes of our critical edition. For this, an examination of the Kavy. Pr. and SD MSS is necessary.)

Bāṇabhaṭṭa (seventh century) describes Vyāsa as a creator of poets and the Bhārata as a shower of the goddess of learning (namaḥ sarvavide tasmai vyāsāya kavivedhase / cakre puṇyaṃ sarasvatyā yo varṣam iva bhāratam, Harṣacarita 1.3). He further says that no poetry is poetry unless it covers the three worlds as does the *bhāratī kathā* (kiṃ kaves tasya kāvyena sarvavṛttāntagāminī / kathe 'va bhāratī yasya na vyāpnoti jagattrayam, *ibid.* 1.9). In his Kādambarī there is a reference to the Mahābhārata recitation by Nārada's daughter, as follows:

mahāśvetāṃ pṛṣṭhataś ca samupaviṣṭena kiṃnaramithunena madhukaramadhurābhyāṃ vaṃśābhyāṃ datte tāne kalagirā gāyantyā nāradaduhitrā paṭhyamāne ca sarvamaṅgalamahīyasi mahābhārate dattāvadhānām (kādambarīm).[11]

Candrapida saw Kādambarī attentively listening to the Mahābhārata, that transcends all good omens, being recited by Nārada's daughter, who was singing in a sweet gentle voice, the accompaniment being with two bamboo-flutes, sweet as bees, by a pair of Kiṃnaras sitting behind Mahāśvetā.

This corroborates the long continuous tradition of *vīṇāgāthins* of Śatapathabrāhmaṇa 13.4.3.3 and 5 as referred to by Weber in support of his views regarding the origin of epic poetry.[12]

Thus Johannes Nobel's impression that "The Mahābhārata . . . is not called a Kāvya by Indian tradition" is not borne out by facts. He rather supports the Indian tradition when he further remarks, "but can anybody deny that also in this great epic there are many passages to be found showing very closely all the characteristics of the Kāvya style?"[13] I am yet unable to understand Hopkins' remark that "a Bhāratavid in India is even now more scorned than honoured."[14]

In fact, there are several passages in the body of the Mahābhārata manuscripts which clearly describe the epic as a *kāvya*. Of course, they have all been proved by the critical edition to be interpolations. But their value as representative of the traditional point of view with regard to the poetry of the Mahābhārata cannot be ignored. The following passages (quoted in Ādi, Appendix I, pp. 884–885) may be specially noted:

kṛtaṃ maye 'daṃ bhagavan 13
kāvyaṃ paramapūjitam /

[11] Bāṇabhaṭṭa, Kādambarī, ed. by Peter Peterson (Bombay, 1889), p. 209; cf. p. 61.

[12] *Vide* E. W. Hopkins, "The Social and Military Position of the Ruling Caste in Ancient India, as Represented by the Sanskrit Epic," *JAOS*, XIII (1885), 323–324.

[13] Johannes Nobel, *The Foundations of Indian Poetry* (Calcutta, 1925), p. 5

[14] *The Great Epic*, p. 400.

This highly adored poem has been composed by me, i.e., Vyāsa.

tvayā ca kāvyam ity uktaṃ 34–36
tasmāt kāvyaṃ bhaviṣyati /
asya kāvyasya kavayo
na samarthā viśeṣaṇe
viśeṣaṇe gṛhasthasya
śeṣās traya ivā 'śramāḥ /

As you (Vyāsa) have called it Kāvya, this will be a Kāvya. Poets cannot excel this poem, as the remaining three āśramas cannot excel the gṛhasthāśrama.

Immediately after 34–36, some manuscripts have:

kāvyasya lekhanārthāya
gaṇeśaḥ smaryatāṃ mune /

Gaṇeśa should be called to mind for the writing of this poetry.

The reference to writing makes this interpolation part of the scribe's tradition.[15]

Winternitz describes the Mahābhārata as "a whole literature rather than one single and unified work"; but he admits that "there shoots forth much true and genuine poetry" in it.[16] He points out (p. 461) the stylistic diversity in the Mahābhārata in the sense that it is more archaic in some parts than in other parts, and also distinguishes between what we call popular linguistic phenomena reminiscent of Pāli, and what he thinks are solecisms "such as are often committed by uneducated and inferior authors like the Purāṇa composers." In his opinion, the style can be said "to be far removed from the so called 'Kāvya style,' i.e., the style of the later ornate poetry, which is characterized by the *excessive* use of embellishments (Alaṃkāras)," though there are also many "passages in the Mahābhārata which remind us of the Kāvya style."

Emeneau in his "Oral Poets of South India: The Todas" recognizes, for the first time in the history of Indological research, the value of the recognition of the implications of oral poetic techniques for the study of the poetry of the Mahābhārata and similar Indian literature. He finds an amalgam of at least three oral poetic genres in the Mahābhārata, viz., heroic, theological or moralistic, and legal, and is of the opinion that in all probability "the same composers worked in all or most of the techniques." If "Bowra excluded this enormous corpus from his study" (*Heroic Poetry*, 1952) upon the plea that "a truly heroic foundation is overlaid with much literary and theological matter," he "was really

[15] *Vide* M. B. Emeneau, "Signed Verses by Sanskrit Poets," *Indian Linguistics* (Chatterji Jubilee Volume), XVI (Nov., 1955), 50–52.

[16] M. Winternitz, *A History of Indian Literature*, vol. I, trans. from original German by Mrs. S. Ketkar (Calcutta, 1927), pp. 326–327.

defeated by the complexities of the Hindu epic, rather than justified logically in excluding it from his work."[17]

Any study of the Mahābhārata would have been less complicated had the original version said to have been taken down by Gaṇeśa at the instance of Vyāsa been preserved! Rather we are told that Vyāsa "taught his Bhārata to his five pupils: Sumantu, Jaimini, Paila, Śuka, and Vaiśampāyana; and the five rhapsodists, the direct pupils of the author, it is reported, published five separate versions of the epic" (saṃhitās taiḥ pṛthaktvena bhāratasya prakāśitāḥ 1.57.75). Vaiśampāyana is said to have recited it for the first time at a sacrificial session, "before King Janamejaya and the assembled guests." Sūta committed the whole Bhārata to memory at the very first recitation and recited it, as we are told, at the next session (Prolegomena to Ādi, p. lxxv).

This tradition of oral recitation stands us in good stead with regard to Vedic texts, thanks to the *prātiśākhyas* and *śikṣās*. But the Bhārata recitation was not so well-organized. As a result, we find a great amount of fluidity and contamination in our texts. The editor, taking all these points into account, rightly remarks: "To conceive of the Epic of the Bhāratas—or for that matter, of any true epic—as a rigid or fixed composition like the dramas or poems of Goethe or Milton, or even of Kālidāsa or Bhavabhūti, would be manifestly grotesque" (*Ibid.*). The editor's pedigree of Ādiparvan versions (Prolegomena, p. xxx) shows how diversified our recensions of the Mahābhārata are:

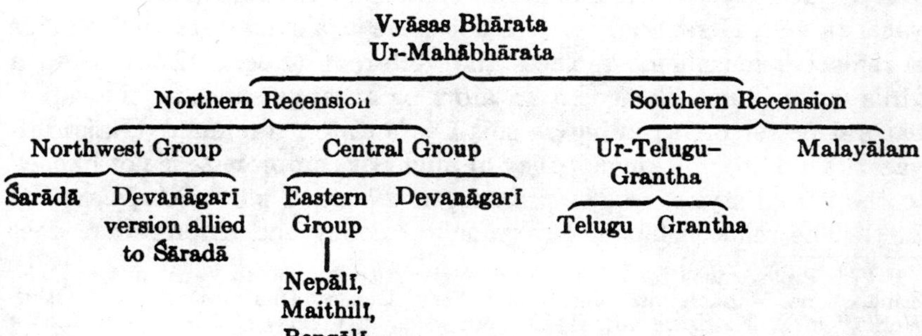

A study of the elements of poetry of the Mahābhārata is the study of the typical poetic expressions of the epic, although it is yet very difficult to reconstruct any typical epic material for want of similar critical editions of other ancient works, which in many instances have

[17] M. B. Emeneau, "Oral Poets of South India: The Todas," *Journal of American Folklore*, LXXI, No. 281 (1958), 313–314.

materials parallel to those in the Mahābhārata.[18] For this study, the critical edition has been taken for granted as the only available unitary source, without going into the controversies regarding the overall pattern of this poetry.[19]

As distinguished from such prosaic expressions as gor apatyaṃ balīvardaḥ tṛṇāny atti mukhena saḥ, "the cow's child, the ox, eats grass with his mouth," the poetic expressions represent mainly those linguistic features which we may call *alaṃkāra*. As Raghavan remarks, "This expressional deviation, this striking disposition of words and ideas, is alaṃkāra; this constitutes the beautiful poetic form. It will be easier to dissociate love from its physical aspect than to keep the concept of poetry aloof from its form."[20] Jayadeva says: One who regards poetry as word and meaning without alaṃkāra, why does he not regard fire as without heat? (aṅgīkaroti yaḥ kāvyaṃ śabdārthāv analaṅkṛtī / asau na manyate kasmād anuṣṇam analaṃ kṛtī, Candrāloka 1.8).

The poetic expressions of the corpus as arranged and presented in the following chapters speak for themselves. We may, however, take a bird's-eye view of the general structure of these stylistic features.

As in the prosaic matter-of-fact expressions, so in poetic expressions, the Mahābhārata displays an extreme simplicity and elegance of style (vaidarbhī rīti). Such complicated compounded constructions as in 3.155.51 ff. are very rare. The same is true of the figures of speech. In the Mahābhārata, there is no dust arising from the march of a king's army that sticks to the moon and creates spots there (*vide* Naiṣadhīyacarita 1.8). Here, Sugrīva does not come as a substitute for Vālin, as a replacive morpheme replaces the verb-root (Ragh. 12.58). Here a girl's waist is not likened to an atom or an appearance of the supernatural power of becoming as small as an atom (aṇiman) (Naiṣadhīyacarita 1.41,64). A king's policy of might or compromise is not likened to the varied styles, *ojas* or *prasāda*, of a learned poet (Śiśupālavadha 2.83). The relationship of governmental policy and ambassadors does

---

[18] *Vide* Prolegomena to Ādi, pp. xxviii–xxix; Introduction to Vana, p. xiv; P. V. Kane, "The Mahābhārata Verses and Very Ancient Dharmasūtras and Other Works," in S. M. Katre and P. K. Gode, eds., *A Volume of Eastern and Indian Studies Presented to Professor F. W. Thomas . . . on His 72nd Birthday . . .*, New Indian Antiquary, extra series I (Bombay, 1939), pp. 128–133; Louis Renou, L'Hymne aux Aśvin de l'Ādiparvan," *ibid.*, pp. 177–187; S. K. Belvalkar, "The Cosmographic Episode in the Mahābhārata and Padmapurāṇa," *ibid.*, pp. 19–28; V. S. Sukthankar, "The Rāma Episode (Rāmopākhyāna) and the Rāmāyaṇa," and "The Nala Episode and the Rāmāyaṇa," both in *Sukthankar Memorial Edition*, vol. I, *Critical Studies in the Mahābhārata* (Bombay, 1944–1945), pp. 387 ff. and 406 ff.

[19] *Vide* Vittore Pisani, "The Rise of the Mahābhārata," in Katre and Gode, eds., *A Volume of Eastern and Indian Studies . . .*, pp. 166–176.

[20] V. Raghavan, *Some Concepts of the Alaṃkāra Śāstra*, Adyar Library Series No. 33 (Adyar, 1942), p. 50.

not compare here with the knowledge of grammar and the *Paspaśāhnika* (introductory chapter) of the Mahābhāṣya (*ibid.* 2.112). Here a heroine's red feet are not likened to Pāṇini's Grammar (having "red colophons" after the *pāda* divisions of the books, so Gray, or refer to Aṣṭādhyāyī 4.2, Vāsavadattā, Gray's edition, 1913, p.180 [234]). The necklace lying on the breast of a heroine does not give a picture of an auspicious jar full of water with the customary mango leaves floating on it as a welcome to her lover to enter her heart (Harṣacarita in Führer's edition, 1909, p. 51, ll. 3–5).

The similes are simple, mostly collected from the spheres of the Vedic gods, nature, and items of material culture. One special feature of the epic similes is the occasional use of more than one synonym for the same object of comparison (e.g., kālāntakayamopama- 3.23.30; vajrāśanisamasparśa- 6.114.55, *vide* chapter 1,I,2,12). Sometimes, the same *tertium comparationis* is denoted by a long list of objects of comparison in the one compounded form (e.g., cow's milk, jasmine flower, the moon, fibers of the lotus stalk, and silver simultaneously symbolizing whiteness: gokṣīrakundendumṛṇālarajataprabha- 3.21.30; *vide* chapter 1,VI). It would be interesting to study the similes and metaphors as representative of standards of the community's contemporaneous taste. Thus, among the gods, Brahmā (Pitāmaha) is the standard, not of might, but of prominence. Śiva's son Kārtikeya symbolizes command; his other son Gaṇeśa does not appear at all. Among animals, the bull is the most conspicuous standard of prominence, might, and honor. The occurrences of *munipuṃgava* and *puruṣarṣabha* are too numerous to count. The same descendent of the cow, the bull or the ox, slowly and gradually became a standard of foolishness in later times. Of course, in some instances we have a foreshadowing of this lowering of the standard of the bull or ox (nasyota iva govṛṣaḥ 3.31.25, *vide* chapter 1,XX; cf. Bhāravi, Kirātārjunīya 4.13).

Sometimes the similes reflect the poet's general knowledge about various aspects of material culture and his keen observation of facts. An army contracts like leather placed on the fire (chapter 1,XL,16). A king's diplomacy is likened to the activity of a porcupine that gives its tongue to many small greedy creatures in order to get food through deceit (chapter 1,XXVI). Vasiṣṭha's cow's eyes are likened to those of a frog (chapter 1,XXVI). A person trembles with fear like a leaf of the Pipal tree (*Ficus religiosa*) disturbed by the wind (like the leaves of the aspen) (chapter 1,XXX,10; cf. Rāmacaritamānasa 2.45.2). Spectators suddenly stand up to witness an exciting spectacle as if raised (or shot) up by a machine (chapter 1,XL,6). The color of good horses is likened to that of peacocks (chapter 1,XXVII,5). The strength of the unity of the weak is likened to that of the bees (chapter 1,XXVIII,2).

What is true of Sanskrit verb-roots in conjunction with prepositions (upasargeṇa dhātvartho balād anyatra nīyate / prahārāhārasaṃhāra-vihāraparihāravat // quoted by Bhaṭṭojidīkṣita in Siddhānta Kaumudī: "The meaning of a verb root is as if forcibly altered by the respective prepositions, as is the case with the words pra+hāra "blow," ā+hāra "food," sam+hāra "destruction, contraction," vi+hāra "enjoyment," pari+hāra "exception") is true also of the objects of comparison in conjunction with other situations. The snake, the standard of fear and terror in isolation, when in conjunction with five-headedness, is compared with well-shaped, exceedingly delicate arms ending in five-fingered hands (pañcaśīrṣā ivo 'ragāḥ 3.54.6; *vide* chapter 1,XXV). Thus it may be interesting to study the object of comparison (upamāna) in isolation, as distinct from that in conjunction with something else; for example, Droṇa surrounded by the five Pāṇḍavas compared to the moon in conjunction with the asterism Sāvitra (Hasta) in 1.125.30 (chapter 1,VI), and Draupadī in her bewildered state of mind compared to a river situated between five mountains in 3.12.17 (chapter 1,XIX).

It seems that many of the similes, like other epic expressions, will prove to be constituents of the traditional stock. Some of them are definitely 'borrowed plumes,' as Sukthankar would put it; that is to say, they do not quite fit the contexts in which they appear.[21] Many others are found to be common in the two great epics.[22] In some instances, both the contents and the expressions of the Mahābhārata have been adopted by later writers (cf. chapter 1,I,3, "Śiva chasing the sacrificial deer," 1.36.12: 3.262.19, with ABHS I.6 and Ragh. 11.44). The expression of insult tṛṇam antarataḥ kṛtvā, 'placing a straw in between . . .' occurring in the Rāmāyaṇa 3.56.1; 5.21.3 and the Mahābhārata 3.265.17 (cf. Adhy. Ram. 5.2.31) continues down to the sixteenth century (Tulasī, Rāmacaritamānasa 5.9.3). It may be possible some day to compile a concordance of poetic expressions of Sanskrit literature or Indian literature as a whole that will show where a poet has adapted his expressions from the traditional stock and where he is out-and-out original. This will be possible only when our compilation is complete from the Ṛgveda down to present times. Any attempt to show parallelism in the later poets (e.g., Kālidāsa and Aśvaghoṣa) and to prove the originality of the one over the other would be premature unless we have

---

[21] *Vide* Sukthankar, "The Nala Episode . . .," in *Sukthankar Memorial Edition*, vol. I, *Critical Studies in the Mahābhārata*, pp. 406 ff.; Mahābhārata 3.65.7–25, especially 3.65.19; and Rāmāyaṇa 5.19.26cd–27ab.

[22] Hopkins, *The Great Epic*, Appendix A, pp. 403–445.

the complete picture beforehand (cf. Emeneau, "The Sinduvāra Tree in Sanskrit Literature," referred to earlier).

No less important is the study, through an internal concordance, of the epic's poetic expressions. As the discussion on the clause māghamāse gavām iva (chapter 1,XX) will show, lack of understanding of the concordance and the oral technique of improvisation has resulted in such divergent and far-fetched readings and interpretations as māghamā segavām iva or māghamāṃ segavā iva . . .!

We have, however, to mark the difference between living and petrified figures. For example, such forms of address as puruṣarṣabha, 'bull among men,' munipuṃgava, 'bull among the sages,' and kamalapatrākṣa, 'lotus-petal-eyed,' though originally living, are in the epics no longer specimens of living figures. They are just the easiest equipment the poet has to fill in the metrical harmony. Such is the case with some adjectival similes as well, e.g., vātaraṃhasaḥ (3.43.7, 69.12, etc., for horses, chariots, she-mules, etc.). In all such cases, the poet seems to have a fixed, rigid terminology which he cannot help using, consciously or unconsciously. An example of the unthinking use of such adjectival phraseology would be amarasaṃkāśa (3.153.17), 'godlike' for Ghoṭotkaca, the demon. The clause bhīmo bhīmaparākramaḥ, 'Bhima of terrible might,' occurs in several passages (1.2.184; 114.9; 141.18; 142.32; 150.3; 3.50.5, 9, etc.); in some instances, it also qualifies Bhīma, Damayantī's father, who does not seem to have any terrible might compared to Arjuna, Karṇa, and other warriors.

A study of stylistic diversity as apparent in the three oral poetic genres referred to by Emeneau may be found interesting. For that, a quantitative study of the poetic expressions arranged according to the contexts where they occur would be necessary. It seems that the portion of the epic which we may call 'heroic poetry' has the greatest number of figurative expressions, the theological or moralistic portion has less, and the legal portion still less. This is, however, an a priori conclusion that needs further investigation.

All possible care has been taken to make the study of the similes of the corpus exhaustive, in the sense that almost all the relevant representative passages are collated or referred to in chapter 1. This was necessitated by the fact that the similes are very well developed in the Mahābhārata. In fact, as S. K. De points out, the name *upamā* occurs "as early as the *Ṛg-veda* (V.34.9; I.31.15)," and "Yāska quotes (iii 13) the grammarian Gārgya's definition of *upamā*" (yad atat tat-sadṛśam iti gārgyaḥ).[23] Even according to the philosophy of *alaṃkāra*, the simile

[23] S. K. De, *Studies in the History of Sanskrit Poetics*, vol. I (London, 1923), pp. 4–6.

stands at the root of almost all the other figures of meaning. The following passage from Appayya Dīkṣita's Citramīmāṃsā may specially be noted in this connection:

> tad idaṃ citraṃ viśvam
> brahmajñānād ivo 'pamājñānāt
> jñātaṃ bhavatī 'ty ādau
> nirūpyate nikhilabhedasahitā sā /
> upamai 'kā śailūṣī
> saṃprāptā citrabhūmikābhedān
> rañjayati kāvyaraṅge
> nṛtyantī tadvidāṃ cetaḥ //[24]

As this diversified universe is known by the knowledge of Brahman, so all the figures are known by the knowledge of the simile. Thus the simile with all its varieties is described in the very beginning. The simile alone, an actress dancing in different kinds of costumes on the stage of poetry, taking different shapes of figures, delights the heart of those who know it.

This justifies a detailed discussion of the representative passages of the similes in our corpus.

Chapters 2 through 9 deal with a brief study of some specimens of other figures of speech, viz., metaphor (rūpaka), poetical fancy (utprekṣā), hyperbole (atiśayokti), inference from circumstances (arthāpatti), antithesis (virodha), exclusion by specification (parisaṃkhyā), excellence (vyatireka), converse (pratīpa), poetical doubt (saṃdeha), mistaker (bhrāntiman), equal pairing (tulyayogitā), accompaniment (sahokti), poetical reason (kāvyaliṅga), description of nature (svabhāvokti), incongruity (viṣama), modal metaphor (samāsokti), and idioms. It is doubtful if this covers all the figures of meaning that are found in this corpus. But this can be said with some amount of certainty, that the *alaṃkāras* like *apahnuti*, *vibhāvanā*, *viśeṣokti*, and *aprastutapraśaṃsā* are not found here. Quite a few examples of *paryāyokta*, *nidarśanā*, *arthāntaranyāsa*, *dṛṣṭānta*, and *dīpaka* have been noted under idioms in chapter 9.

The only *alaṃkāras* that are well developed from the point of view of later *kāvya* style are metaphor, poetical fancy, and antithesis. We will see how some of the usages of the metaphor and poetical fancy have been drawn upon by later poets. The few examples of *svabhāvokti* we have are undoubtedly very good specimens of poetic description of nature. But the poet's imagination seems to be confined to forest life and battle scenes. We find kings bringing their elephants and horses to Damayantī's *svayaṃvara*, but we do not know how the elephants and horses behave normally. We know more about the normal behavior of the animals from their occurrences as *upamānas* than from their natural description, as Kālidāsa or Māgha would have done it.

[24] Appayya Dīkṣita, Citramīmāṃsā (Bombay, 1941), p. 6.

The chapter on idioms includes specimens of all expressions of the Mahābhārata that can be called popular idioms. Epic idioms were probably based on the living tradition of the contemporaneous popular speech. Thus most of the idioms listed in this chapter are still living in our colloquial dialects.[25] Such expressions as 'crying in the wilderness' (1.68.34), 'letting loose the poison' (3.9.3), 'swallowing the hook' (3.154.35), 'cutting off the root' (1.34.27), 'placing a straw between' (3.265.17), 'rubbing one hand on the other' (1.46.33), and 'biting the lips with the teeth' (1.140.20) may especially be noted.

The idioms are specimens of the expressions (anubhāvas) of the various emotions as well. Besides the last three items noted in the preceding paragraph, 'the red eyes' (1.140.20), 'the frowning face' (6.44.41), 'looking sideways' (1.68.21), 'eyes wide open' (1.122.18), 'licking the corners of the mouth' (6.90.5) are good examples.

Two of the idioms, prakṣālanād dhi paṅkasya dūrād asparśanaṃ varam (3.2.47), 'prevention is better than cure,' and śivās te santu panthānaḥ (3.292.11), 'goodbye,' are very common among the students of Sanskrit in India.

Chapter 10 deals with the figures of sound (sabdālaṃkāra). Its five sections cover the repetition of consonants (anuprāsa), chime (yamaka), paronomasia (śleṣa), indirect mode of expression (vakrokti), and repetition of words or phrases in a set of verses respectively. Sampling (sthālīpulākanyāya) was especially necessary for this chapter, because there is hardly a page in our corpus that does not have at least half a dozen striking examples of the figures of sound.

According to a pre-Bhāmaha school of rhetoricians, the excellence of words (sauśabdya) was the main constituent of poetic beauty,[26] the excellence of meaning being considered 'something exterior.' As opposed to this, Bhāmaha, Daṇḍin, and their successors regarded both figures of sound and figures of meaning as equally important.

Quantitatively speaking, the repetitions of sound (alliterative or otherwise) far surpass other kinds of figures in the Mahābhārata. This was normally not expected of a poem like the Mahābhārata, which is primarily a work of the *vaidarbhī* style. This seems to have puzzled Hopkins for a while. But he finds his way through by recognizing the difference between the "classical affectations and epic style." He also recognizes the fact that in the epics, "alliteration is a common trick, but is not so overdone as it is in the works of later poets."[27]

---

[25] *Vide* John Christian, *Behar Proverbs* (London, 1891), p. xxix; Mahābhāṣya on 1.3.1 (pṛṣṭham kuru, pādau kuru-).

[26] *Vide* Bhāmaha, Kavyālaṅkāra 1.14.15; Mammaṭa, Kavy. Pr. 6.48; J. Nobel, *The Foundations of Indian Poetry*, pp. 85–87.

[27] *The Great Epic*, p. 203.

Hopkins does not seem to be very clear in the second clause of his statement. What he seems to intend to convey is the fact that unlike the condensed jingling effect of alliteration in compounded or well-set expressions of later poems (e.g., cañcadbhujabhramitacaṇḍagadābhighāta- or latākuñjaṃ guñjan madavad alipuñjaṃ capalayan), the effect of most of the alliterative expressions of the epics is somewhat disorderly or apparently unevenly distributed. But he cannot mean that the *anuprāsas* are less common in the epics. In fact, nowhere in classical Sanskrit literature are occurrences of *lāṭānuprāsa* so numerous as in the Mahābhārata.

Repetition is the very essence of an oral poem like the Mahābhārata. Thus *anuprāsa*, as a repetition of sounds, may be an artificial feature of a written poem but it is a natural phenomenon with our epics. The chime (yamaka), paronomasia (śleṣa), or indirect mode of expression (vakrokti) is not well developed from the point of view of classical *kāvya*.

One point worth noting with regard to the epic versification is that unlike the written poems of later times, in which, on the whole, single verses form the basic unit, the whole continuum of epic verses in a given context generally seem to have been composed as a unit. The *yugmakas* or *kulakas* of Sanskrit *kāvya* may be said to be somewhat similar to this kind of versification, but they are by no means based on the same principles. It will often be observed that the long chain of epic verses in a given context, especially when the poet seems to be highly emotional in his recitation, are woven together by a set of repetitive words or phrases (as discussed in chapter 10,V) used according to fixed principles. It seems that the grammarian-philosopher's *vākyasphoṭa* is involved here; i.e., the vehicle or the wave of the central idea goes on repeating itself in a given context. The rhetoricians have given the name *dhvani* to the content side of it. But how the waves of emotions find expression in a natural or normal oral tradition has still to be worked out.

For the time being, we may describe this phenomenon by taking recourse to the principle of repetition—concatenative, chiasmic, or otherwise.

Thus the present study is a sort of structural approach to the study of poetry based on the words of the poet himself. A similar approach to other aspects of the Mahābhārata (e.g., philosophy, sociology, ethics, or grammar) might also be enlightening.

1. SIMILE (UPAMĀ)

JAYADEVA DEFINES THE SIMILE (upamā) as a figure of speech in which the beauty of similarity exists between two objects, as between the two breasts of a woman (upamā yatra sādṛśyalakṣmīr ullasati dvayoḥ / hṛdaye khelator uccais tanvangīstanayor iva // Candrāloka 5.3).

The simile (upamā) normally consists of four parts: (*a*) the subject of comparison (upameya), (*b*) the object of comparison (upamāna), (*c*) the *tertium comparationis* (upamānadharma), and (*d*) the linking word or morpheme between the subject and the object of comparison, such as *iva, yathā, -vat,* etc. (aupamyavācaka). It is possible, however, to get the effect of the simile even without explicit mention of the *tertium comparationis* and/or the linking word, e.g., kamalapatrākṣaḥ, 'one having lotus-petal-like eyes.'

The following sections are mainly devoted to the study of the objects of comparison (upamāna) as standards or symbols of the respective *tertia comparationis* (upamānadharmas).

I. THE GODS (DEVA)

1. The Gods in General

The gods, in general, symbolize brillance. A brilliant child is thus described as one with splendor like that of a god or a divine child (kumāro devasaṃnibhaḥ 1.155.37; cf. 3.104.18; kumāro devagarbhābhaḥ 1.68.4; cf. 1.8.7; 44.17; 68.13; 77.27; 92.31; 100.30; 213.82: 3.73.25; 112.1; 123.9). A beautiful girl is described as god-complexioned (amaravarṇinī 1.73.16) or divine-child-like (surasutopamā 1.99.34); cf. 1.100.22; 155.42; 157.14; 198.4: 3.62.24; 62.43; 65.36; 277.31. A king, a sage, or a priest is godlike (amarapratimaṃ nṛpam 1.3.189; amaraprakhyo (rājā) 1.38.25; surasaṃkāśa 1.109.22; devā iva suvarcasaḥ 1.131.9; devasamānarūpaḥ 1.185.2; cf. 1.187.7: 3.32.13; 49.42; 58.32; 62.33; 79.25; 145.43; devakalpa- 1.54.9; cf. 1.69.50; 69.51; 89.55: 3.153.28; 154.58; 197.23; 276.7; 281.58; 292.4: 6.15.2; 105.22; 115.31; 117.13; 1.84.16[?]).

An assembly of kings is compared either to the assembly of the gods or to the mystery of the gods guarded by the gods (asmin rājasamāvāye devānām iva saṃnaye 1.180.5; tāṃ devaguptām iva devamāyām 3.24.12).

One's command to his subordinates is likened to the command of the gods (vaśyān iva divaukasaḥ 3.229.26).

Two or more friends rejoice or roam about like the gods (vijahrāte 'marāv iva 1.204.5; cf. 1.57.14; 116.5; 211.9: 3.54.37; 123.23; 225.14; 229.6; 248.1).

Two fighting warriors shine like two gods (putrau tau devasaṃkāśau vyarocetāṃ mahābalau 6.69.22).

Cyavana, after the Aśvins' treatment, becomes ever-young, free from old age like a god (vṛndārakam ivā 'jaram 3.124.10). Those who recite or listen to the recitation of the Mahābhārata attain godhood (prāpnuyur devatulyatām 1.56.14).

A terrific war is likened to that between the gods and demons (devadānavayor iva 3.154.46; cf. 3.269.10: 6.43.81; 53.28; 54.12; 65.33; 79.11; 81.16; 83.31; 96.30; 97.10; 113.49; 114.22).

Even a demon and a mountain are compared to the gods (amarasaṃkāśa- 3.153.17 for the demon Ghaṭotkaca; devasame girau 3.86.14). Brilliance seems to be the *tertium comparationis* in both these examples.

The gods in the above figurative sense occur in at least 81 passages in this corpus; *deva, sura, amara, vṛndāraka, divaukas, tridaśa,* and *īśvara* (?1.84.16) are the synonyms generally used.

2. Indra

Indra, the lord of the gods and heaven, symbolizes valor, splendor, and prominence, in general (e.g., śakrapratimatejasaḥ 1.1.164; 89.4: 3.1.3; devarājasamadyutiḥ 1.61.62; 71.3: 3.48.2; 61.76; devendrasamānarūpa- 1.83.11; sākṣād indra ivā 'parah 1.80.5; balabhid yathā vā 1.32.23; amararājakalpa 1.83.12; cf. 1.2.161; 50.12,14; 55.14,34; 61.65; 69.47; 81.7; 88.9; 94.11,24,32; 99.48; 114.29; 163.21; 179.22; 190.18: 3.13.108; 26.1,9,10; 44.22; 46.14; 79.3; 94.5,6; 113.19; 126.3,10,23; 157.21; 161.19,24; 166.23; 173.2,6; 225.10; 229.13; 241.16; 248.3; 252.2; 253.15, 17,25; 254.21; 265.57; 297.1: 6.14.12; 15.1,20; 17.36; 22.4,12; 55.35; 56.22; 58.34; 67.5; 69.24; 75.26; 77.8; 79.25; 81.32; 86.80; 91.15; 93.20; 96.11; 97.17; 102.25; 103.27,31). Thus, the *tertia comparationis* (upamānadharmas) referred to in compounds are brilliance (tejas, dyuti, prabha-, and rūpa), might (parākrama, vīrya, vikrama, and karma), and prominence (prabhāva and gaurava). Those in uncompounded forms are (*a*) knowledge of moral laws (e.g., devarājasadṛśo dharmajñaḥ 1.94.11), (*b*) bravery (e.g., tridaśeśasamo vīraḥ 3.46.14), (*c*) invincibility (e.g., yaḥ sa śakra ivā 'kṣobhyaḥ 6.14.12), (*d*) uproarious noise (e.g., śakrasye 'vā 'bhigarjataḥ 6.67.5), (*e*) shining splendor (e.g., vibabhau sa mahendravat 6.93.20), and (*f*) archery (e.g., śakreṇe 'va dhanuṣmatā 6.22.4).

An encounter between two warriors is likened to that between Indra and (*a*) Vṛtra (at least six times), (*b*) Maya (twice), (*c*) Prahlāda (twice), (*d*) Śambara (once), (*e*) Bali (once) (i.e., (*a*) vṛtravāsavayor iva 6.43.34; 96.49; cf. 3.13.96; 40.46: 6.86.54; 107.41; (*b*) Mayaśakrau yathā purā 6.106.29; cf. 6.112.34; (*c*) śakraprahlādayor iva 3.273.18; cf. 3.270.12; (*d*) śakraśambarayor iva 6.96.51; (*e*) balivāsavayor iva 3.18.11). It may be noted in this connection that Prahlāda and Prahrāda are synonyms for the name of one of Hiraṇyakaśipu's sons, who "was an enemy of Indra and friend of Viṣṇu" (MW), and who "got Indra's power from him by character," i.e., by piety (*Epic Myth.*, p. 134).

Besides the above typical epic phraseology putting two fighting enemies together in a *dvandva* compound, references to Indra's wars with the demons in general, and Vṛtra, Maya, Tāraka, Namuci, and Bala in particular, are numerous. Thus, Duryodhana requests Bhīṣma to kill the sons of Pāṇḍu, as Indra killed the demons (jahi pāṇḍusutān vīrān mahendra iva dānavān 6.93.36; cf. 1.185.3: 3.83.111; 152.219; 158.6; 234.18: 6.15.25; 43.61; 68.30; 73.11,30; 75.26; 78.50; 79.27; 82.37; 90.28). Cekitāna throws a mace, desirous of killing Gautama, as Indra was desirous of killing Vṛtra (gautamasya vadhākāṅkṣī vṛtrasye 'va purandaraḥ 6.80.25; cf. 3.120.6). Abhimanyu delights his friends by terrifying the Kaurava army, as Indra delighted his friends by defeating Maya (nandayām āsa suhṛdo mayaṃ jitve 'va vāsavaḥ 6.96.19; cf. 6.97.20). Bhīṣma asks Bhagadatta to defeat Ghaṭotkaca as Indra defeated Tāraka in times of yore (yathe 'ndras tārakaṃ purā 6.91.17). Mahodara strikes Bhīma with nine arrows as Indra struck Namuci (with a special kind of missile) (namuciṃ vṛtrahā yathā 6.84.16). Ghaṭotkaca attacks Alambusa as Indra attacked Bala in battle (balaṃ śakra ivā 'have 6.43.39).

A contrast between the Pāṇḍava and Kaurava army is shown by referring respectively to the army of the lord of the gods (devendrasenā) and that of the lord of the demons (daityendrasenā); 6.20.5.

Members of Indra's family are referred to. Thus, Pāṇḍu is united in wedlock with Kuntī as Indra was united with Śacī (paulomyā maghavān iva 1.105.3; cf. 3.54.34; 180.7; and 275.38). Subhadrā gives birth to a brilliant son as Śacī gave birth to Jayanta (jayantam iva paulomī dyutimantam ajījanat 1.213.58). Kausalyā is delighted to embrace her son Pāṇḍu as Śacī was delighted to embrace Jayanta (jayantam iva paulomī pariṣvajya nararṣabham 1.106.4). Hundreds of companions wait upon Damayantī as many maids wait upon Śacī (śatam sakhīnaṃ ca tathā paryupāste śacim iva 3.50.11; cf. 1.55.34). Sukanyā is likened to Indra's daughter (devarājasutām iva 3.123.2).

Indra symbolizes protection, generosity, and command as well. Thus, Duḥśāsana is asked to look after his brothers as Indra looks after the gods (maruto vṛtrahā yathā 3.238.23; cf. 1.199.25). Kinsmen should depend upon Duḥśāsana in the same way as the gods depend upon Indra (bāndhavās tvo 'pajīvantu devā iva śatakratum 3.238.23). Yudhiṣṭhira bestows donations upon the Brāhmaṇas as Indra bestows donations upon the gods (śakra ivā 'marebhyaḥ 6.22.8). Droṇa guards the Kaurava army from the rear as Indra guarded the gods' army (paścāc camūm indra ivā 'bhirakṣan 6.20.11). Like Indra, Bhīṣma leads his great army (vāhinīm surarāḍ iva 6.47.11).

A king or a warrior being accompanied by his retinue is likened to Indra being accompanied by the gods. Thus, Bhīṣma accompanied by great kings shines like Indra accompanied by the gods (rarāja rājottama rājamukhyair vṛtaḥ sa devair iva vajrapāṇiḥ 6.56.3; cf. 1.125.32; 134.4; 206.4: 3.7.12; 80.3; 118.21; 154.61; 158.37; 226.10; 235.25; 249.13: 6.19.11; 58.54; 93.18,23; 95.15).

Indra honored by others symbolizes the highest honor. Sages honor Yudhiṣṭhira as they honor Indra (ajātaśatrum ānarcuḥ purandaram iva 'rṣayaḥ 3.27.25). All the warriors guard Bhīṣma as the gods guard Indra in the war between the gods and the demons (yathā devāsure yuddhe tridaśā vajradhāriṇam 6.95.20; cf. 1.105.15: 3.89.2: 6.93.25).

Indra's paying honor to Bṛhaspati, the teacher of the gods, is a still more conspicuous symbol of honor, e.g., Janamejaya offers a seat to Vyāsa as Indra does to Bṛhaspati (āsanaṃ kalpayām āsa yathā śakro bṛhaspateḥ 1.54.11).

Viṣṇu as an accessory of Indra is referred to. Thus, Yayāti's brilliant sons, Yadu and Turvasu, are likened to Indra and Viṣṇu (śakraviṣṇū ivā 'parau 1.78.9; cf. 6.79.55). In prominence, Yayāti is, however, likened to Indra, Viṣṇu, and also the sun god (śakrārkaviṣṇupratimaprabhāvam 1.83.9).

Indra's enemies also have gained symbolic prominence. The Pāṇḍavas attack Bhīsma as the demons attack Indra (vajrapāṇim ivā 'surāḥ 6.104.33). Hiḍimba attacks Bhīma as Bala attacks Indra (balo vajradharaṃ yathā 3.154.41). Abhimanyu chases the Kaurava army as Vṛtra chases the gods' army (vṛtro devacamūm yathā 6.96.22). Kumbhakarṇa is likened to Vṛtra (vṛtrasaṃkāśam 3.271.18).

Indra's heaven (svarga) symbolizes extreme delight and grace. Having reached the beautiful mountain, the Pāṇḍavas are as happy as the gods are happy to reach heaven (yathā divaṃ prāpya marudgaṇānām 3.161.3. Duryodhana is advised to enjoy the rulership of the earth, as Indra enjoys heaven (divaṃ śambarahā yathā 3.226.2). Yudhiṣṭhira enters the Dvaita-woods as Indra enters heaven (triviṣṭapaṃ śakra ivā 'mitaujāḥ 3.25.21). The mountain, with the Pāṇḍavas, shines as heaven shines with the gods (divaṃ devavarair iva 3.158.8). Ayodhyā, full of contented and healthy people, shines with the king Kalmāṣapāda as heaven shines with Indra (tuṣṭapuṣṭajanākīrṇā sā purī kurunandana / aśobhata tadā tena śakreṇe 'vā 'marāvatī 1.168.20; cf. 1.55.14). After the day's suspension of arms (avahāra), the place of the army's retirement, without any talk of war, looks like heaven for a moment (muhūrtam iva tat sarvam abhavat svargasaṃnibham / na hi yuddhakathāṃ kāṃcit tatra cakrur mahārathāḥ 6.83.55). Cf. 1.64.19; 77.1; 94.38; 199.27,35; 213.35; 214.18: 3.16.18; 87.6; 98.17; 145.35; 170.25; 173.11.

Indra's divine garden (Nandana) is a standard par excellence of pleasure and comforts. Nala, after a long separation, lives with Damayantī happily as Indra lives in Nandana (devarāḍ iva nandane 3.78.3). The Pāṇḍavas enjoy a lotus-pond as the sages, free from fear, enjoyed living in Nandana (te remire nandanavāsam etya dvijarṣayo vītabhayā yathai 'va 3.174.10). Cf. 1.63.12; 64.28: 3.155.36; 264.41: 6.7.29.

Indra's rainbow and banners symbolize charm and auspiciousness. A banner is, thus, auspicious like a rainbow (śakrāyudhasamā śubhā 1.216.12; cf. 6.46.43). Kings' banners shine like Indra's banners in Indra's homes (mahendraketavaḥ śubhra mahendrasadaneṣv iva 6.16.31; cf. 6.18.7).

Hanumān's tail is, moreover, raised like (*a*) Indra's banner, and (*b*) the rainbow (śakradhvajam ivo 'cchṛtam 3.146.60; indrāyudham ivo 'cchṛtam 3.147.18; cf. 1.64.12; 162.2; 179.2: 3.61.36: 6.114.84).

Indra's release of showers of rain symbolizes a release of arrows. Bhagadatta, sitting on the elephant Supratīka, casts thousands of arrows upon Bhīma as Indra, sitting on his elephant Airāvata, releases showers of rains (kirañ śarasahasrāṇi supratīkaśirogataḥ / airāvatastho maghavān vāridhārā ivā 'nagha 6.91.33; cf. 3.17.12).

Indra's elephant Airāvata symbolizes prominence too. Pāṇḍu, living with Kuntī and Mādrī in a forest, looks like beautiful Airāvata standing between two female elephants (kareṇor iva madhyasthaḥ śrīman paurandaro gajaḥ 1.106.9). An elephant is extolled as like Airāvata (gajam airāvaṇopamam 6.58.42; cf. 6.112.55).

Indra's thunderbolt (vajra, aśani, or kuliśa) symbolizes terror. Terrific missiles, terrific noise, and terrific blows are the main subjects of comparison of this figure. Ghoṭotkaca hurls his spear upon Duryodhana as Indra hurls his thunderbolt upon the enemy (aśanīṃ maghavān iva 6.88.5; cf. 3.12.43; 40.24,44; 157.68: 6.91.59,61). A missile with terrific noise, a trumpeting elephant, or a demon making uproar is likened to the thunderbolt (indrāśanisamasvanam 6.58.57; cf. 3.12.40; 48.9: 6.59.16; 60.55; 69.11; 87.23; 90.2; 90.31; 91.66; 102.14; 112.70; 116.20);

niṣpeṣa and *visphūrjitam* are the other synonyms used for the noise of the thunderbolt. Similarly, a missile which delivers a terrific blow is described as *indrāśanisamasparśa* 3.13.94: 6.49.9; 112.98; 167.27; cf. 1.40.4, 125.27; 218.40: 3.146.57; 154.53: 6.42.19; 55.29; 75.24; 84.16.

A brave warrior is described as having an heroic nature like that of the thunderbolt (vajrasamānavīryaḥ 1.180.14).

A brilliant missile is likened to the brilliant or burning thunderbolt (mahāśanisamaprabha 6.75.9; cf. 3.225.20: 6.88.14; 97.41; jvalantīm aśanīm iva 6.114.27; cf. 3.12.44).

Sometimes, two synonyms of the thunderbolt are simultaneously used in order to emphasize the intensity of terror, e.g., Arjuna's arrows are described as delivering a thunderbolt-thunderbolt-like blow (vajrāśanisamasparśaḥ 6.114.55; cf. 3.40.15).

Thus, apart from occurrences of the word *indra* in such compound forms as *rājendra*, *munīndra*, *mṛgendra*, *gajendra*, and others, where it does not always seem to be alive as a figure, Indra occurs in its symbolic figurative use in at least 247 passages in this corpus. *Indra*, *devendra*, *mahendra; śakra; vajradhara*, *vajrapāṇi*, *vajrabhṛt*, *vajrāyudha*, *vajrin; devarāja*, *amararāja*, *surarāja; purandara*, *maghavan*, *sahasranetra*, *sahasradṛk; vāsava*, *śatakratu*, *harihaya*, *tridaśeśa*, *vṛtrahan*, *balabhid*, *balavṛtrahan*, and *śambarahan* are the synonyms used.

3. Śiva

Primarily, Śiva is the standard of invincibility, might, and terror. Skanda is invincible like Lord Śiva (ajeyas tvaṃ raṇe 'rīṇam umāpatir iva prabhuḥ 3.221.75). Garuḍa breaks through his enemy like the mighty wielder of Pināka, enraged at the time of the destruction of the universe at the end of an age (yugāntakāle saṃkruddhaḥ pinākī 'va mahābalaḥ 1.28.20). Bhīma with his bloodstained mace looks like Rudra (rudravat pratyadṛśyata 6.98.36; cf. 6.58.52). Bhīma stands in the battlefield like the wielder of Pināka standing in a cemetery (atiṣṭhat tumule bhīmaḥ śmaśāna iva śūlabhṛt 6.58.61). Bhīma, moving around in the battlefield with his mace, looks like dancing Śaṃkara (nṛtyantam iva śaṃkaram 6.58.56).

Śiva's weapon adds to the intensity of horror. Saubha, killed by Kṛṣṇa's weapon, falls down on the ground, as the three cities destroyed by the arrows of Śiva fell down (maheśvaraśaroddhūtaṃ papāta tripuraṃ yathā 3.23.34). Bhīma's mace, smeared with hair and marrow, looks like the Pināka of Śiva, destroying animals (pinākam iva rudrasya kruddhasyā 'bhighnataḥ paśūn 6.58.58).

Śiva is also a standard of extreme honor, delight, and brilliance.

People honor Vasiṣṭha, as the gods honor Śiva (divaukasa ive 'śvaram 1.168.15). Āstīka, the child, delighted his family of snakes as Lord Śiva, the bestower of gold, delights all (bhagavān iva deveśaḥ śūlapāṇir hiraṇyadaḥ 1.44.22). The Pāṇḍavas are described as shining like Śiva (bhūtapatiprakāśāḥ 3.24.2).

Śiva's family: Kṛṣṇa accompanied by Arjuna looks like Lord Śiva accompanied by Kārtikeya (babhau yathā bhūtapatir mahātmā sametya sākṣād bhagavān guhena 3.180.13). The Kṣatriyas (desirous of winning Draupadī in the Svayaṃvara) surrounding Draupadī shine like the gods surrounding the daughter of the lord of mountains (te kṣatriyā rangagatāḥ sametā jigīṣamāṇā drupadātmajāṃ tām / cakāśire parvatarājakanyām umāṃ yathā devagaṇāḥ sametāḥ 1.178.4).

Śiva, as a symbol of hunting, is already known to the students of Kālidāsa (cf. ABSH 1.6; Ragh. 11.44). Parīkṣit hunts the deer as Lord Śiva with a bow in his hand hunts the sacrificial deer (yathā hi bhagavān rudro viddhvā yajñamṛgaṃ divi / anvagacchad dhanuṣpāṇiḥ paryanveṣaṃ tatas tataḥ 1.36.12; cf. 3.262.19).

It has been suggested that Śiva as a hunter allegorically represents the constellation Ārdrā chasing the constellation Mṛgaśiras (Orion) in the firmament. In fact, 3.262.19 reads: rudras tārāmṛgaṃ yathā.

Śiva appears as the *upamāna* in at least 14 passages, as Īśvara (1.168.15), Umāpati (3.221.75), Pinākin (1.28.20: 6.58.52), Bhūtapati (3.24.2; 180.13), Maheśvara (3.23.34), Rudra (1.36.12: 3.262.19: 6.58.58; 98.36), Śaṃkara (6.58.56), Śūlapāṇi (1.44.22), and Śūlabhṛt (6.58.61).

4. Viṣṇu

Viṣṇu symbolizes conquest, protection, prominence and delight.

Māndhātṛ conquers the three worlds by means of his virtuous acts as Viṣṇu conquered the three worlds with three steps (dharmeṇa vyajayal lokāṃs trīn viṣṇur iva vikramaiḥ 3.126.32).

Duḥśāsana is advised to look after his kinsmen as Viṣṇu looks after the troops of the gods (jñātīṃś cā 'py anupaśyethā viṣṇur devagaṇān iva 3.238.25).

The three worlds are obedient to Māndhātṛ as they are to Lord Viṣṇu (yasya lokās trayo vaśyā viṣṇor iva mahātmanaḥ 3.126.2).

Nothing is difficult for Arjuna, accompanied by Kṛṣṇa, as nothing was difficult for Viṣṇu, endowed with firm resolution, in the destruction of the enemy (vyavasāyasahāyasya viṣṇoḥ śatruvadheṣv iva 1.55.36).

As Viṣṇu was among the Ādityas, so Arjuna is among his brothers (ādityānāṃ yathā viṣṇus tathai 'va pratibhāti me 3.79.2; cf. 6.32.21). As Aditi's affection was caused to grow by Viṣṇu, so Viṣṇu-like Arjuna will cause Kuntī's affection to grow (adityā viṣṇunā prītir yathā 'bhūd abhivardhitā / tathā viṣṇusamaḥ prītiṃ vardhayiṣyati te 'rjunaḥ 1.114.30).

Viṣṇu's friendship with Indra is referred to. The Śini chief comes to Arjuna's aid as Viṣṇu comes to Indra's aid (viṣṇur yathā vṛtraniṣūdanasya 6.55.77). Pārṣata being advised by Arjuna is like Viṣṇu being advised by Indra (viṣṇur vajrabhṛtā iva 6.46.41).

Mt. Mandara's fall from Viṣṇu's hand (after the churning of the ocean was over, where Viṣṇu, in the form of a tortoise, kūrma, was holding up Mt. Mandara) is alluded to. Vṛtra, struck by Indra's thunderbolt, falls down as great Mt. Mandara fell down released from Viṣṇu's hand (yathā mahān śailavaraḥ purastāt sa mandaro viṣṇukarāt pramuktaḥ 3.94.14).

Viṣṇu symbolizes the heroic qualities of a king as well. Duḥṣanta is like Viṣṇu in valor (bale viṣṇusamaś cā 'sīt 1.62.13; cf. 1.50.14, 114.34).

Viṣṇu appears as the *upamāna* in at least 12 passages, as Viṣṇu, Nārāyaṇa, and Upendra. The synonym Viṣṇu, is, however, the most common.

5. Brahmā

Brahmā, as the *upamāna*, appears in at least 12 passages as Pitāmaha, grandfather, (parameṣṭhi) Prajāpati, Lord of Creatures, and Svayaṃbhū, self-born.

Primarily, Brahmā symbolizes prominence and honor. The assembly of kings attending upon Bhīṣma shines like that of the gods attending Pitāmaha (vibabhau ca nṛpāṇāṃ sā pitāmaham upāsatām / devānām iva deveśaṃ pitāmaham upāsatām 6.116.8; cf. 1.214.8: 6.115.28). Rāvaṇa's father is Prajāpati-like (prajāpatisamo vipro 3.265.22; cf. 1.14.6: 3.210.2; 262.22). Bhīṣma is likened to Parameṣṭhi-Prajāpati, the lord of all the worlds (sarvalokeśvarasye 'va parameṣṭhi-prajāpateḥ 6.15.35; cf. 1.71.57).

Prajāpati's sense of equality is referred to. King Parīkṣit is equal to all like Prajāpati (samaḥ sarveṣu bhūteṣu prajāpatir ivā 'bhavat 1.45.8).

The following passages are somewhat obscure:

a) jājvalyamānaṃ vapuṣā
yathā lakṣmyā pitāmaham 3.98.18.

(The gods saw Dadhīca) exceedingly shining with his body like Brahmā shining with Lakṣmī (?).

Gonda in his *Aspects of Early Visnuism*[1] shows how Śrī Lakṣmī, "before being constantly described as specially connected with Viṣṇu," "was associated with" Kubera, Dharma, and Indra. He refers to Rāmā-

[1] J. Gonda, *Aspects of Early Visnuism* (Utrecht, 1954), pp. 223 f.

yaṇa 2.60.13G: rāmalakṣmaṇayor madhye sītā rājati te snuṣā / viṣṇuvāsavayor madhye padmā śrīr iva rupiṇī, i.e., Daśaratha's daughter-in-law Sītā shines between Rāma and Lakṣmaṇa as charming Śrī shone between Viṣṇu and Indra. Gonda's list of Śrī's associates, however, should have included Pitāmaha as well, as attested from our stanza at least. In fact, traditionally speaking, both are regarded as abiding in the lotus; this distinctive common feature may be found interesting in this connection (cf. synonyms: Kamalālaya for Brahmā and Kamalālayā for Lakṣmī).

According to our edition, all the southern manuscripts read *sākṣāt* ("like Brahmā before one's very eyes"), apparently their ancestor having found *lakṣmyā* a *lectio difficilior*. The edition marks *lakṣmyā* with the wavy line of uncertainty, perhaps unnecessarily.

b) tena ratnavatā pārthaḥ
sa ca gāṇḍīvadhanvanā /
babhūva paramopetaḥ
svayaṃbhūr iva bhānunā 6.46.44.

Arjuna was well complemented with the banner decked with precious stones, and the banner was well complemented with Arjuna, as Brahmā is complemented by the sun (?).

Vide Hopkins, *Epic Myth.*, p. 87, "Surya is also said to be born of Brahman ("son of the self-existent").

6. The Aśvins

The Aśvins are referred to in four passages as comparisons for (*a*) charm and beauty, (*b*) delight, and (*c*) invincibility.

a) sa cā 'śvirupasadṛśo
devasattvaparākramaḥ /
sarvāsām eva nārīṇāṃ
cittapramathano 'bhavat // 1.96.56.

And he (Vicitravīrya), like the two Aśvins in beauty, having the valor and strength of the gods, became the agitator of the hearts of all women (cf. 3.50.26).

b) tatro 'paviṣṭau muditau
nākapṛṣṭhe 'śvināv iva // 1.214.29.

Kṛṣna and Arjuna, sitting there, were delighted like the two Aśvins sitting in the uppermost heaven.

c) aśvināv iva duḥsahau 3.48.4.

Bhīma and Arjuna are invincible like the Aśvins.

7. Savitṛ

Lomapāda giving his daughter in marriage to Ṛśyaśṛṅga is likened to Savitṛ giving his daughter Sūryā in marriage to the Aśvins (lomapādo duhitaraṃ sāvitrīṃ savitā yathā 3.110.5).

8. Mitrāvaruṇā

The gods Mitra and Varuṇa (in *dvandva* form *mitrāvaruṇā*) probably symbolize might and charm, e.g.,

bhrātuḥ putrān pradāsyāmi
mitrāvaruṇayoḥ samān 1.99.38.

I (Vyāsa) will give to my deceased brother sons like Mitra and Varuṇa.

It may be noted in this connection that even though *putrān* is plural, the duality Mitra and Varuṇa may conceivably be used because two wives are involved.

9. Kubera

Kubera, the god of wealth, symbolizes wealth and grandeur. A study of the related *upamānas* shows that his home, his wealth, and his *caitraratha*-forest are more significant than his personality.

śuśubhe dhanasampūrṇaṃ
dhanādhyakṣakṣayopamam 1.199.36

The house of the Kauravas shone, full of wealth, like the house of the lord of wealth (Kubera).

maṇipravekān sumanoharāṃś ca
yathā bhaveyur dhanadasya rājñaḥ 3.161.6

(The Pāṇḍavas saw) on Mt. Gandhamādana exceedingly charming, excellent gems as if they belonged to King Kubera.

A delightful forest is described as *caitraratha*-like (vane caitraratho pame 1.73.4; cf. 1.64.25: 3.174.17,20). The forest without Arjuna looks like the *caitraratha*-forest without Kubera (kubereṇa yathā hīnaṃ vanaṃ caitrarathaṃ yathā 3.79.6).

At one place, in a long list of *upamānas* of conjugal love, Kubera's wife Bhadrā is referred to (yathā vaiśravaṇe bhadrā 1.191.6).

Kubera, Dhanādhyakṣa, and Vaiśravaṇa are the synonyms used.

10. Kārtikeya

Kārtikeya, Śiva's son and commander-in-chief of the gods' army, symbolizes bravery and powers of command. Dhṛṣṭadyumna is requested to become the commander of the Pāṇḍava army as Kārtikeya was the commander of the gods' army (kārtikeyo yathā nityaṃ devānām abhavat purā / tathā tvam api pāṇḍūnāṃ senānīḥ puruṣarṣabha 6.46.33). Nakula and Sahadeva are likened to Kārtikeya (yau tau kumārāv iva kārtikeyau 1.180.21).

The story of Kārtikeya's splitting of Mt. Krauñca, referred to in Megha. 58, is alluded to in one instance. Bhīma with an arrow stuck in his breast, shines like Mt. Krauñca shining with Kārtikeya's spear (uraḥsthena babhau tena bhīmasenaḥ pratāpavān / skandaśaktyā yathā krauñcaḥ purā nṛpatisattama 6.107.44).

Bhīṣma lying on the bed of arrows is compared to Kārtikeya, lying on the bed of reeds where he was born (sa dadarśa mahātmānaṃ śaratalpagataṃ tadā / janmaśayyāgataṃ devaṃ kārtikeyam iva prabhum 6.117.3).

Kārtikeya, Guha, and Skanda are the synonyms used (cf. section I.3, *guha*). It may be interesting to note that the passage from book 1 reads *kārtik°*, those from book 6, *kārttik°*. The latter is of course etymologically correct. Phonemically *v rt v* and *v rtt v* have no contrast. *kartik°*, however, gives a simpler reading.

11. Kāma

Kāma, the god of love, symbolizes beauty. Nala is described as Kāma himself, because of his beauty (kandarpa iva rūpeṇa mūrtimān abhavat svayam 3.50.14; cf. 3.51.26. *Vide* section II,4.

Kāma's weapons are standards of amorous excitement. The blooming Kurabakas look like the multitudes of Kāma's arrows (kāmasye 'va śarotkarān 3.155.58). So are the mango trees likened to Kāma's arrows (tathā 'naṅgaśarākārān 3.155.60).

The excellent sindhuvāra trees are compared to Kāma's darts (sindhuvārān atho 'dārān manmathasye 'va tomarān 3.155.57). It may be noted here that the critical edition has the reading *'ddāmān*, with a wavy line underneath, instead of *'dārān* as adopted in the passage quoted last. But as Emeneau has shown,[2] the reading *'dārān* is justified inasmuch as this is in agreement with the versions of the "all-important" Śāradā and Malayālam manuscripts, and "the 'K' version, the Bengali version, the Devanāgarī version in its three groups, and one of the two manuscripts of the Telugu version." Moreover, "*uddāma* is far less common than the banal *udāra*, but hardly a *lectio difficilior*." "Restoration to the passage of *'dārān* yields an effect of sound (*°vārān . . . 'dārān . . . tomarān*)" too.

Kāma, Kandarpa, and Manmatha are the synonyms used.

---

[2] M. B. Emeneau, "The Sinduvāra Tree in Sanskrit Literature," *University of California Publications in Classical Philology*, XII (1944), 335.

12. Yama

Yama, the god of death, with or without his rod, fire, open mouth, or other accessories, symbolizes destruction and terror. Yama (restrainer), Antaka (destroyer), Kāla (time), Daṇḍapāṇi (one with a rod in his hand), Pretarāja (the king of the deceased), and Mṛtyu (death) are the synonyms used. Yama as the *upamāna* appears in at least 104 passages in this corpus.

Kṛṣṇa kills his opponents like Kāla (nighnaṃś carati vārṣṇeyaḥ Kālavat tatra bhārata 1.219.6, cf. 1.26.9: 3.2.38; 12.20; 41.18; 46.18; 117.7; 124.22; 174.18: 6.58.55; 59.18; 82.11; 92.28; 100.30; 114.59).

A weapon meant for killing the enemy is likened to Yama's rod (kāladaṇḍopamam 1.9.21; cf. 1.167.19; 180.16: 3.12.43; 152.15; 274.27: 6.43.8,30; 49.9; 76.5; 81.30,33; 90.21; 96.4; 97.18; 102.5; 106.39; 107.11; 112.47). In one instance, Yama's rod and the thunderbolt are simultaneously used as figurative epithets of arrows (yamadaṇḍāśaniprabhān 6.70.20).

Two or more synonyms of Yama are simultaneously used in compounds to emphasize the intensity of fear or destruction. Thus, a sword is described as Kāla, Antaka, and Yama (kālāntakayamopamam 3.23.30; cf. 3.28.23; 138.12; 175.15: 6.50.42; 51.38; 87.7; 90.20; kālāntakopamaḥ 3.154.40; antakakālakalpa(ḥ) 3.225.20; kālamṛtyusama(ḥ) 6.60.18; 66.58). Kāla and poison (viṣa) come together once in a similar situation (kālaviṣopamaḥ 3.142.14).

Yama with his mouth open adds to the frightful situation. Bhīma attacking the elephants is likened to Yama with his mouth open (vyāditāsyam ivā 'ntakam 6.58.33; cf. 6.59.20; 102.18; 110.38; 112.74; vyāttānanam (ivā 'ntakam) 6.55.45; 59.23; 78.23; 80.19; 103.93; 104.37; cf. 3.125.1: 6.101.32).

A terrifying warrior is likened to Yama with his rod, or a mace, or a noose (daṇḍapāṇim ivā 'ntakam 3.153.25; cf. 6.50.2; 58.51; 59.11; 76.57; 98.35; 103.68; gadāhastam 6.73.37; pāśahastam . . . 6.105.10).

Kāla's fire which destroys the universe stands as a comparison for an all-destroying warrior or weapon (kālānalasama- 3.195.21; 216.14; 6.78.34; 96.50). So also is the universe-destroying sun (yugāntāditya); cf. 3.23.32; 42.11.

A large-scale destruction by a warrior is likened to the destruction of the universe by Kāla at the end of the age (kālene 'va yugakṣaye 6.53.2; 98.14; 100.74; 102.75; cf. 1.218.38: 6.55.127; 59.12,17; 102.52).

Kāla's cloud which destroys the universe at the end of the age is also referred to in a similar situation (yugānte jalado yathā 6.88.15; yugāntameghaughanibham 6.76.19).

Kāla, hungry or enraged, symbolizes immediate destruction (bubhukṣitaḥ kāla ivā 'ntako mahān 1.24.10; kālaṃ kruddham ivā 'ntakam 3.142.10; kruddhaḥ kāla ivā 'parah 6.85.24; kruddho 'ntakaḥ prāṇabhṛto yathai 'va 1.185.5; daṇḍapāṇir iva kruddhaḥ 3.12.46).

Kāla created by another Kāla is all the more frightful. Ghaṭotkaca, proceeding towards Duryodhana, is likened to a Kāla created by Kāla (kālasṛṣṭam ivā 'ntakam 6.87.24; cf. 6.60.43; 104.39; kālaṃ yathā mṛtyukṛtaṃ kṣaṇena 6.81.20).

Kāla's blow stands as a comparison for the battlefield, full of slain men, elephants, and horses (raṇāṅgaṇaṃ tad abhavan mṛtyor āghātasaṃnibham 6.59.15).

In one passage, a spear is likened to Kāla's terrifying sister (mṛtyor ghorām iva svasām 6.112.3; note *svasām* instead of *svasāram*). Traditionally, Yamī or the Yamunā River is regarded as Yama's sister. But the above passage has nothing to do with Yamī or the river. It, in fact, represents a specimen of the figurative use of kinship terms to give a sense of emphatic reality to the object of comparison (i.e., Kāla).

Kālarātri, the night of the destruction of the universe at the end of the age, stands as a comparison for Vārṣṇeya's terrific spear directed towards Bhīṣma (abhidudrāva vegena kālarātrir yathā naram 6.100.33).

Kāla, as the king of the deceased (Pretarāja), along with his town (Pretarājapura), the Vaitaraṇī River, and the dead or ghosts (preta), is referred to. The river of the battlefield carries away timid warriors, as the Vaitaraṇī River carries the dead towards the town of the king of the dead (apovāha raṇe bhīrūn kaśmalenā 'bhisaṃvṛtān / yathā vaitaraṇī pretān pretarājapuraṃ prati 6.99.38). The town, devoid of king Saṃvaraṇa, surrounded by hungry, unhappy, corpselike men, looks like the town of the king of the dead surrounded by the dead (tat kṣudhārtair nirānandaiḥ śavabhūtais tadā naraiḥ / abhavat pretarājasya puraṃ pretair ivā 'vṛtam 1.163.16). Frightening sounds like those of the ghosts are heard (śuśruve dāruṇā vācaḥ pretānām iva bhārata 6.44.19).

Yama, in one passage, stands as a comparison for an upright judge; viz., Janamejaya, as a judge for the ascertainment of the law of virtue, is likened to Yama (yamo yathā dharmaviniścayajñaḥ 1.50.15). So is the anger of an ideal king (Śantanu) compared to that of Kāla (antakapratimaḥ kope 1.94.12).

II. THE GODDESSES (DEVĪ)

1. Aditi

Aditi, the mother of the gods, who is sometimes described as a personified universe in its various aspects (áditir dyáur áditir antárikṣam áditir mātā́ sá pitā́ sá putraḥ / víśve devā́ áditiḥ páñca jánā́ áditir jātám áditir jánitvam, RV 1.89.10. Aditi is heaven; Aditi is the airspace; Aditi is the mother, the father, and the son; all the gods and men are Aditi; Aditi is that which was born and that which is to be born), is the symbol of motherhood. Draupadī gives birth to her sons as Aditi gave birth to the gods (pāñcālī suṣuve virān ādityān aditir yathā 1.213.73). Cf. section I,4.

2. Umā

Vide section I,3, Śiva's family.

3. Śrī

Śrī, the goddess of beauty and wealth, symbolizes feminine beauty. Damayantī, Śakuntalā, Draupadī, Sāvitrī, Śantanu's wife Gaṅgā, and Vasu's wife Girikā are all charming like Śrī (śrīr ivā 'yatalocanā 3.50.12; kanyā śrīr iva rūpiṇī 1.65.3; śriyam iva rūpiṇīm ca 1.189.39; devī śrīr iva rūpiṇī 3.277.29; gaṅgā śrīr iva rūpiṇī 1.92.2; sākṣāc chriyam ivā 'parām 1.57.38; cf. 1.92.26; 203.6: 3.65.3; 277.25).

The boy in the midst of the deluge, however, looks like the abode of Lakṣmī before one's eyes (sākṣāl lakṣmyā ivā 'vāsaḥ sa tadā pratibhāti me 3.186.86).

Lakṣmī is the *upamāna* of conjugal love as well (yathā nārāyaṇe lakṣmīḥ 1.191.6). Subhadrā is united in marriage with Arjuna as Lakṣmī was united with Kṛṣṇa (śrīḥ kṛṣṇene 'va saṃgatā 1.55.34).

Śrī and Lakṣmī are the synonyms used. In 1.92.26, *padmā* also appears along with Śrī (Sākṣāt padmām iva śriyam 1.92.26). Note also Lakṣmī in section I,5.

4. Ratī

Ratī, Kāma's wife, is the symbol of fascination. Charming-lotus-petal-eyed Damayantī is fascinating to the whole world as Ratī is fascinating to Kāma (cārupadmapalāśākṣīṃ manmathasya ratīm iva / iṣṭāṃ sarvasya jagataḥ 3.65.11). *Vide* section I,11.

5. Kiṃnarī and Apsaras

The Kiṃnarīs, a class of female spirits having human head and equine body or vice versa "who live chiefly in the mountains" and dance and sing, symbolize feminine loveliness (*Epic Myth.*, p. 159).

Yavakrī sees Raibhya's daughter-in-law wandering about like a Kiṃnarī (vicarantīṃ snuṣāṃ tasya Kiṃnarīm iva bhārata 1.137.2); cf. Kumārasambhava 1.11.

Apsarases, like Kiṃnarīs, are divine nymphs, but more individualized and of greater mythological importance. Thus, we have such personal names of Apsarases as Menakā, Urvaśī, Tilottamā, and the like.

In Ketumāla, a country towards the west of Mt. Meru, men are gold-complexioned and women are like the Apsarases (suvarṇavarṇāś ca narāḥ striyaś cā 'psarasopamāḥ 6.7.33; cf. 3.115.10).

III. SACRIFICIAL OBJECTS (YAJÑA)

Sacrificial objects as the *upamāna* already appear in the Ṛgveda (RV 4.51.2).

A son is compared to the Āhavanīya fire taken out of the Gārhapatya fire, and the father consequently is made into two (yathā hy āhavanīyo 'gnir gārhapatyāt praṇīyate / tathā tvattaḥ prasūto 'yaṃ tvam ekaḥ san dvidhā kṛtaḥ 1.68.65).

Kaikeyī's slim waist is likened to the hourglass-shaped sacrificial altar or *vedī* (vedīvilagnamadhye 'va bibhratī rūpam uttamam 3.261.19; cf. 3.213.43). Also the earth covered with slain heads of warriors is compared to the *vedī* covered with *kuśa* grass (kīrṇām kuśair vedim ivā 'dhvareṣu 3.120.17).

Yudhiṣṭhira with his four brothers looks like a great, widely spread sacrifice with the four Vedas being recited (bhrātṛbhiḥ sahito rājā caturbhir adhikaṃ babhau / prayujyamānair vitato vedair iva mahādhvaraḥ 1.214.7).

Abhimanyu shines like the fire god on the sacrificial altar with its garland of flames into which the sacrifice is made with powerful mantras (babhau mahāmantrahutārcimālī sadogataḥ san bhagavān ivā 'gniḥ 6.56.24).

The sacrificial food eaten by a dog or a crow stands as a comparison for something or somebody being exploited by an unworthy person. Thus Karṇa, supposedly of low pedigree, is as unworthy to enjoy the kingdom of the Aṅgas as a dog is unworthy to eat sacrificial food (aṅgarājyaṃ ca nā 'rhas tvam upabhoktuṃ narādhama / śvā hutāśasamīpasthaṃ puroḍāśam ivā 'dhvare 1.127.7). Rāma is not ready to accept Sītā after her return from Rāvaṇa's home because she is like sacrificial food licked by a dog (no 'tsahe paribhogāya śvāvalīḍhaṃ havir yathā 3.275.13). Yudhiṣṭhira is warned lest some wicked person should touch the auspicious face of Draupadī, like a dog eating sacrificial food (spṛsyāc chubhaṃ kaścid akṛtyakārī / śvā vai puroḍāśam ivo 'payuñkṣīt 3.253.20). A girl, uncared for, may be taken away by some wicked persons as sacrificial food is carried away by crows (havir dhvāñkṣā ivā 'dhvarāt 1.146.17).

The Pāṇḍavas are warned lest Draupadī should surrender herself to some unworthy person like a ladle filled with good ghee being offered to the ashes (dadāti kasmai cid anarhate tanuṃ varājyapūrṇām iva bhasmani srucam 3.253.18).

The Sarasvatī River is likened to the sacrificial gift for the gods (āyāgabhutām iva devatānām 3.174.24).

People find the proper means of release by counseling among themselves as the gods found the fire-god hidden in a cave (api mantrayamāṇā hi hetuṃ paśyāma mokṣaṇe / yathā naṣṭaṃ purā devā gūḍham agnim guhāgatam 1.33.8).

In one instance a nonvedic sacrificial object is referred to. Śakuntalā is described by Duḥṣanta in court as one cast out by Menakā on the Himālayas, like flowers left at a sacrificial ceremony (yayā himavataḥ pṛṣṭhe nirmālye 'va praveritā 1.68.73).

IV. FIRE (AGNI)

The fire symbolizes brilliance in general; *agni*, *pāvaka*, *anala*, *jvalana*, *havyavāh*, *Kṛṣṇavartman*, *vahni*, *hutāśana*, *vaiśvānara*, *dhūmaketu*, and *vibhāvasu* are the synonyms used. Apart from its occurrence (21 times) jointly with *sūrya* (the sun), it occurs in isolation in at least 125 passages.

Thus, a king, an ascetic, a Brāhmaṇa, or a missile is likened to fire (vibhāvasusamadyutiḥ 1.43.18; 81.7; cf. 1.1.3, 54,83; 2.4; 17.23,28; 20.5; 24.3,6; 25.1; 26.8,46; 28.3; 29.5; 38.37; 43.18,38; 88.12; 155.7; 175.9; 183.3; 185.7; 212.4,13; 213.46; 217.10: 3.3.31,4.1; 18.15; 40.13; 42.19; 60.35; 80.2,79; 132.8; 134.2; 145.3; 146.70; 158.53; 168.3; 197.22; 218.24; 233.3; 235.19; 249.6,9; 254.13; 273.21: 6.16.30; 18.6; 22.9; 44.31; 45.16; 46.5; 50.39; 55.21,111; 69.29; 75.10,35; 81.15,36; 91.52,60,66; 95.33; 100.31; 103.14,27; 105.25; 107.12; 112.137).

Fire burning a heap of cotton or a forest stands as a comparison for one dispersing his opponents in general. Thus, Droṇa disperses the Pāṇḍava army as fire burns cotton (vyadhamat pāṇḍavīṃ senāṃ tūlarāśim ivā 'nalaḥ 6.71.31; cf. 3.27.17; 40.3; 141.3; 225.1; 252.15: 6.45.56; 46.4; 50.107; 55.106; 82.20; 82.38; 91.7; 98.7; 102.9; 112.66; 112.88; (kṛṣṇavartme 'va kānanam 6.104.38; 105.15); cf. ABHS 1.10.

Abhimanyu, after having dispersed his enemy, stands in the battlefield, shining like fire devoid of smoke (vidhūmo 'gnir iva jvalan 6.96.9; cf. 1.96.28: 3.161.18: 6.7.9; 45.56; 105.33; 112.122).

Fire is also a favorite simile for illustrating various philosophical or moralistic ideas.

koṭarāgnir yathā 'śeṣaṃ
samūlaṃ pādapaṃ dahet /
dharmārthināṃ tathā 'lpo 'pi
rāgadoṣo vināśayet // 3.2.29.

As fire in a hollow can burn the whole tree along with the root, so even a little of attachment and hatred can destroy the one aspiring for virtuous life.

yathai 'dhāṃsi samiddho 'gnir
bhasmasāt kurute 'rjuna
jñānāgniḥ sarvakarmāṇi
bhasmasāt kurute tathā // 6.26.37.

As the kindled fire burns pieces of fuel to ashes, so the fire of knowledge burns all actions to ashes.

mānasaṃ śamayet tasmāj
jñānenā 'gnim ivā 'mbunā 3.2.25.

One should extinguish mental worry by means of knowledge, as one extinguishes fire by water.

anādyantā hi sā tṛṣṇā
antardehagatā nṛṇām /
vināśayati saṃbhūtā
ayonija ivā 'nalaḥ // 3.2.36.

That desire without beginning and end, living inside the body of men, when born, destroys them like fire not produced in the ordinary course of generation (i.e., 'self-produced fire').

yathai 'dhaḥ svasamutthena
vahninā nāśam ṛcchati /
tathā 'kṛtātmā lobhena
sahajena vinaśyati // 3.2.37.

As fuel is destroyed through fire arising out of itself, so one with indisciplined spirit perishes by means of his own inborn greed.

dhūmenā 'vriyate vahnir
yathā.................
....
tathā tene 'dam āvṛtam 6.25.38.

As fire is covered with smoke, so knowledge is covered with desire.

sarvārambhā hi doṣeṇa
dhūmenā 'gnir ivā 'vṛtāḥ 6.40.48.

All the activities of life are covered with apparent defect as fire is covered with smoke.

brahma kṣatreṇa saṃsṛṣṭam
kṣatraṃ ca brahmaṇā saha /
udīrṇau dahataḥ śatrūn
vanānī 'vā 'gnimārutau 3.27.10.

The Brāhmaṇa caste combined with the Kṣatriya caste and the Kṣatriya caste with the Brāhmaṇa caste destroy the enemy as fire and the wind burn forests; cf. 3.27.16.

prakṛtiḥ sā hi kāmasya
pāvakasyā 'raṇir yathā // 3.34.28.

As the fire drill is the origin of fire, so virtue and wealth constitute the origin of desire.

Fire being fed with sacrificial food symbolizes anger being fanned by some external circumstances. Thus, being excited by the (sacrificial food of the) words of Uttaṅka, Janamejaya got angry with Takṣaka as fire fed with the sacrificial object burns high (uttaṅkavākyahaviṣā dīpto 'gnir haviṣā yathā 1.3.193).

The flame of fire appears, at times, as the *upamāna* of beauty. Lopāmudrā is likened to the auspicious flame of fire (agner iva śikhā śubhā 3.94.22).

Fire symbolizes prominence and prosperity also. The warriors occupy the thrones as fires occupy the subordinate altars (dhiṣṇyānī 'va hutāśanaḥ 1.212.14). Kṛṣṇa wishes that the Pāṇḍavas may prosper like fire being kindled (jvalana ive 'dhyamānaḥ 1.183.9).

Fire hidden by smoke or ashes signifies sometimes beauty, sometimes brilliance, covered with some casual external circumstances. Damayantī, spending her life separated from her husband, is likened to the light of fire covered with much smoke (pinaddhāṃ dhūmajālena prabhām iva vibhāvasoḥ 3.65.7). The Pāṇḍavas in Pāñcāla appear like fires covered with ashes (bhasmāvṛtāṅgān iva havyavāhān 1.178.9).

But, as the hidden fire is known by its heat, so is Damayantī recognized by Sudeva on the basis of her bodily splendor and various signs (pihito 'gnir ivo 'ṣmaṇā 3.66.8).

The close association of the wind with fire is referred to as a standard of ideal friendship. Thus, friendship between Hanumat and Sugrīva is established like that between the wind and fire (anilasyā 'gninā yathā 3.147.26).

Warriors, missiles, or armor, when devoid of their usual spendor, are likened to fires with flames extinguished (śāntārciṣa ivā 'gnayaḥ 1.169.23; cf. 6.92.61).

Fire and the sun taken together add to the intensity of the brilliance of a king, a god, a warrior, or a missile. Yayāti and Kṛṣṇa in his Virāṭ form are each likened to fire and the sun (vaiśvānarārkadyutim aprameyam 1.83.8 [Yayāti]; dīptānalārkadyutim aprameyam 6.33.17 [Kṛṣṇa]; cf. 3.222.21). Karṇa, because of his brilliance, beauty, splendor, and good qualities, is likened to the sun, the fire, and also the moon (dīptikāntidyutiguṇaiḥ sūryendujvalanopamaḥ 1.126.4); *vide* sections V and VI.

V. SUN (SŪRYA)

The sun (sūrya) primarily symbolizes brilliance, power, and might. Arka, Bhāskara, Āditya, Sūrya, Tapana, Raśmimat, Sahasraraśmi, Vivasvat, Bhānumat, Divākara, Gharmāṃśu, Aṃśumat, and Ravi are the synonyms used. It is only in this primary sense that this figure occurs in 92 passages in this corpus, e.g., Duḥṣanta is likened to the sun in brilliance (tejasā bhāskaropamaḥ 1.62.13; cf. 1.3.140; 6.3; 20.12; 26.47; 28.12,23; 50.13; 59.36; 62.13; 65.23; 78.6; 94.12,37; 114.25; 160.17; 165.34; 169.21; 189.19; 204.19; 208.17; 215.16; 216.10: 3.4.8; 23.6; 28.13; 42.15; 43.26,27; 50.2; 51.27; 54.35; 77.28; 112.2; 116.30; 126.25,42; 130.7; 146.6; 149.7,13; 156.26; 162.3,16; 164.6; 180.49; 194.11; 195.20; 210.4; 221.1,62,64,71; 226.9,13; 278.15; 263.36; 281.8; 292.18: 6.15.7,62; 17.18; 19.42; 30.9; 47.56; 55.64,86; 57.7; 59.28; 67.29; 69.19; 75.15,32; 76.16; 78.11; 79.24; 80.34; 81.18; 84.1; 96.16; 102.51,74,77; 103.61; 105.34; 107.45; 112.123; 113.29; 114.10; 116.7; 117.17; repeated passages such as rathenā 'dityavarcasā, 'by a chariot having splendor like that of the sun' 3.23.45; 170.29; 221.1; 273.12; 275.49: 6.48.18; 59.22, and divākarasamadyuti- 3.4.8; 98.18 may specially be noted).

The rising sun symbolizes a special kind of splendor that is shared in this corpus by a brilliant child (taruṇādityasaṃkāśam [Karṇa as a child] 3.293.6; cf. 1.68.14; 107.10; 214.30: 3.150.27; 214.19; 214.26; 218.39; sa bālārkasamadyutiḥ 3.214.23 [Skanda]), people of Jambūdvīpa (taruṇādityavarṇās te jāyante tatra mānavāḥ 6.8.25), and monkeys (taruṇādityasadṛśaiḥ 3.268.27).

A warrior's overpowering brilliance is likened to the dazzling heat of the sun (duṣprekṣyo raśmivān iva 6.102.38; cf. 1.1.83: 6.19.33; 45.57; 55.47).

King Vyuṣitāśva shines surpassing human beings and all creatures as the sun shines towards the close of winter (vyuṣitāśvas tato rājann atimartyān vyarocata / sarvabhūtāny ati yathā tapanaḥ śiśirātyaye 1.112.10). Duryodhana, with bright splendor, shines like the sun in the autumn (śuśubhe vimalārciṣmān śaradī 'va divākaraḥ 6.93.22).

Sātyaki harasses Aśvatthāman as the sun at the passing away of clouds harasses living beings (vimukto meghajālena yathai 'va tapanas tathā 6.97.51; cf. 1.72.6: 3.23.19).

If accompanied by cloud and lightning, the sun gives a picture of charm, rather than mere brilliance. The Lord of creatures (Śiva), sitting in a chariot with Umā, shines like the sun accompanied by lightning, shining in a cloud with the rainbow (tasmin rathe paśupatiḥ sthito bhāty umayā saha / vidyutā sahitaḥ sūryaḥ sendracāpe ghane yathā 3.221.4).

But, Bhīma, charming to look at, surrounded by the demons, looks like the sun covered with multitudes of clouds (pracchādyamānaṃ rakṣobhiḥ pāṇḍavaṃ priyadarśanam / dadṛśuḥ sarvabhūtāni sūryam abhragaṇair iva 3.157.47; cf. 1.181.40: 3.268.8: 6.22.16). Likewise, a warrior whose body is covered with arrows is likened to the sun covered with clouds (chādayantaḥ śaravrātair meghā iva divākaram 6.42.14).

The son of the fire god, wearing two speckless red garments, shines like the sun accompanied by two red clouds (araje vāsasī rakte vasānaḥ pāvakātmajaḥ / bhāti dīptavapuḥ śrīmān raktābhrābhyām ivā 'ṃśumān 3.218.31; cf. 1.168.6: 3.214.19).

Bhīsma, standing in a shining chariot, is likened to the sun in the midst of a white cloud (śvetābhra iva tīksṇāṃśum 6.164.1).

Viṣṇu is compared to one thousand suns (sahasrasūryapratimam 3.194.15). But when it is said: if there be a simultaneous light emanating from one thousand suns, that light may compare with that of Kṛṣṇa in his Virāṭ form (divi sūryasahasrasya bhaved yugapad utthitā / yadi bhāḥ sadṛśī sā syād bhāsas tasya mahātmanaḥ 6.33.12), this constitutes *atiśayokti* (hyperbole); cf. Magha 3.8, *vide* chapter 4,III.

Sometimes, the sun and the moon are named together to signify extreme brilliance and charm. Thus, Bhīma's son, Sutasoma, is likened to the moon and the sun in splendor (somārkatejasam 1.213.75; cf. 1.87.1; 185.6; 189.34; 209.7; 218.49: 3.44.27; 61.77; 175.13; 194.11; 254.17; 267.17; 272.26: 6.19.26; 54.23; 106.28; 111.37). Cf. section VI.

So does the sun accompanied by the planet Mars (Maṅgala) or the asterism Puṣya symbolize a brilliant pair. The Ācārya, entering the assembly with his son, is likened to the sun accompanied by Mars (sāṅgāraka ivā 'ṃśumān 1.124.18). King Saudāsa, accompanied by Vasiṣṭha, is likened to the sun rising at the proper time, accompanied by the asterism Puṣya (puṣyeṇa sahitaṃ kāle divākaram ivo 'ditam 1.168.17). Cf. sections VII and IX.

The sun's rays are referred to in various ways. Bhīṣma takes away the glory of his enemy as the sun takes away water with his rays (jalaṃ sūrya ivā 'ṃśubhiḥ 6.105.31; cf. 3.157.48: 6.102.72). Bhīma hits the enemy with arrows, as the sun covers everything with his rays (sa raśmibhir ivā 'dityaḥ 3.157.48; cf. 3.40.33; 46.16). As the sun's rays purify everything, so the fire god's flames will purify everything (yathā sūryāṃśubhiḥ spṛṣṭaṃ sarvaṃ śuci vibhāvyate / tathā tvadarcirnirdagdhaṃ sarvaṃ śuci bhaviṣyati 1.7.21).

As the sun effaces the stars, so Aṣṭāvakra is going to destroy the bard (nakṣatrāṇī 'va savitā nāśayāmi 3.133.18). Kārtikeya defeats the enemy as the sun destroys darkness (tamāṃsī 'va yathā sūryo 3.221.70).

The sun symbolizes also honor and distinction. People approach dying Bhīṣma as all the creatures approach the sun (bhūtānī 'va tamonudam 6.116.3; cf. 1.160.18). As it is impossible for the sun to live incognito in the sky, so it is impossible for the Pāṇḍavas to live incognito (divī 'va pārtha sūryasya na śakyā carituṃ tvayā 3.36.23).

An enemy attacking a warrior is likened tc Rāhu or the inauspicious great planets attacking the sun (svarbhānur iva bhāskaram 3.12.52; cf. 1.168.5: 6.97.34; prajāsaṃharaṇe sūryaḥ krūrair iva mahāgrahaiḥ 6.73.10). Cf. section VII.

The setting sun is the standard of death or invisibility. Vicitravīrya dies like the setting sun (jagāmā 'stam ivā 'dityaḥ Xauravyo yamasādanam 1.96.58). Lord Śiva goes out of sight, as the sun sets for the world (tasya sampaśyatas tv eva pinākī vṛṣabhadhvajaḥ / jagāmā 'darśanaṃ bhānur lokasye 'vā 'stam eyivān 3.42.1; cf. 1.39.15).

The following are examples of the sun symbolizing some philosophical or moralistic ideas.

> yasya dharmo hi dharmārthaṃ
> kleśabhāñ na sa paṇḍitaḥ /
> na sa dharmasya vedā 'rthaṃ
> sūryasyā 'ndhaḥ prabhām iva // 3.24.23.

By whom virtue is practised for virtue's sake, he has troubles; he is not a wise man; he does not know the meaning of virtue, as a blind man does not know the light of the sun.

> yathā rājan prajāḥ sarvāḥ
> sūryaḥ pāti gabhastibhiḥ
> atti cai 'va tathai 'va tvaṃ
> savituḥ sadṛśo bhava // 3.34.69.

O king! as the sun protects all the creatures, and also eats them (i.e., takes away their moisture) with his rays, so you should become like the sun (and protect all your subjects and also collect taxes).

ādityo divi deveṣu
tamo nudati tejasā /
tathai 'va nṛpatir bhūmāv
adharmaṃ nudate bhṛśam // 3.184.26.

As the sun, by his brilliance, removes darkness in heaven among the gods, so does a king remove unrighteousness on the earth.

yathā 'dityaḥ samudyan vai
tamaḥ sarvaṃ vyapohati /
evaṃ kalyāṇam ātiṣṭhan
sarvapāpaiḥ pramucyate // 3.198.53.

As the rising sun removes all darkness, so a person performing virtuous acts is released from all sins.

yathā prakāśayaty ekaḥ
kṛtsnaṃ lokam imaṃ raviḥ /
kṣetraṃ kṣetrī tathā kṛtsnaṃ
prakāśayati bhārata // 6.35.33.

As the sun, all alone, illuminates this entire world, so does the Spirit illuminate the entire sphere of matter.

jñānena tu tad ajñānaṃ
yeṣāṃ nāśitam ātmanaḥ /
teṣām ādityavaj jñānaṃ
prakāśayati tat param // 6.27.16.

For them, whose ignorance has been destroyed by the knowledge of self, that knowledge discloses the supreme being, as the sun discloses the world; cf. 3.198.45.

Taken altogether, the sun as a figure occurs in at least 166 passages in this corpus.

VI. MOON (CANDRA)

The moon symbolizes charm and beauty. It appears in isolation in at least 74 passages in this corpus. Candra, Candramas, Soma, Śaśin, Indu, Śītāṃśu, Tārādhipa, Tārāpati, Tārakārāja, Nakṣatrarāj, Niśākara, and Uḍupa are the synonyms used.

As opposed to the sun's dazzling brightness (duṣprekṣya; cf. 6.102.38), delightfulness to the eyes (sudarśa 1.45.10) is the moon's distinguishing feature.

King Yayāti is of delightful appearance like the moon (somavat priyadarśanaḥ 3.278.18; the same clause repeated in 1.94.12; 115.26; cf. 1.45.10: 3.71.9; 222.21).

Duryodhana shines like the moon (bhāsi nakṣatrarāḍ iva 3.226.10).

The wives of the sages are bright like the digits of the moon (candralekhā ivā 'malāḥ 3.213.43); the face of the moon is made up of sixteen crescent-shaped parts, which are often translated 'digits.' So, Tārā is moon-faced (tārāṃ tārādhipānanām 3.264.18; cf. 3.250.9 candramukhī; 264.20.

Having plunged into the river at a pilgrimage center, one being devoid of all pains always shines like the moon (sarvaduḥkhaiḥ parityakto dyotate śaśivat sadā 3.81.151; cf. 3.80.80,98,122; 82.109; 83.6,59).

Hanumat's face, which had the points of his teeth in a circle and was adorned with white rays which were within his mouth, was like the moon with its rays (vadanaṃ vṛttadaṃṣṭrāgraṃ raśmivantam ivo 'ḍupam / vadanābhyantaragataiḥ śuklabhāsair alaṃkṛtam 3.146.68–9. The *upamānadharma* is whiteness.

A fish is likened to the rays of the moon in splendor (candrāṃśusadṛśaprabham 3.185.11). Menakā's garment is moonlike (śaśisaṃnibham 1.66.3; cf. 1.91.4).

When the moon is full, the charm is intensified (pūrṇacandranibhānanām 3.60.31; 65.25: 6.8.16; pūrṇendusadṛśānanā 1.161.10; 213.19; cf. 1.71.49; 140.13; 164.1; 213.19: 3.61.76; 65.10,11; 186.83; 218.4,36: 6.16.26,36).

The moon sometimes appears together with the swan (haṃsa), cow's milk (gokṣīra), the jasmine (kunda), the fibers of the lotus stalk (mṛṇāla), and silver (rajata), as symbols of the whiteness of an object. Nándinī, the white cow, shines like a swan and the moon (haṃsacandrapratīkāśām 1.164.22). White-complexioned Balarāma and the conch shell, Pāñcajanya, are each likened to cow's milk, the jasmine flower, the moon, the fibers of the lotus stalk, and silver, in splendor (tato gokṣīrakundendumṛṇālarajataprabha- 3.21.30; 119.4). A girl's charming face is likened to the moon and the lotus (padmendusadṛśānane 1.161.10; cf. 6.92.74).

The moon accompanied by various stars presents different pictures in different situations. Karṇa with his two brilliant earrings shines like the bright moon between the two stars of the constellation Viśākhā in the firmament (śobhase kuṇḍalābhyāṃ hi rucirābhyāṃ mahādyute / viśākhayor madhyagataḥ śaśī 'va vimalo divi 3.2.85). Emeneau in his paper "Notes on Śrīharṣa's Naiṣadhacarita"[3] has examined this passage along with the similar passages in Naiṣadhacarita 19.57; 22.22; Vikramorvaśīya 1.10.6 (i.e., act 1, 6th line after the 10th verse), and ABHS 3.11.12 (probably interpolated), and has rightly proved that, unlike Rohiṇī who is mythically related to the moon-god as his favorite wife, Viśākhā, being a constellation of two stars, symbolizes nothing more than the duality (of charming females or of brilliant earrings), and the shape (of a *śaṅkha* or shell as in the Naiṣadhacarita) involved in the above passages.

Śāntā duly serves Ṛśyaśṛṅga as the constellation Rohiṇī, the faithful one, serves the moon in the sky (śāntā cai 'naṃ paryacarad yathāvat khe rohiṇī somam ivā 'nukūlā 3.113.22). Rohiṇī literally means 'a red female.' This is a constellation consisting of five stars of which "Aldebaran or principal star" (MW) is red, and is personified as Dakṣa's daughter and the moon's favorite wife.

Droṇa surrounded by the five Pāṇḍavas shines like the moon in conjunction with the asterism Sāvitra with its five stars (pañcatāreṇa saṃyuktaḥ sāvitreṇe 'va candramāḥ 1.125.30). PW refers to this passage to illustrate the meaning of Sāvitra as "das unter Savitar stehende Nakshatra Hasta." We learn from Bṛhat saṃhitā 98.16 (referred to by PW) that the moon in conjunction with the asterism Sāvitra (= Hasta, among others) is auspicious for undertaking any preparations for a ceremony or vow, etc. (dīkṣāvratamekhalādi). Thus, this simile may serve the double purpose here of indicating both the conjunction of the moonlike Droṇa with the Hasta-like five Pāṇḍavas, and the auspiciousness of the feats of archery undertaken. The five stars of which the constellation Hasta (= hand) consists help to render this simile perfect in all details. Cf. section IX.

Duryodhana, surrounded by the auspicious golden lamps, shines like the moon accompanied by the brilliant great planets (śuśubhe candramā yukto dīptair iva mahāgrahaiḥ 6.93.31). We do not know if anything more than brilliance is intended by the great planets in this context. The meaning Saturn or Rāhu (MW) is out of the question in view of the plural number (mahāgrahaiḥ) used.

The attack of Rāhu (the eclipse demon) on the moon is referred to in order to illustrate an attack by the enemy or mental grief. Śini's son attacks Aśvatthāman, as Rāhu attacks the moon in the sky (abhyadravad raṇe drauṇim rāhuḥ khe śaśinaṃ yathā 6.97.42; cf. 6.97.53; 106.35). Damayantī, perturbed by the pangs of separation from her

[3] Emeneau, "Notes on Śrīharṣa's Naiṣadhacarita," *University of California Publications in Semitic Philology* (Semitic and Oriental Studies Presented to William Popper), XI (1951), 101–102.

husband, is likened to the full-moon night in which the moon is eclipsed by Rāhu (paurṇamāsīm iva niśāṃ rāhugrastaniśākarām 3.65.13).

The moon accompanied by a mere fragment of cloud symbolizes a beautiful face or facial object in certain situations.

Lakṣmaṇa envies those who will at the time of coronation see Rāma's face, full of bits of *kuśa*-grass, fried rice, and the *śamī*, looking like the moon covered with fragments of cloud (drakṣyanty āryasya dhanyā ye Xuśalājaśamīlavaiḥ / abhiṣiktasya vadanaṃ somaṃ sābhralavaṃ. yathā 3.263.30). The mole on Damayantī's forehead, covered with dirt, like the moon covered with a little cloud, was made by the creator as a sign for her prosperity (malena saṃvṛto hy asyās tanvabhreṇe 'va candramāḥ / cihnabhūto vibhūtyartham ayam dhātrā vinirmitaḥ 3.66.6).

Different colors of clouds illustrate different situations. Damayantī, endowed with the quality of beauty and grace, worthy of decoration, (but) not decorated, is likened to a new crescent moon in the sky, covered with black cloud (rūpaudāryaguṇopetāṃ maṇḍanārhām amaṇḍitām / candralekhām iva navāṃ vyomni nīlābhrasaṃvṛtām 3.65.16). Indra with his white umbrella shines like the moon in the neighborhood of a white cloud (śuśubhe tārakārājaḥ sitam abhram ivā 'sthitaḥ 3.42.4).

But the mole on Damayantī's forehead, with dirt removed, shines like the moon in a cloudless sky (damayantyās tadā vyabhre nabhasī 'va niśākaraḥ 3.66.10).

Damayantī, meeting Nala after a long separation, devoid of affliction, shines as the night shines with the rising moon (sai 'vaṃ sametya vyapanītatandrī śāntajvarā harṣavivṛddhasattvā / rarāja bhaimī samavāptakāmā śītāṃśunā rātrir ivo 'ditena 3.75.27).

Bhīṣma, with his lofty banner made of silver on his great chariot, the banner with its device of a palmyra and five stars, shines like the moon with Mt. Sumeru (babhau bhīṣmas tadā rājaṃś candramā iva meruṇā 6.44.48).

King Kalmāṣapāda fills his kingdom with wealth as the moon when risen fills the sky with the cool rays in autumn (sa hi tāṃ pūrayām āsa lakṣmyā lakṣmīvatāṃ varaḥ / ayodhyāṃ vyoma śītāṃśuḥ śaratkāla ivo 'ditaḥ 1.168.18).

The mole on Damayantī's forehead, covered with dirt, does not shine very much, like the crescent of the moon, dim because it is the first day of the month (pratipatkaluṣe 've 'ndor lekhā nā 'tivirājate 3.66.7).

A child's growth is likened to the moon's growth in the bright (i.e., waxing) half of the lunar month (sa cā 'pi vavṛdhe bālaḥ śuklapakṣe yathā śaśī 1.213.64; cf. 1.44.16: 3.292.1).

A child (e.g., Abhimanyu) is lovable to his parents and other kinsmen as the moon is to all creatures (dayito vasudevasya bālyāt prabhṛti cā 'bhavat / pitṛṇāṃ cai 'va sarveṣāṃ prajānām iva candramāḥ 1.213.63).

The following are examples of the moon illustrating moralistic ideas:

pāpaṃ cet puruṣaḥ kṛtvā
kalyāṇam abhipadyate /
mucyate sarvapāpebhyo
mahābhrair iva candramāḥ // 3.198.52.

If one has recourse to a virtuous path even after committing sins, he is released from all sins as the moon is released from massive clouds.

brāhmaṇebhyo dadad grāmān
gās ca rājan sahasraśaḥ /
mucyate sarvapāpebhyas
tamobhya iva candramāḥ // 3.34.76.

One who gives gifts to the Brāhmaṇas is released from all sins as the moon is released from darkness.

VII. PLANETS (GRAHA)

1. Planets in General

The planets, in general, symbolize terror and war.

The wicked planets (Krūragraha).—Bhīma surrounded by his Kaurava brothers shines like the sun surrounded by the great wicked planets at the time of the destruction of creatures (prajāsaṃharaṇe sūryaḥ krūrair iva mahāgrahaiḥ 6.73.10).

Draupadī's sons attack the demon as the five planets attack the sun (rākṣasaṃ dudruvuḥ sarve grahāḥ pañca yathā ravim 6.96.35). Cf. section V.

A demon harassed by the five sons of Draupadī in battle is likened to the moon surrounded by a group of five planets at the time of the destruction of the world (vīryavadbhis tatas tais tu pīḍito rākṣasottamaḥ / yathā yugakṣaye ghore candramāḥ pañcabhir grahaiḥ 6.96.36). PW cites another passage (te 'pīḍayan bhīmasenaṃ . . . prajāsaṃharaṇe rājan somaṃ sapta grahā iva 7.112.22) where warriors harassing Bhīma are likened to the seven planets attacking the moon at the destruction of the creatures.

So far as the above five planets are concerned, they are the five 'star-planets' (tārāgrahas) that are auspicious when in a favorable position (cf. Ragh. 3.13), and inauspicious (krūra) when in an unfavorable one.

Varāhamihira shows in his chapter on planetary conflicts (Grahayuddhādhyāya XVII) how the planets fight among themselves in different situations and what the consequences are for human life. In the above passages, the conflict between the moon or the sun on the one side, and the five star-planets, Mars (Maṅgala), Mercury (Budha), Jupiter (Guru), Venus (Śukra), and Saturn (Śani) on the other, is referred to as an *upamāna* of one prominent warrior being attacked by many others. The two lesser planets, Dragon's Head (Rāhu) and Dragon's Tail (Ketu), may be added to the list in order to explain the passage quoted from PW above. Cf. section VI.

The same figure holds good in the passages where warriors in general are likened to the planets in the firmament (grahā iva nabhastale 6.53.30; 68.19; cf. 3.22.24; 111.9; 216.10: 6.18.8; 42.22; 67.27). As there is no mention of an object of attack, the sun or the moon is not referred to.

2. Specific Planets

a) Mars and Mercury (Maṅgala-Budha).—Cedirāja and Bāhlīka, enraged, fight together like Mars (Aṅgāraka) and Mercury (Budha) (samīyatūḥ susaṃkruddhāv aṅgārakabudhāv iva 6.43.38).

b) Venus (Śukra).—The Pāṇḍavas cannot look at Bhīṣma with his white steed and white bow, looking like the rising planet Venus (śvetagraha = Śukra) (na śekuḥ pāṇḍavā draṣṭuṃ śvetagraham ivo 'ditam 6.78.12).

c) Venus and Mars (Śukra-Maṅgala).—The encounter of Saindhavaka and Drupada arouses delight in the spectators, like that between Venus and Mars (īkṣitṛprītijananaṃ śukrāṅgārakayor iva 6.43.54).

d) Mercury and Venus (Budha-Śukra).—Droṇa and Arjuna fight together as Mercury and Venus fight in the firmament (tato droṇaś ca pārthaś ca sameyātāṃ mahāmṛdhe / yathā budhaś ca śukraś ca mahārāja nabhastale 6.97.57).

e) Saturn (Śanaiścara).—A demon coming near Sīta is likened to Saturn (Śanaiścara) coming near Rohiṇī (sa tasyās tanumadhyāyāḥ samīpe rajanīcaraḥ / dadṛśe rohiṇīm etya śanaiścara iva grahaḥ 3.264.6; cf. sections VI and IX).

f) Mercury and Saturn (Budha-Śanaiścara).—Citrasena and Abhimanyu come together to fight like Mercury and Saturn (samāgatau tau tu raṇe mahāmātrau vyarocatām / yathā divi mahāghorau rājan budhaśanaiścarau 6.100.20).

It may be interesting to note that neither the sun nor the moon is ever shown as attacking any other planet, although it is possible according to Varāhamihira. The absence of Jupiter (Guru), from the list of fighting planets in similes is not accounted for. *Vide* section V.

VIII. COMET (DHŪMAKETU)

Arjuna's banner, raised, is likened to a comet (dhūmaketum ivo 'tthitam 6.67.3). Saturn (grahas tīvro = Śanaiścara) in the constellation of the Kṛttikās by his brilliance takes away their beautiful appearance as a comet would (kṛttikāsu grahas tīvro nakṣatre prathame jvalan / vapūṃṣy upaharan bhāsā dhūmaketur ivo 'tthitaḥ 6.3.26). This forms a part of the description of the indications of the coming Mahābhārata war; cf. Br. saṃ. 11.39–40 (tribhāgaśeṣāḥ prajāḥ Kurute, i.e., the comet, coming closer to the constellation of the Kṛttikās, destroys two-thirds of population). The fact that Saturn's appearance among the Kṛttikās has been likened to that of a comet shows that the latter was more famous as an indication of impending destruction than the former.

IX. CONSTELLATION AND STARS (NAKṢATRA, TĀRĀ)

The asterisms or stars symbolize charm and brilliance.

The faces of the kings attending Damayantī's Svayaṃvara shine like the stars in the sky (mukhāni rajñāṃ śobhante nakṣatrāṇi yathā divi 3.54.7). The Pāṇḍava army shines like the night shining with stars (śuśubhe pāṇḍavī senā nakṣatrair iva śarvarī 6.71.26; cf. 1.190.8: 6.71.27; 92.75).

In one passage, the immortality of the stars is referred to. The Pāṇḍavas are not destroyed any more than the multitudes of stars in the sky (yena kṣayaṃ na gacchanti divi tārāgaṇā iva 6.61.5).

The stars also symbolize innumerability. Gaya's gifts to the priests are as innumerable as the stars in the sky (yathā vā divi tārakāḥ 3.121.9; *vide* section XII).

The poet's minute observation may be seen in the description of conch shells under the water which look like stars covered by a thin cloud at night (śankhānāṃ ca sahasrāṇi magnāny apsu samantataḥ / dṛśyante sma yathā rātrau tārās tanvabhrasaṃvṛtāḥ 3.166.4; cf. 3.66.6; 263.30).

Among the specific asterisms, only Rohiṇī appears in isolation, as a symbol of charm and love (cf. section VI). Lopāmudrā is a brilliant girl like Rohiṇī in heaven (āste tejasvinī kanyā rohiṇī 'va divi prabho 3.94.24). Sudeva looks forward to the day when Damayantī will meet Nala as the asterism Rohiṇī comes closer to the moon (kadā nu khalu duḥkhasya pāraṃ yāsyati vai śubhā / bhartuḥ samāgamāt sādhvī rohiṇī śaśino yathā 3.65.21). It may be mentioned in this connection that among the 27 asterisms personified as the moon's wives, Rohiṇī is mythically regarded as his favorite one. Cf. sections I,3 (tārāmṛga) and VI (viśākhā).

X. THE EARTH (PṚTHIVĪ)

The earth is primarily the standard of patience, endurance, and forgiveness, e.g., Duḥṣanta is like the earth in endurance (sahiṣṇutve dharāsamaḥ 1.62.13; cf. 1.94.12: 3.222.39; 278.15: 6.14.8). Again, if there were no earthlike patient people, there would be no peace among men; for war originates from anger (yadi na syur manuṣyeṣu kṣamiṇaḥ pṛthivīsamāḥ / na syāt saṃdhir manuṣyāṇāṃ krodhamūlo hi vigrahaḥ 3.30.25; cf. 3.30.31).

The productive earth is the *upamāna* for a wife:

damayanty api bhartāram
avāpyā 'pyāyitā bhṛśam /
ardhasaṃjātaśasye 'va
toyaṃ prāpya vasuṃdharā // 3.75.26.

Also, Damayantī was exceedingly delighted when she had recovered her husband, like the earth with crops half-grown on getting a shower.

A clod of earth symbolizes physical immobility and, consequently, spiritual tranquillity. The wise Cyavana, practising penance, is covered all over with ants, like a clod of earth (immobile and calm):

tathā sa saṃvṛto dhīman
mṛtpiṇḍa iva sarvaśah 3.122.4.

Cf. ABHS 6, between verses 8–9 (mae vi mippiṇḍabuddhiṇā taha ebba gahīdam), where the clod of earth symbolizes stupidity.

XI. SKY (ĀKĀŚA)

The sky symbolizes, primarily, brightness. A clear lake or sharp swords are thus likened to the sky (ambaraprakāśam 1.19.16–17; vimalāmbarasaṃnibhaḥ 6.83.29).

The autumn sky is regarded as the most picturesque. The battlefield strewn with bright armor, flags, and umbrellas shines like the sky in autumn (vikīrṇaiḥ kavacaiś citrair dhvajaiś chatraiś ca māriṣa / śuśubhe tad raṇasthānam śaradī 've nabhastalam 6.55.15; cf. 3.275.20).

The army, thronging with chariots, elephants, and infantry, is likened to the sky when the clouds of the rainy season have dispersed and the signs of autumn are not yet fully developed (rathair nāgaiḥ padātaiś ca śuśubhe 'tī 'va saṃkulā / vyapetābhraghane kāle dyaur ivā 'vyaktaśāradī 3.240.43). The *tertium comparationis* is not very clear.

The sky symbolizes expansiveness and detachment also. The Niṣādas blinded by the clouds of dust raised by the wind entered the wide open, immeasurable mouth of Garuḍa as birds in great affliction by thousands ascend to the sky when the forest has its trees shaken by a great wind (tadānanaṃ vivṛtam atipramāṇavat samabhyayur gaganam ivā 'rditāḥ khagāḥ / sahasraśaḥ pavanarajobhramohitā mahānilapracalitapādape vane 1.24.13). Though present everywhere, the sky, on account of its subtlety, is not attached to anything. So the Soul, though covering every part of the body, is not attached to it (yathā sarvagataṃ saukṣmyād ākāśaṃ no 'palipyate / sarvatrā 'vasthito dehe tathā 'tmā no 'palipyate // 6.35.32).

XII. CLOUD (MEGHA)

Cloud occurs as an *upamāna* in at least 158 passages in this corpus. *Megha*, *ambuda*, *jalada*, *toyada*, *parjanya*, *jīmūta*, *abhra*, *balāhaka*, and *stanayitnu* are the synonyms used.

The great noise and deep sound of the thundercloud seem to be the primary connotations of this figure, e.g., babhūvā 'tra mahāghoṣo mahāmegharavopamaḥ (i.e., there was a great noise like the sound of the massive cloud); cf. 1.16.18; 125.6; 185.11; 215.16; 217.22; 219.36: 3.12.9; 13.28; 41.3; 42.3,16; 71.4; 126.40; 162.4; 166.8; 214.22; 252.17: 6.42.11,13; 43.6; 45.47; 55.52,54; 65.27; 66.11; 78.9; 89.6,33; 91.21; 92.14; 96.14,20,25; 98.33; 99.26; 102.43,45; 107.48. The chariot, the elephant, the army, the bow, arrows, and a roaring person—all make noise like the cloud.

Damayantī is, however, pining to hear the nectar-like voice of the king of Niṣadha, smooth and deep like the sound of a cloud (kadā nu snigdhagambhīraṃ jīmūtasvanasaṃnibham / śroṣyāmi naiṣadhasyā 'haṃ vācam tām amṛtopamām 3.61.54; cf. 1.96.7; 126.8; 176.33: 3.297.21). Thus, the cloud sometimes symbolizes loudness, sometimes deepness of sound.

When the thundercloud is accompanied by *dundubhi* (a kind of drum) or a peacock (barhin), the loudness of the noise is intensified. Thus, Baladeva roars like the cloud and the drum (meghadundubhinisvanaḥ 3.42.35; cf. 1.212.32).

The cloud sometimes symbolizes a huge, massive substance. Mt. Mandara, covered with creepers, is decorated with peaks like pinnacles of cloud (tato 'bhraśikharākārair giriśṛṅgair alaṃkṛtam / mandaraṃ parvatavaraṃ latājālasamāvṛtam 1.16.1; cf. 1.17.24; 28.21; 102.8; 140.2; 199.31: 3.12.68; 155.36; 174.2; 221.59; 255.17; 268.6: 6.6.13). An army (e.g., vyūhaṃ mahāmeghasamam 6.56.7) a cloud of dust (e.g., mahābhrasadṛśaṃ rajaḥ 6.67.17), an army of elephants (e.g., gajānīkaṃ ca saṃprekṣya meghavṛndam ivo 'dyatam 6.87.13), and a stalwart king (e.g., Bhīma's warrior friend Nīla, nīlam abhracayopamam 6.90.34), are each likened to a massive cloud.

The white cloud, particularly the autumn cloud (śaradabhra), symbolizes white splendor. White-complexioned Baladeva is likened to a spotless cloud (nirmalatoyadābho 1.180.22; cf. 3.43.6). Silver ores look like an autumn cloud (śaradabhraghanopamaḥ 3.155.79; cf. 1.216.8: 3.267.11: 6.17.28).

Similarly, a huge, dense forest is likened to a black cloud (nīlameghanibhaṃ mahat 1.142.5; cf. 3.40.12; 42.25: 6.50.84; 90.27).

Various kinds of minerals look like white or black clouds (sitāsitābhrapratimā 3.155.82). Caves of red arsenic shine like a mass of evening clouds (manaḥśilāguhāś cai 'va saṃdhyābhranikaropamāḥ 3.155.81; cf. 1.219.5: 6.112.130).

When the cloud is accompanied by a mountain, it adds to the hugeness of an object. Thus Kabandha, the demon, looks like a cloud and a mountain (meghaparvatasaṃkāśam 3.263.25; cf. 3.221.32: 6.44.24; 99.26).

Shining snakes, herds of mad elephants, and the warrior shooting showers of arrows, all look like massive showering clouds (varṣanta iva jīmūtāḥ 1.3.139; cf. 3.118.7; 150.19; 154.47; 268.38: 6.15.14; 50.20; 54.24; 59.22; 67.6; 70.4; 96.1). Warriors fill Arjuna with showers of arrows, as the cloud fills a pond with showers of rain (taḍāgam iva dhārābhir yathā prāvṛṣi toyadaḥ 6.77.37). Warriors shower forth showers of arrows, as the clouds shower forth rain on the mountain (vavarṣuḥ śaravarṣeṇa varṣeṇe 'vā 'drim ambudāḥ 1.96.21; cf. 6.43.47; 49.25; 58.12; 58.37; 70.19; 73.41; 75.25; 78.40; 81.5; 87.30; 89.4; 90.16; 91.34; 92.20; 92.29; 102.71). One who would defeat Bhīṣma is likened to a cloud extinguishing a forest fire by its showers (dāvāgniṃ jalado yathā 6.46.23).

A warrior covering his enemy with arrows is likened to a cloud covering the sun (meghā iva divākaram 6.112.87; 113.48; yathā megho divākaram 6.82.5; 97.49; cf. 6.43.48; 60.38; 78.5; 79.43; 80.50). A brilliant warrior seated on the back of an elephant or surrounded by warriors or elephants is also compared to the sun in the midst of or surrounded by a cloud or clouds (meghastha iva bhānumān 6.17.35; cf. 6.60.42; 96.38; 98.31; 101.1). *Vide* section V.

A cloud accompanied by lightning is a standard of expansiveness and brilliance. Indraprastha, heaven-like, shines like a rising massive cloud covered with lightning (tat triviṣṭapasaṃkāśam indraprastham vyarocata / meghavṛndam ivā 'kāśe vṛddhaṃ vidyutsamāvṛtam 1.199.35).

Flames of fire surrounding Mt. Mandara look like lightning surrounding the black cloud (vidyudbhir iva nīlābhram āvṛṇon mandaraṃ girim 1.16.22; cf. 1.3.139; 26.24: 3.62.23: 6.56.5; 67.4). Draupadī illuminates her part of the forest as lightning illuminates a black cloud (bhrājayantīṃ vanoddeśaṃ nīlābhrām iva vidyutam 3.248.9). Arjuna with his golden armor and missiles looks like the evening cloud accompanied by the sun, the rainbow, and lightning (sārkaḥ sendrāyudhataḍit sasandhya iva toyadaḥ 6.77.37).

A brilliant warrior, missiles, elephants, and an army are each likened to a cloud or clouds accompanied by lightning (meghā iva savidyutaḥ 6.16.25; 18.5; 87.14; 89.32; savidyud iva toyadaḥ 3.146.40). The gilded bow of Abhimanyu, roaming about in all directions, shines like lightning shining amidst clouds (hemapṛṣṭham dhanuś cā 'sya dadṛśe carato diśaḥ / toyadeṣu yathā rājan bhrājamānāḥ śatahradāḥ 6.96.12).

The Kauravas shake their great bows as clouds cause lightning flashes to dart (mahācāpāni dhunvanto jaladā iva vidyutaḥ 6.42.7).

Lightning in the midst of a cloud sometimes symbolizes yellow color amidst dark color. Sītā's yellow garment falls among the monkeys, and looks like lightning amidst a cloud (tat teṣāṃ vānarendrāṇām papāta pavanoddhutam / madhye supītam pañcānāṃ vidyun meghāntare yathā 3.263.9; cf. 6.55.88; 76.17; 102.57).

Lightning from a cloud symbolizes the suddenness or sharpness of a flight of missiles or the fall of a flag, e.g., the flag suddenly falls down from the chariot, as lightning darts from the cloud (papāta sahasā bhūmau vidyuj jaladharād iva 6.75.14; cf. 6.83.28; 114.29).

In one passage, lightning in a cloud stands as a comparison for invisibility, e.g., the girl suddenly becomes invisible before the kings like lightning hiding itself amidst clouds (saudāminī 'va sā 'bhreṣu tatrai 'vā 'ntaradhīyata 1.160.39).

Lightning and cloud mixed together symbolize brown color. Thus, the sage's twisted locks of hair are likened to lightning and cloud (vidyudambhoruhanibhā jaṭās tasya mahātmanaḥ 3.39.24).

The demon Kirmīra biting his lips with his teeth, with red coppery eyes, with his hair flaming, shines like a cloud accompanied by the sun's rays, a wheel of lightning, and a row of cranes (daṣṭoṣṭhadaṃṣṭraṃ tāmrākṣaṃ pradīptordhvaśiroruham / sārkaraśmitaḍiccakraṃ sabalākam ivā 'mbudam 3.12.8). This presents the most complex cloud imagery in this corpus. Cf. sections V, XIII, XXVII, 9, and chapter 9,A,I,3.

The clouds also represent that which is long awaited. The Pāṇḍavas await Arjuna as those (farmers, etc.) desirous of rain await the cloud (pratīkṣāmo 'rjunaṃ vīraṃ varṣakāmā ivā 'mbudam 3.84.18).

The broken cloud symbolizes destruction. Arjuna is curious to know if one fallen from the yogic path does not perish like a broken cloud (kaccin no 'bhayavibhraṣṭaś chinnābhram iva naśyati 6.28.38; cf. 3.221.46; 263.6).

Gaya's gifts to the priests are as innumerable (asaṃkhyeya) as the showers of the rain cloud (yathā vā varṣato dhārā 3.121.9). *Vide* section IX.

A sudden inrush is compared to clouds impelled by the wind. The mahoutless elephants rushed into battle like clouds impelled by the wind (meghā vātahatā iva 6.50.79). Cf. section XIV.

Interdependence of two objects is compared to that of the cloud and the ocean. Thus, virtue and wealth are described as originating from one another, as the cloud and the ocean originate from one another (itaretarayonī tau viddhi meghōdadhī yathā 3.34.29). Cf. section XV.

XIII. LIGHTNING (VIDYUT)

As in association with the cloud (section XII), so in isolation, lightning primarily symbolizes brilliance and charm. Damayantī, Lopāmudrā, and Sukanyā are each likened to lightning from the cloud (vidyut saudaminī yathā 3.50.12; 94.19; 123.6). Sukanyā is also described as a girl like moving lightning (carantīm iva vidyutam 3.122.10).

Chariots and missiles also shine like lightning (vidyutprabha- 3.161.17: 6.55.109).

Ṛśyaśṛṅga views the ornament appearing on the false brahmacarin's neck as something shining like lightning in the space between heaven and earth (vibhrājate vidyud ivā 'ntarikṣe 3.112.3).

Lightning serves in this corpus as a standard of *cañcalatā* in the sense of 'trembling' and motion, not in the sense of 'inconstancy or fickleness,' as in the works of later writers; e.g., Mada's tongue, which repeatedly licks his lips, is described as restless and trembling like lightning (vidyuccapalalolayā 3.124.23). Contrast Bhāravi, Kirātārjunīya 2.19 acirāṃśuvilāsacañcalā . . . lakṣmīḥ . . ., i.e., wealth, fickle like a lightning flash.

Hanumān (the monkey god) is difficult to look at, (brownish) red, and all-trembling like a lightning flash (vidyutsaṃghātaduṣprekṣyaṃ vidyutsaṃghātapiṅgalam / vidyutsamghātasadṛśaṃ vidyutsaṃghātacañcalam 3.146.65). *Vide* chapter 10,V,2,A.

XIV. THE WIND (VĀYU)

The wind primarily symbolizes speed. Warriors, horses, she-mules (aśvatarī), chariots, monkeys, and others moving speedily are likened to the wind. The number of passages describing horses with this simile is, however, by far the largest. A favorite terminology for describing horses is vātaraṃhas-, 'having velocity like that of the wind'; 1.215.16: 3.43.7; 69.12,22; 176.50: 6.75.34; 86.4; 92.12; cf. the same terminology occurring in the description of Bhīma, 1.36.19: 3.146.38; of chariots 3.167.7; of monkeys 3.268.23; and of she-mules 1.213.43. Other similar expressions are anilaraṃhasaḥ 3.79.24; vātajava- 3.72.9: 6.86.5; anilopama- 1.133.1; anilaughavega- 3.253.6; vātāyamāna- 6.50.106; 99.28; 112.72; vāyusama- 6.86.23.

Bhīma is further likened to the blowing wind (yaḥ sa vāta ivo 'ddhūto 6.19.8). Warriors (including the sons of the gods born on this earth and the Yakṣas) are described as having speed like the velocity of the wind (vāyuvegasamo jave 1.2.124; 94.12: 3.38.28; 140.7; 153.18; 260.13). The sons of King Saubala charge with force like the momentum of the wind (vāyuvegasamasparśāḥ 6.86.23).

Speed is more emphatically compared to the wind and the mind in a double *upamā*. Thus, running horses are described as having speed like that of the mind and the wind (manomārutaraṃhasaḥ 6.68.27; cf. 1.6.1; 26.6; 216.8: 3.164.35). Cf. section XXXIX.

The wind dispersing clouds is a comparison for a warrior dispersing his enemy. Arjuna disperses many troops as the wind blows away clouds in the sky in the proper season (arjuno vyadhamat kāle divī 'vā 'bhrāṇi mārutaḥ 6.112.62; cf. 1.219.23: 6.58.61; 98.17,32; 110.36).

Similar is the wind shaking or breaking trees or the woods. Bhīma shakes Kirmīra with force, as a terrible wind shakes a tree (dhūnayām āsa vegena vāyuś caṇḍa iva drumam 3.12.59; cf. 6.73.32; 91.48). The armies, because of the noise of conch shells and drums, tremble like woods shaking in the wind (cakampire śankhamṛdaṅganisvanaiḥ prakampitānī 'va vanāni vāyunā 6.42.6; cf. 6.95.52). In this case, trembling motion is the *upamānadharma*.

In one passage, a storm uproots and carries along a tree. Kṛṣṇa goes carrying Arjuna along with him (by the hand) by force as a storm carries along a tree by its velocity (ādāya vegena jagāma viṣṇur jiṣṇuṃ mahāvāta ivai 'kavṛkṣam 6.55.97). Here, the storm appears as a symbol of overpowering might and uncheckable velocity.

Or the wind blows away a heap of cotton. Abhimanyu, dispersing those troops, shines exceedingly like the wind tossing a heap of cotton in all directions (tāny anīkāni saubhadro drāvayan bahv aśobhata / tūlarāśim ivā 'dhūya mārutaḥ sarvatodiśam 6.96.7). Cf. section IV.

The noise of the storm or the wind is a simile for the noise of an army. Thus, at the time of the departure of King Duryodhana with his army, there is an exceedingly great noise like that of a violent storm in the rainy season (tataḥ prayāṇe nṛpateḥ sumahān abhavat svanaḥ / prāvṛṣī 'va mahāvāyor uddhatasya viśāṃ pate 3.229.28).

The wind also symbolizes strength. Thus, Bhīma, the son of the wind, is likened to the wind in might (samīraṇenā 'pi samo balena samīraṇasyai 'va suto balīyān 3.225.15; vāyuvegaparākramaḥ 3.13.81; cf. 1.137.22).

Bhīma makes the earth tremble with his feet, as a *nirghāta*, 'hurricane,' occurring on the full moon and new moon days, makes the earth tremble (kampayan medinīṃ padbhyāṃ nirghāta iva parvasu 3.146.38). According to Varāhamihira, when a wind struck by another rushes upon the earth from the sky, then there is a *nirghāta* (pavanaḥ pavanābhihato gaganād avanau yadā samutpatati / bhavati tadā nirghātaḥ . . . Br. sam. 39.1). We do not know, however, how '*nirghāta*' causes an earthquake. Varāhamihira says nothing more about it except that the direction from which issues the noise of the *nirghāta*, 'hurricane,' terrific and hollow like that of a breaking pot, is destroyed (bhairavajarjaraśabdo yāti yatas tāṃ diśaṃ hanti, Br. sam. 39.5).

The following are examples of the wind symbolizing philosophical concepts:

a) *Absolute freedom:—*

nirmuktaḥ sarvapāpebhyo
vyatītaḥ sarvavāgurāḥ /
na vaśe kasyacit tiṣṭhan
sadharmā mātariśvanaḥ // 1.110.8.

(Pāṇḍu intends to live a life of renunciation where he would be) free from all sins, beyond all snares, not under the subordination of anybody, sharing the characteristics of the wind.

b) *Domination:—*

yathā vāyos tṛṇāgrāṇi
vaśaṃ yānti balīyasaḥ /
dhātur evaṃ vaśaṃ yānti
sarvabhūtāni bhārata // 3.31.28.

As the tips of grass come under the control of the wind, the powerful one, so all the creatures come under the command of God, O descendant of the Bharatas!

c) *Uncertainty:*—

anyathā parivartante
vegā iva nabhasvataḥ 3.31.32.

Things turn out differently from what one expects, like gusts of wind.

d) *Perturbation:*—

indriyāṇāṃ hi caratāṃ
yan mano 'nuvidhīyate /
tad asya harate buddhiṃ
nāvaṃ vāyur ivā 'mbhasi // 3.202.24; cf. 6.24.67.

If mind is subjected to the roving sense organs, it carries away a person's wisdom, as the wind a boat on the water.

e) *Uncontrollability:*—

tasyā 'haṃ nigrahaṃ manye
vāyor iva suduṣkaram 6.28.34.

I think that control of the mind is as difficult of accomplishment as that of the wind.

f) *Omnipresence:*—

yathā 'kāśasthito nityaṃ
vāyuḥ sarvatrago mahān /
tathā sarvāṇi bhūtāni
matsthānī 'ty upadhāraya // 6.31.6.

As the great all-pervading wind always resides in the ether, so all beings reside in Me; understand this!

g) *Impression:*—

śarīraṃ yad avāpnoti
yac cā 'py utkrāmatī 'śvaraḥ /
gṛhītvai 'tāni saṃyāti
vāyur gandhān ivā 'śayāt // 6.37.8.

When the soul (lit. 'the lord') assumes or quits a body, he goes taking along these things (the senses), as the wind blows, taking along odors from their place (i.e., flowers, etc.).

The wind as a figure appears in at least 62 passages in this corpus. *Vāyu*, *vāta*, *anila*, *māruta*, *mātariśvan*, *satataga*, *samīrana*, and *nabhasvat* are the synonyms used. *Nirghāta* occurs in the sense of 'hurricane.'

XV. OCEAN (SAMUDRA)

An ocean primarily symbolizes an unfathomable expanse, deepness, and also richness. A city is decorated with ocean-like moats (sāgarapratirūpābhiḥ parikhābhir alaṃkṛtam 1.199.29). The moon coming out of the ocean is as if equal to the ocean (samāna iva sāgarāt 1.16.33). As the ocean and the Himālayas are both famous as treasuries of gems, so is the (Mahā)-Bhārata a treasury (yathā samudro bhagavān yathā ca himavān giriḥ / khyātāv ubhau ratnanidhī tathā bhāratam ucyate 1.56.27). Draupadī alone knows her husband's treasury, inexhaustible like Varuṇa's ocean, full of treasures (adhṛṣyaṃ varuṇasye 'va nidhipūrṇam ivo 'dadhim 3.222.54). A lake is described as (deep) ocean-like (sa hradaḥ sāgaropamaḥ 6.7.27). The hugeness of the army and its various parts are compared to the ocean (te sene sāgaraprakhye 6.41.6; cf. sāgarapratima- 6.48.2; 78.2; 83.2,5; sāgaropama- 6.83.13,16; samudrakukṣipratimam 6.72.15; 108.36; dvitīyasāgaranibham 3.267.22; *vide* 3.267.13). Duḥṣanta is like an ocean in his imperturbability (deepness or gravity) (akṣubdhatve 'rṇavasamaḥ 1.62.13). The end of grief is as hard to see as is the far shore of an ocean by a man crossing just with his two arms (na hi pāraṃ prapaśyāmi duḥkhasyā 'sya kathaṃ cana / samudrasye 'va mahato bhujābhyāṃ pratarann iva 6.61.8; cf. Br. sam. 2.4).

The prominence of the ocean among bodies of water is referred to; e.g., the Mahābhārata is described as the best of all texts as an ocean is the best among all the bodies of water (hradānām udadhiḥ śreṣṭho 1.1.201).

A dynasty's growth is likened to that of the ocean into which all the streams flow (vardhate tad idam putra kulaṃ sāgaravad yathā 1.103.4).

Surging waves of the ocean in general and those in various situations (e.g., the time of the full moon, the mythical churning of the ocean, or in storms, etc.) are used as a simile for turmoil and uproarious noise. The demons come back to the battlefield like the waves of the ocean (te yuddhe saṃnyavartanta samudrasya yatho 'rmayaḥ 3.170.31). Kārtikeya roars like an ocean (vyanadat sāgaro yathā 3.216.7). With musical instruments being played upon and with the curiosity of the people, an assembly looks disturbed like an ocean (mahārṇava iva kṣubdhaḥ samājaḥ so 'bhavat tadā 1.124.16; cf. 1.25.15; 125.3: 3.220.25). The army of the gods is like the agitated ocean (samuddhūtodadhiprabham 3.216.8; cf. 6.1.23; 50.11; 73.70). The ocean being filled by rivers or being churned in the beginning of creation is a standard of military turmoil (mahodadhim ivā 'pūrṇam āpagābhiḥ samantataḥ

6.72.14; cf. 6.54.30; 96.26; samudrasye 'va mathyataḥ 1.217.13; cf. 6.78.18). For a moment, of the armies fighting and cutting down one another there was a vortex (a whirling motion) as of the confluence of the Gangā and the ocean (āsīd gāñga ivā 'varto muhūrtam udadher iva 6.114.7). Likewise, the ocean on the full-moon day or the new-moon day (parvan) is referred to; e.g., a military array is thick with the troops of great warriors like the ocean at the full moon or the new moon (samudra iva parvaṇi 6.20.19; cf. 6.59.3; 89.11; 92.13; 96.21). The noise of the armies resembles that of the oceans agitated by the wind (babhūva ghoṣas tumulaś camūnāṃ vātoddhutānām iva sāgarāṇām 6.42.7; 95.53).

The ocean of the deluge at the end of the world stands as a comparison for terribleness. Often two oceans agitated (through the wind of destruction) are referred to. Thus, two fighting warriors or armies are likened to two oceans agitated at the time of the destruction of the world (yugāntānilasaṃkṣubdhau mahāvegāv ivā 'rṇavau 1.125.5; dvayoḥ sāgarayor iva 6.1.24; dṛśyete sāgarāv iva 6.16.45 or 6.114.17). The two oceans seem to denote the upper ocean (uttara-samudra) of the air-space (antarikṣa) and the lower ocean (adharasamudra) of the earth (pṛthivī).[4] Cf. RV 10.136.5 ubháu samudrā́v ā́ kṣeti; RV 10.98.5.

The seashore (velā) as related to the sea presents two pictures. One is of restraint and the other is of nontransgression. The seashore restrains the rising waves of the ocean, and the waves do not go above the seashore. Thus, although basically the same, the figurative meaning presents itself in two somewhat different forms. One cannot override the command of the god of death, as the ocean cannot go above the shore (kṛtāntaṃ nā 'ticakrāma velām iva mahodadhiḥ 1.164.8; cf. 1.218.27). But Yudhiṣṭhira and his army restrain the speed of the cavalry of the opponents, as the seashore restrains the pressure of the ocean, swelling, being filled up in the rainy season on the full-moon day (udvṛttasya mahārāja prāvṛṭkālena pūryataḥ / paurṇamāsyām ambuvegam yathā velā mahodadheḥ 6.101.17; cf. 6.59.5; 91.43; 101.27; 104.57; 106.23,27).

Rivers running towards the ocean symbolize speediness, tumult, or turmoil. Yet the ocean receiving these rivers automatically running towards it symbolizes tranquillity and quietude of mind. Thus, warriors about to die enter the mouth of Kṛṣṇa speedily like the rivers running towards the ocean (yathā nadīnaṃ bahavo 'mbuvegāḥ samudram evā 'bhimukhā dravanti / tathā tavā 'mī naralokavīrā viśanti vaktrāṇy abhivijvalanti 6.33.28; cf. 1.29.1). But, he into whom all objects of desire enter as the waters enter the ocean, which is constantly being

[4] *Vide* A. A. Macdonnell and A. B. Keith, *Vedic Index of Names of Subjects* (London, 1912), p. 432.

filled but still has its stability (or foundation) unchanged, he alone attains peace, rather than one longing for the objects of desire (āpūryamāṇam acalapratiṣṭhaṃ samudram āpaḥ praviśanti yadvat / tadvat kāmā yaṃ praviśanti sarve sa śāntim āpnoti na kāmakāmī 6.24.70).

One picture of the relation between a river and the ocean is altogether different from the preceding ones. As the sweet water of the Gaṅgā, the river of the gods, becomes salty because of contact with the saltiness of the ocean, likewise that prowess of Dhṛtarāṣṭra's mighty sons, having come up against the brave sons of Pāṇḍu, becomes of no profit (useless) in the battlefield (gaṅgāyāḥ suranadyā vai svādubhūtaṃ yatho 'dakam / mahodadhiguṇābhyāsāl lavaṇatvaṃ nigacchati // tathā tat pauruṣaṃ rājaṃs tāvakānāṃ mahātmanām / prāpya pāṇḍusutān vīrān vyarthaṃ bhavati saṃyuge 6.79.5–6).

Though of vast expanse, the ocean can be crossed by means of a boat. Likewise, the vast story of the Mahābhārata can be made easily accessible through the Parvasaṃgraha (the summary of the contents) (ākhyānaṃ tad idam anuttamaṃ mahārthaṃ vinyastaṃ mahad iha parvasaṃgraheṇa / śrutvā 'dau bhavati nṛṇāṃ sukhāvagāhaṃ vistīrṇaṃ lavaṇajalaṃ yathā plavena 1.2.243).

The ocean as a figure occurs in at least 62 passages in this corpus. *Sāgara*, *samudra*, *udadhi*, *arṇava*, *makarālaya*, and *lavaṇajala* are the synonyms used.

XVI. LAKE (SARAS)

The following are the passages in which the lake (saras) is used as an *upamāna* in various contexts.

a) vidhvastaparṇakamalāṃ
vitrāsitavihaṃgamām /
hastihastaparikliṣṭāṃ
vyākulām iva padminīm 3.65.14.

(Sudeva saw Damayantī) appearing like a lotus-lake, perturbed, with the leaves and lotuses destroyed, with birds frightened, lashed into confusion by the trunk of an elephant.

b) saraḥ suparṇena hṛtoragaṃ yathā
rāṣṭraṃ yathā 'rājakam āttalakṣmi /
evaṃvidhaṃ me pratibhāti kāmyakaṃ
śauṇḍair yathā pītarasaś ca kumbhaḥ 3.253.5.

Like a lake with its snakes carried away by Garuḍa, like a kingdom full of wealth without a king, the Kāmyaka woods appear to me (i.e., Yudhiṣṭhira) like a pot with all its water drunk by the thirsty.

c) sukhāt sukham anuprāptā
hradād dhradam ivā 'gatā 3.287.25.

Coming from one happiness to another happiness, (you, Pṛthā) have come as if from one lake to another lake.

d) bhīmasenabhayatrastaṃ
sainyaṃ ca samakampata /
kṣobhyamāṇam asambādhaṃ
grāheṇe 'va mahat saraḥ 6.50.80.

The army trembled being frightened for fear of Bhīma, like a big wide lake being disturbed by a crocodile.

XVII. RIVER (NADĪ)

Rivers in general (or the Gaṅgā and/or the Yamunā in particular) primarily symbolize the motion and vastness of an army, e.g., a huge army was moving like the stream of the Gaṅgā (gaṅgaughapratimā rājan prayātā sā mahācamūḥ 3.240.43; cf. 6.19.17; 56.6). Eleven *akṣauhiṇīs* of the Kaurava army appeared like the Gaṅgā amidst the Yamunā (akṣauhiṇyo daśai 'kā ca tava putrasya bhārata / adṛśyanta mahārāja gaṅge 'va yamunāntare 6.18.18).

The Kaurava army, being perturbed by Arjuna, looks like the exceedingly great mouth of a river covered with high waves (since it is agitated) by the Timi fish (mahorminaddhaṃ sumahat timine 'va nadīmukham 6.108.34).

The noise of rivers and their swelling in the rains are also referred to. Sugrīva roars with a sound like that of a stream (nanādau 'ghanibhasvanaḥ 3.264.16). People thrive in Śākadvīpa like rivers in the rainy season (prajās tatra vivardhante varṣāsv iva samudragāḥ 6.12.29).

Draupadī, moving about in the forest with the five Pāṇḍavas, being terrified at Kirmīra's demonical magic, became perturbed like a river situated between five mountains (pañcaparvatamadhyasthā nadī 'vā 'kulatāṃ gatā 3.12.17; cf. Kumārasaṃbhavam 5.85). Cf. section XVI,*a* and chapter 2,I,4.

XVIII. WELL, WATER (UDAPĀNA, JALA)

Water primarily stands as an *upamāna* for soothingness and comfort.

Being burnt by mental agony or suffering from diseases, wise men are glad in the company of their wives as those distressed by the heat of the sun feel relieved in water (hlādante sveṣu dāreṣu gharmārtāḥ salileṣv iva 1.68.49). A soothing word is, likewise, compared to water offered to a thirsty person (pipāsitasye 'va yathā bhavet payas tathā tvayā vākyam idaṃ samīritam 3.281.36).

A fish dying out of water symbolizes a person who has taken no thought for the primary objects of human endeavor. One devoid of virtue and wealth who indulges in pleasure at will surely perishes at the end of his period of indulgence as a fish perishes when water dries up (tasya dharmārthahīnasya kāmānte nidhanaṃ dhruvam / kāmatô ramamāṇasya mīnasye 'vā 'mbhasaḥ kṣaye 3.34.27).

A boat plunged into unfathomable water is a standard of extreme shock and bewilderment. The Kauravas are extremely shocked to see Bhīṣma's death as persons going to the opposite shore get bewildered upon seeing the boat plunged into unfathomable water (agādhe salile magnāṃ nāvaṃ dṛṣṭve 'va pāragāḥ / bhīṣme hate bhṛśaṃ duḥkhān manye śocanti putrakāḥ 6.15.52).

The well (udapāna) amidst a flood of water symbolizes uselessness: Just as much profit as there is in a well when there is a flood of water on all sides, so much (and no more) profit is there for a Brāhmaṇa in all the Vedas when he truly understands (the teaching of the Gīta)[5] (yāvān artha udapāne sarvataḥ saṃplutodake / tāvān sarveṣu vedeṣu brāhmaṇasya vijānataḥ 6.24.46).

XIX. MOUNTAIN (PARVATA)

The mountain primarily symbolizes hugeness as contrasted with the broad expanse of the ocean, e.g., the huge head of a demon is likened to a mountain summit (tac chailaśṛṅgapratimaṃ dānavasya śiro mahat 1.17.7). A huge body is described as like a mountain (mahīdharapratimavapuḥ 1.25.33; cf. 1.26.7; 52.21; 142.16; 152.9; 213.47: 3.25.19; 26.24; 40.14; 149.5; 158.23; 166.19; 185.36; 266.46; 267.45; 271.16: 6.17.33; 55.14; 58.47,49,50; 83.29; 84.12; 88.6; 91.42,73; 92.55; 112.36–7).

Sometimes specific mountains are mentioned in this connection; e.g., the elephant Airāvata (of white color) is described as like Mt. Kailāsa (kailāsam iva śṛṅgiṇam 3.43.36). So is Baladeva (kailāsaśikharopamaḥ 1.212.20). So are great white palaces (kailāsaśikharaprakhyaiḥ 1.176.19; cf. 6.58.30; 90.22).

The following are examples of elephants being compared to mountains in different situations. The primary *upamānadharma* of hugeness is supplemented with various subsidiary elements. One hundred elephants having red spots on their skins look like one hundred mountains having

[5] Edgerton.

golden summits (śataṃ girīṇām iva hemaśṛṅgiṇam 1.190.16). Elephants in rut, decorated with gold nets, shine like shining mountains (dīpyamānā ivā 'calāḥ 6.19.30; cf. 6.96.39; 97.16). An elephant with his shoulders broken falls like a mountain with its slopes broken by the current of the river (ārugṇah sindhuvegena sānumān iva parvataḥ 6.50.37). The battlefield covered with slain elephants looks like the earth covered with fallen mountains (patitair bhūr nagair iva 6.50.51). Slain elephants, again, look like either mountains destroyed by a thunderbolt, or the mountains with their wings cut off (girīn vajrahatān iva 6.58.46; cf. 6.58.45; chinnapakṣā ivā 'drayaḥ 6.89.34). Elephants with their mahouts killed look like summitless mountains (viśṛṅgā iva parvatāḥ 6.89.36). With the elephants trumpeting, the battlefield seemed as if it had mountains being blown like conch shells (dhamyamānair iva 'calaih 6.92.66); the *upamānadharma* is not very clear.

Bhīṣma shines like the Himālayas (śvetaśailaprakāśaḥ 6.20.9). Hanumat's body is like Mts. Vindhya and Mandara (vindhyamandarasaṃnibham 3.149.10). Palaces, again, look like the summits of the Himālayas (himavacchikharair iva 1.176.22).

Sometimes a mountain symbolizes might, e.g., Draupadī gave birth to five auspicious, brave sons who were like five mountains (lebhe pañca sutān vīrān śubhān pañcā 'calān iva 1.213.71; cf. 1.126.17). Duryodhana and Bhīma, ready to fight with their maces, look like two mountains with one peak (ekaśṛṅgāv ivā 'calau 1.124.25). This one peak probably refers to the customary joining of the two raised maces in the beginning of the encounter.

A warrior's resistance to his opponent's attacks is compared to the firm endurance of a mountain, and sometimes specific names (Maināka, etc.) are mentioned in this connection (tasthau girir ivā 'calaḥ 1.179.14; 181.4: 3.11.23; 40.27; 157.39; 230.25; 255.19: 6.49.11; 88.12; 90.21; bhidyamāna ivā 'calaḥ 6.48.26; 74.7; 79.33,48; himavān iva niścalaḥ 3.17.13; 270.2; 284.10; merur ivā 'calaḥ 6.59.8; 74.24; cf. 3.23.39; 40.2; maināka(m) iva parvata(m) 3.12.15: 6.43.64; 45.19; 88.23). The mountain's endurance of earthquakes (kṣitikampa 6.114.42), showers of rains (toyavṛṣṭi 6.98.15; cf. Tulasi, Rāmacaritamānasa 4.14.2, for its converse), and showers of stones (śilāvarṣaṃ 3.40.34) are also referred to in similar situations.

Vasiṣṭha, however, bears the grief of his sons' death as a great mountain sustains the earth (dhārayām āsa taṃ śokaṃ mahādrir iva medinīm 1.166.39); cf. *Epic Myth.*, p. 79. There is the story of Indra cutting off the wings of the mountains and with the mountains pinning down and making firm the earth, which previously had been unstable. That is what is meant by such synonyms for a mountain as *mahīdhara*, *bhūdhara*, etc. Thus, *dhārayām āsa* is a good example of paronomasia (śleṣa) too.

Warriors ready to fight, surging waves of the ocean, and elephants in rut are compared to moving mountains (e.g., caladbhir acalair iva 6.19.24; jaṅgamāḥ parvatā iva 6.17.17; calanta iva parvatāḥ 3.166.2: 6.19.31; 47.33; pādacārī 'va parvataḥ 1.126.2).

The splitting mountain symbolizes the loud, uproarious noise of arms, etc.; e.g., of bows resounding, of bowstrings being twanged, loud was the uproar like that of the splitting mountains (mahān samabhavac chabdo girīṇām iva dīryatām 6.55.6; cf. 6.55.8; 82.22; 88.27; 89.26).

The noise of falling heads, arms, and the like is compared to that of a shower of stones (aśmavṛṣṭir ivā 'bhāti 3.234.14; cf. 6.58.39; 66.6).

Mt. Meru or Mt. Mandara in conjunction with massive clouds, high summits, or the sun is the standard of ornamentation. Thus, a warrior with a garland shines like Mt. Malaya decorated with wreaths of cloud (śrīmān iva mahāśailo malayo meghamālayā 3.264.34). Aśvatthāman, with three arrows piercing his head, shines like Mt. Meru with three lofty golden summits (śikharaiḥ kāñcanamayair merus tribhir ivo 'cchritaiḥ 6.78.26; cf. 6.106.33). A mountain with auspicious woods, graced by a warrior (Kārtikeya), shines like Mt. Mandara with charming caves, accompanied by the sun having bright rays (ādityene 'vā ṃśumatā mandaraś cārukandaraḥ 3.220.22).

Sometimes, the permanent relationship between Mt. Meru and the light of the sun is referred to. Draupadī, with her sense of virtue, did not divorce the Pāṇḍavas as the light of the sun never leaves Mt. Meru (na jahau dharmataḥ pārthān merum arkaprabhā yathā 3.80.4).

Mt. Kailāsa and Mt. Meru are also the standards of excellent abodes or seats. The Pāṇḍavas entered the beautiful house as the Yakṣas enter Mt. Kailāsa (kailāsam iva guhyakāḥ 1.134.12). The ladies ascend the platforms at a contest of arms as the divine ladies ascend Mt. Meru (meruṃ devastriyo yathā 1.124.14).

Each of the remaining *upamānas* involving mountains depends upon a different image. Thus, big crocodiles in a river are likened to mountains submerged in water (jale magnā ivā 'drayaḥ 3.165.3). The demons with their bodies besmeared with blood look like the summits of mountains colored with red minerals (adrīṇām iva kūṭāni dhāturaktāni śerate 1.17.14; cf. 3.22.8; 213.9: 6.74.28; 89.35; 91.41). Two warriors covered with dust look like two mountains covered with fog (vibhrājetāṃ yathā śailau nīhāreṇā 'bhisaṃvṛtau 1.142.16). Soma's chariot shines like a mountain and cloud (nagameghapratīkāśaṃ 1.216.11). The great tree with the Pāṇḍavas, who had come to it to rest, looked like a huge mountain with five leaders of a herd of elephants (mahādrumaḥ epañcabhir ugradhanvibhiḥ . . . mahāgirir vāraṇayūthapair iva 3.25.26). The Kāleyas, gold-armored, iron-bar-weaponed, attacking the gods, look like mountains burning with forest fires (dāvadagdhā ivā 'drayaḥ 3.99.6). The limbs of slain warriors emit blood, as the summits of mountains having excessive rains during the rainy season emit reddish water (prāvṛṣī 'vā 'tivṛṣṭāni śṛṅgāṇī 'va dharābhṛtām 3.168.26; cf. 3.263.4: 6.91.32; 109.26). The demon (Alambusa) with all his limbs pierced with arrows, shines like a mountain covered with blooming *kiṃśuka* trees (puṣpitaiḥ kiṃśukai rājan saṃstīrṇa iva parvataḥ 6.97.15; cf. section XXX,2, Kiṃśuka). Bhīṣma, surrounded by many enemy warriors, shines like a mountain surrounded by black clouds (śailo meghair ivā 'sitaiḥ 6.105.36; cf. 3.154.52: 6.79.31). The curses of the sages directed towards Sunda and Upasunda are not effective as arrows are not effective on rocks (nā 'krāmanti yadā śāpā bāṇā muktāḥ śilāsv iva 1.202.16; cf. Ragh. 2.34). Elephant warriors falling from the backs of the elephants look like mountains falling from the top of a mountain (giriśṛṅgān nagā iva 6.83.34). He who, being prosperous, looks upon his enemies who are in misfortune as one standing on a mountain looks down on the people living on the surface of the earth—what happiness is greater than that? (samastho viṣamasthān hi durhṛdo yo 'bhivīkṣate / jagatīsthān ivā 'dristhaḥ kiṃ tataḥ paramaṃ sukham 3.226.17; cf. Dhammapada 2.8; also chapter 2,I,9). All the kings are inferior to King Janaka as the other mountains are inferior to Mt. Maināka (mainākasye 'va parvatāḥ 3.134.5).

The mountain as an *upamāna* occurs in at least 110 passages in this corpus. *Parvata, Śaila, Mahīdhara, vasudhādhara, adri, giri,* and *acala* are the synonyms used.

XX. CATTLE: COW, BULL, OX (GO)

W. Norman Brown summarizes the Vedic use of cattle in similes as follows:

> No symbol of fecundity or maternity or source of nourishment compares in the Veda to the cow. No symbol of virility compares to the bull. Any female at all, whether a deity like Uṣas, or a cosmic element like the waters (āpas) or a human queen or just a beautiful young woman (RV 10.95.6) seems flattered if she is called a cow or compared to a cow or is characterized as a mother of cows (RV 4.52.2). And, of course, a heroic god like Indra or Agni or a human being is gratified to be lauded as a bull.[6]

[6] W. Norman Brown, "The Sanctity of the Cow in Hinduism," *Journal of the Madras University*, XXVIII, No. 2 (1957), 40.

The cow as a mother, however, appears just once in this corpus. Kuntī, with a view to alleviating the trouble of the Brāhmaṇa, hurriedly enters his inner apartment like a cow entering the cow-pen where her calf is tied up (viveśa kuntī tvaritā baddhavatse 'va saurabhī 1.145.18). This, in fact, symbolizes the hurry of a mother running towards her child, and thus Kuntī's motherly affectionate haste in her effort to rescue the Brāhmaṇa family from some impending danger.

Cow's milk symbolizes white color. Thus, white conch shells are likened to cow's milk (śaṅkhāṃś ca gokṣīranibhān 6.42.104; cf. section VI, Moon).

Cattle primarily symbolize weakness. The helpless Pāṇḍavas being chased by Bhīṣma are likened to cattle sunk in the mire (trātāraṃ nā 'dhyagacchanta gāvaḥ paṅkagatā iva 6.102.76; cf. 3.36.7). The Pāṇḍavas' helplessness is again compared to that of cattle troubled by cold (trātāraṃ nā 'dhyagacchanta gāvaḥ śītārditā iva 6.45.58; cf. 6.15.49; 113.7; 114.60). In 6.114.60, the passage kṛntanti mama gātrāṇi māghamāse gavām iva, they (Arjuna's arrows) pierce my (Bhīṣma's) limbs as the cold pierces the vitals of cattle in the month of Māgha (winter), is marked in the critical edition with wavy lines in view of the fact that various commentators have taken it in various ways. Thus, Arjunamiśra takes it as *māgamāṃ segavā iva*, 'as scorpions come out breaking through the stomach of their mother' (māgamā vṛścikī proktā tadapatyāni segavā / vṛścikīṃ mātaraṃ kṛntanti / udarasthāny apatyāni pṛṣṭhaṃ vidārya bahir nirgacchantī 'ty arthaḥ). Vādirāja takes it as *māghamā segavām iva*, 'as a crab breaks open its mother's stomach.' Devabodha, the oldest commentator, however, in his first explanation, in part at least, accepts the reading *māghamāse gavām iva*. Belvalkar in his exegetical note correctly refers to 6.113.7 (yathā hi śaiśiraḥ kālo gavāṃ marmāṇi kṛntati), which goes against any such presumed reading as *māgamām* or *māghamā*.

A similar passage occurs in 12.137.85 as follows:

gṛhasnehāvabaddhānāṃ
narāṇām alpamedhasām /
kustrī khādati māṃsāni
māghamāse gavām iva //

An evil wife eats up the flesh of men of small intelligence who are captivated by domestic affection as the cold pierces the vitals of cattle in the month of Māgha (winter).

It is strange that the editor, in spite of his inclination to adopt the most obvious correct reading, *māghamāse gavām iva*, in 6.114.60, clearly divides the *pāda* d in 12.137.85 as *māghamā segavām iva*. Had he followed Nīlakaṇṭha, he would have *māghamāṃ segavā iva* in both passages (cf. Nīlankaṇṭha's commentary: māghamāṃ karkatīṃ segavās tadapatyāni / karkatyā nāśahetur garbha eve 'ti prasiddham). He seems definitely to have been misled by the speculative attempts of some redactors and commentators to solve the syntactical incongruity involved here. But there is no doubt about the fact that the whole *pāda* of 6.114.60 is repeated in this passage, although it does not quite fit into either of these two contexts. As Bowra would put it, each of these *pādas* is improvised over the formula: yathā hi śaiśirah kālo gavāṃ marmāṇi kṛntati 6.113.7.[7]

Devabodha's afterthought (athavā . . .) and similar speculative interpretation of the other commentators should not compel us to disregard the techniques of oral poetic composition and thus to adopt such speculative readings simply because they fit neatly in the syntax. The fact that each of the presumed words *māghamā* and *segavā*, if adopted, would be *hapax legomenon* in the whole realm of Sanskrit literature renders such speculation still weaker.

Cattle symbolize sexual promiscuity. Thus, the women of all castes were of old not shut up. As do cattle, so did mankind in all their various castes (anāvṛtā hi sarveṣāṃ varṇānām aṅganā bhuvi / yathā gāvaḥ sthitās tāta sve sve varṇe tathā prajāḥ 1.113.14.

The herd of cattle (gokula) mostly stands as a simile for bewilderment. The Kaurava army, bewildered after Bhīṣma's death, is compared to a bewildered herd of cattle without a cowherd (agopam iva co 'dbhrāntam gokulaṃ tad balaṃ mama 6.15.49; cf. 6.55.39; 102.29). In one instance, the herd of cattle is a standard of overpowering might. As the herd of cattle tramples the harvested grain, so Bhīṣma trampled the Pāṇḍava army (dhānyānām iva lūnānāṃ prakaraṃ gogaṇā iva 6.99.3).

The bull as a standard of might and manliness is so common that it forms a part of many of the forms of address of sages or kings (puruṣarṣabha, munipuṃgava, etc.); cf. chapter 2,II.

Two fighting warriors are likened to two fighting ruttish bulls (samadāv iva govṛṣau 1.124.32; cf. 3.12.53: 6.107.34).

The bellowing of bulls is referred to. Thus, Bhīmasena roars like a bull (prāṇadad govṛṣo yathā 6.42.8; cf. 1.96.31: 3.146.61: 6.66.5; 102.58). Sometimes this bellowing is accompanied by horn-wounds on the faces of fighting bulls. Kṛṣṇa and Arjuna, wounded by Bhīṣma's arrows,

[7] *Vide* Emeneau, "Oral Poets of South India: The Todas," *Journal of American Folklore*, LXXI, No. 281 (1958), 312–324.

shine like two bulls bellowing, marked with scratches of horns (govṛsāv iva nardantau viṣāṇollikhitāṅkitau 6.55.60; 102.49). In one instance, wells roar like bulls as a mark of impending destruction of the world (phenāyamānāḥ kūpāś ca nardanti vṛṣabhā iva 6.3.32).

Bulls symbolize grandeur. The Pāṇḍavas entered the marriage assembly as great bulls enter their pens, rejoicing (maharṣabhā goṣṭham ivā 'bhinandinaḥ 1.190.10).

A bull endures showers of rain falling from the sky. So Bhīma endures showers of arrows (yathā hi govṛṣo varṣaṃ saṃdhārayati khāt patat 6.92.31).

A good ox bears a heavy burden and endures heat, cold, etc. So is a disciple always bound to heavy burdens, enduring all unfavorable circumstances such as hunger, etc., and is uncomplaining everywhere (gaur iva guruṣu dhūrṣu niyujyamānaḥ śītoṣṇakṣuttṛṣṇāduḥkhasahaḥ sarvatrā 'pratikūlaḥ 1.3.81).

But a good ox has no tolerance for blows (i.e., even the slightest blow makes him run faster). So Bhīma does not bear Draupadī's fiery speech and instantly sets out for an encounter with the Yakṣa (nā 'mṛṣyata mahābāhuḥ prahāram iva sadgavaḥ 3.157.25).

The various bodily parts are compared to those of a bull. This is especially so with regard to the eyes of kings and their male children. Pāṇḍu is bull-eyed (ṛṣabhākṣam mahābalam 1.105.2; cf. 1.93.14; 105.60; 186.10). Subhadrā gives birth to Abhimanyu, the mighty one, bull-eyed (ṛsabhākṣam arindamam 1.213.59). It is interesting to note that this simile is very extensively used in Homer.

Abhimanyu is further described as bull-shouldered (durdharṣaṃ ṛṣabhaskandham 1.213.68). Arjuna's gait is likened to that of a ruttish bull (ya eṣa mattarṣabhatulyagāmī 1.180.18).

In one passage, the prominence of a bull is shown by contrast; all kings are inferior to King Janaka, as calves are inferior to a bull (sarve rājño maithilasya mainākasye 'va parvatāḥ / nikṛṣṭabhūtā rājāno vatsā anaḍuho yathā 3.134.5).

An ox led by a nose-rope is a standard of fatalism. Thus, man, like an ox led by a nose-rope, follows the command of God, made of Him, dedicated to Him (. . . nasyota iva govṛṣaḥ / dhātur ādeśam anveti tanmayo hi tadarpaṇaḥ 3.31.25).

This figure of cattle occurs in at least 38 passages in the corpus; *go, ṛṣabha, vṛṣabha, anaḍvan,* (*saurabhī* for a cow only) are the synonyms used.

XXI. HORSES (AŚVA)

Horses are very favorite *upamānas* of fickle sense-organs and human emotions, e.g., even a learned man is misled by the deceitful sense organs as a charioteer, bewildered, is misled by excited disobedient horses (hriyate budhyamāno 'pi naro hāribhir indriyaiḥ / vimūḍhasaṃjño duṣṭāśvair udbhrāntair iva sārathiḥ 3.2.62; cf. 3.202.23). One who controls his rising anger as a charioteer controls his horse is regarded as a charioteer by the virtuous persons—not he who simply holds reins (yaḥ samutpatitaṃ krodhaṃ nigṛhṇāti hayaṃ yathā / sa yante 'ty ucyate sadbhir na yo raśmiṣu lambate 1.74.2); cf. chapter 2,I,12, and chapter 7.

XXII. ELEPHANT (GAJA)

The elephant is primarily a figure of might and vitality.

A warrior is described as having might like that of an elephant in must (mattavāraṇavikramaḥ 1.94.4: 6.45.46; 57.27,108.1; cf. 1.47.24; 124.31; 127.31; 213.69: 3.61.51; 146.21,54: 6.22.13; 112.53), like an elephant with temples exuding must-fluid (prabhinna iva vāraṇa[ḥ] 1.180.13: 3.157.29,30,56: 6.48.20; cf. 3.146.15: 6.88.3), like an elephant sixty years old in must (mattāv iva . . . vāraṇau ṣaṣṭihāyanau 1.141.23), like the Himālayan elephant in must (mattā yathā haimavatā gajendrāḥ 1.178.2), endowed with might like that of ten elephants (daśanāgabalānvitaḥ 1.112.12), or having the vitality equal to that of ten thousand elephants (nāgāyutasamaprāṇa- 1.100.9; cf. 1.150.15; 197.17: 3.11.21,25; 297.68; nāgāyutaprāṇa- 1.56.6; cf. 3.175.1,20; 176.3).

To Kṛṣṇa the five Pāṇḍavas look like five *abhipadma*-elephants, a class of elephants having red spots on the skins (pancā 'bhipadmān iva vāraṇendrān 1.178.9).

One elephant or more attacking another elephant or a group of elephants is the standard of attack on the enemy. A warrior attacks his enemy as a must-elephant attacks another must-elephant (matto mattam iva dvipam 6.43.37,60; 77.28; cf. 1.181.5,23: 3.12.48,56; 154.54: 6.74.10; 75.51; 101.19; 107.27). Sometimes an elephant's fight for the sake of a she-elephant is referred to. Karṇa falls upon Arjuna vigorously, as an elephant desirous of fighting for the sake of a she-elephant falls upon the hostile elephant (yuddhārthī vāśitāhetor gajaḥ pratigajaṃ yathā 1.181.7).

An elephant treading upon lotuses or smashing trees or gardens is a standard of devastation. Bhīma plucks up a tree with his two hands and strips off the leaves like an elephant stripping a tree of its leaves (niṣpatrayām āsa yathā gajendraḥ 1.180.15; cf. 141.8: 3.146.43: 6.59.13). Bhagadatta tramples the army of the Pāṇḍavas as a wild elephant wanders treading upon the lotuses in a pool (pāṇḍavīṃ samare senāṃ saṃmamarda sakuñjaraḥ / yathā vanagajo rājan mṛdnaṃś carati padminīm 6.79.41; cf. 6.96.34; 97.28; 103.13).

The elephant as a standard of prominence appears in various forms. Draupadī follows Arjuna as a she-elephant follows a male elephant (nāgaṃ yathā nāgavadhūḥ prahṛṣṭā 1.185.4). Rāma and Arjuna both have a gait like that of a must-elephant (mattamātaṅgagāminam 3.261.9; cf. vāraṇamattagāmī 3.161.15). Arjuna's hand (kara) is like the trunk (kara) of an elephant (nāgarājakaropamaḥ 1.179.9; cf. 1.17.21; 47.24; 140.9: 6.93.27). Sometimes the thighs of a hero or a heroine are likened to the trunks of elephants (ūrū gajakaropamau 3.143.4; cf. 6.92.59). The shoulders of a warrior are often compared to those of an elephant (gajaskandham 1.105.2,60).

The young elephant is often a figure of reddish color. Thus, the fighting monkeys are of reddish color like young elephants (karabhāruṇagātrāṇām 3.268.25).

The elephant shares many of the figures applied to a mountain. Thus, Duryodhana endures a shower of arrows as a great elephant endures rain (yathā varṣaṃ mahādvipaḥ 6.88.1). Arjuna restrains the heat of his anger as a great elephant does his (mahāhastī 'va yacchati 3.36.13). The clouds are massive like the herd of elephants (tato gajakulaprakhyas 3.186.65; cf. 3.186.68). Cf. section XIX.

The hook used to guide an elephant symbolizes the vigor used in wielding a weapon. Thus, a warrior strikes his enemy with weapons, as one hits an elephant with the hook (tottrair iva mahādvipam) 6.57.35; 60.1; 75.16; 97.12; 102.6; 107.7; 109.12; cf. 3.40.38: 6.86.32; 89.5).

King Janaka, even while being goaded, does not listen to Aṣṭāvakra as an elephant sometimes does not listen to the command of the mahout (hastī 'va tvaṃ janaka vitudyamāno na māmikāṃ vācam imāṃ śṛṇoṣi 3.134.28).

The strength of a kingdom devoid of Brāhmaṇas comes to an end as does the strength of a battle elephant without the mahout (kuñjarasye 'va saṃgrāme 'parigṛhyā 'ṅkuśagraham / brāhmaṇair viprahīnasya kṣatrasya kṣīyate balam 3.27.15).

Elephants sunk in mire and elephants afraid of lions are figures of bewilderment (e.g., trātāraṃ nā 'dhyagacchanta paṅke magnā iva dvipāḥ 6.96.8; siṃhabhītā gajā iva 6.87.5). *Vide* section XX.

In one instance, an elephant serves as an *upamāna* of delight. The Pāṇḍavas with Draupadī, and she with them, are exceedingly delighted, as the Sarasvatī river is pleased with elephants and they with it (babhūva paramaprītā nāgair iva sarasvatī 1.205.3).

In the following, three different figures using an elephant are found in one stanza:

mattavāraṇavikrānto
mattavāraṇavegavān /
mattavāraṇatāmrākṣo
mattavāraṇavāraṇaḥ 3.146.31.

Bhīma, having a gait like a must-elephant, endowed with the speed of a must-elephant, having coppery eyes like those of a must-elephant, capable of restraining a must-elephant.[8]

The elephant as an *upamāna* appears in at least 92 passages in this corpus. *Gaja*, *vāraṇa*, *kuñjara*, *mātaṅga*, *nāga*, and *hastin* are the synonyms used.[9]

XXIII. LION (SIṂHA)

The lion is primarily a figure of might, dignity, and pride, both in such metaphors as *narasiṃhānām* (3.39.3) and in the similes (cf. chapter 2,II). Thus, Bhīma, proud as a lion, free from fear and bewilderment, rushes towards the mountain (kesarī 'va yatho 'tsiktaḥ 3.157.29; cf. 1.142.14: 3.36.25; 48.39; 146.15: 6.12.15; 53.26; 75.54; 81.35; 98.3,28). Kings are proud as lions (siṃhadarpa 1.115.26). Karṇa is likened to a maned lion born in the Himālayan forests (himavadvanasaṃbhūtaṃ siṃham kesariṇaṃ yathā 3.292.21). Citrasena's jumping from the chariot is compared to a lion's jumping from a mountain peak (avaplutaḥ siṃha ivā 'calāgrāt 6.81.35). Bhīma and Arjuna in the battlefield appear like two lions, proud of their might, desirous of flesh, roaming about in the midst of cows (āmiṣepsū gavāṃ madhye siṃhāv iva balotkaṭau 6.110.11). Paurava and Dhṛṣṭaketu, fighting with swords, look like two lions striving as to which shall unite with a lioness in heat (vāśitāsaṃgame yattau siṃhāv iva mahāvane 6.112.20; cf. 1.96.31; 181.7; also sections XX and XXII). About the use of the word *vāśitā* in relation to *siṃha*, the editor remarks: "simhāv iva. The S_1 Ko–2 D_1 reading govṛṣau, or the K_3 reading vṛṣau, would suit vāśitā. But the latter word can be used in the general sense of any female in the mating season. It is used of elephants as in 1.124.31; of gazelles and even of women. We have accepted siṃhau, since a change from that to govṛṣau is likely, but not vice versa" (Critical Notes, p. 795). God Hanumat has all the characteristics of both a lion and a tiger (siṃhaśārdūlalakṣaṇaḥ 1.216.13).

[8] Cf. section XX.
[9] *Vide* Edgerton, *The Elephant Lore of the Hindus* (New Haven, 1931).

The lion's roar is the figure of the uproarious challenging noise of a warrior, e.g., the Pañcālas make an uproarious noise like that of a group of lions (praṇeduḥ siṃhasaṃghavat 1.155.46). The phrase *siṃhavad vinadan muhuḥ* alone occurs at least six times (6.55.49; 75.40; 87.9; 97.9; 102.40,54).

The various parts of the body and the gait of a warrior or a king are compared to those of a lion. Thus Pāṇḍu's teeth are like those of a lion (siṃhadaṃṣṭram 1.105.2). Nala and Pāṇḍu are each *siṃhoraska*, 'having a chest like that of a lion' (1.105.6: 3.61.12). Bhīma's shoulders look like those of a lion (siṃhaskandho 1.139.14). A warrior's gait is like that of a lion (e.g., siṃhavikrānta- 1.80.6: 3.13.105; siṃhavikrāntagati- 1.186.10; siṃhavikrāntagāmin- 3.142.8; siṃham iva gacchantam 3.38.19). Bhīma's gait is like that of a lion and of a bull (siṃharṣabhagatiḥ 3.157.26).

A lion's attack on small animals is the standard of a warrior's successful attack on a weak opponent (e.g., siṃhaḥ kṣudramṛgān iva 1.166.38: 3.221.55; siṃhaḥ kṣudramṛgaṃ yathā 1.141.19: 6.92.23).

Bewilderment and fear among the opponents at the sight of a brave warrior are compared to those of small animals at the sight of a lion (e.g., siṃhaṃ kṣudramṛgā iva 6.19.10; siṃhaṃ mṛgagaṇā iva 6.82.19; siṃhasye 'va mṛgā rājan 6.105.13; cf. 6.14.10; 101.23). If the lion has yawning jaws, bewilderment is emphasized (e.g., jṛmbhamāṇaṃ mahāsiṃhaṃ dṛṣṭvā kṣudramṛgā yathā 6.16.43).

The lion is also the standard of persecution and victory. The demon, killed by Bhīma, is compared to a bull killed by a lion (siṃhene 'va gavāṃ patim 3.157.69). Dhṛṣṭadyumna, desirous of killing Droṇa, looks like a lion desirous of meat, running towards a must-elephant (āmiṣārthī yathā siṃho vane mattam iva dvipam 6.49.31; cf. 1.141.11: 6.55.87,126).

The kings entering the assembly of Damayantī's *svayaṃvara* are compared to lions entering a mountain (viviśus te mahārañgaṃ nṛpāḥ siṃhā ivā 'calam 3.54.3). Here, the lion symbolizes grace and prominence.

A lion's cub is used as a figure of the prowess of a warrior, especially a young warrior. Young Abhimanyu encountering five warriors is likened to a lion's cub fighting with five elephants (saṃsaktam atitejobhis tam ekam dadṛśur janāḥ / pañcabhir manujavyāghrair gajaiḥ siṃhaśiśuṃ yathā 6.57.2). The Pāṇḍavas view Bhīṣma roaming about in the battlefield like a lion's cub in the forest coming into the midst of deer (taṃ carantaṃ raṇe pārthā dadṛśuḥ kauravaṃ yudhi / mṛgamadhyaṃ praviśye 'va yathā siṃhaśiśuṃ vane 6.82.18).

A coward attacking the home of a brave person is compared to a wolf entering a lion's den, as when Jayadratha attacks the Pāṇḍava's home in their absence (sa praviśyā 'śramaṃ śūnyaṃ siṃhagoṣṭhaṃ vṛko yathā 3.251.8). Here not the presence, but the temporary absence of the lion constitutes the required figure. This compares in part with Paṇḍitarāja's *anyokti* referring to a lion's sleep in the cave (svapiti girigarbhe haripatiḥ, Bhaminīvilāsa 1.50).

The lion in his den (on his return from the day's tiresome hunting pursuits) symbolizes extreme affliction. Arjuna (with his brothers) exiled, is exceedingly afflicted like a lion in his den (āste paramasaṃtapto nūnam siṃha ivā 'śaye 3.36.12).

The lion occurs in a simile in at least 65 passages in this corpus. Only two synonyms, *siṃha* and *kesarin*, are used.

XXIV. TIGER (VYĀGHRA)

Like the lion, the tiger stands for might, supremacy, persecution, and pride, both in metaphors such as *puruṣavyāghra* and in similes (cf. chapter 2,II). Bhīma kills his opponent as a tiger kills a small animal (vyāghraḥ siṃhaśiśuṃ yathā 3.11.24; cf. 1.166.36: 6.92.33). Sātyaki pierces Śāradvata with arrows as tigers kill an elephant (śārdūla iva kuñjaram 6.97.39). The encounter between Kirmīra and Bhīma was like that between two proud tigers (vyāghrayor iva dṛptayoḥ 3.12.54; cf. 3.255.3: 6.92.21; 93.19). Bhīma makes an uproarious noise like a tiger in the forest (śārdūla iva kānane 6.100.18). Cekitāna chases Bhīṣma as a tiger's cub chases a bull (vṛṣaṃ vyāghraśiśur yathā 6.106.8). An assembly of kings full of tigers among men (i.e., the kings) looks like a mountain cave full of tigers (saṃpūrṇāṃ puruṣavyāghrair vyāghrair giriguhām iva 3.54.5).

The tiger occurs in a simile in at least 11 passages in this corpus. Only two synonyms, *vyāghra* and *śārdūla*, are used.

XXV. SNAKE (SARPA)

The snake primarily symbolizes terror. Arrows and other missiles are compared to snakes (śarāṃś cā 'śīviṣopamān 3.23.2; 40.9; 146.15; 273.20: 6.70.2,9; 78.20; 88.38; cf. 3.17.31; 34.83; 40.16,25: 6.44.21,30; 45.38,60; 50.26; 55.19; 57.9; 69.35; 75.27; 82.9). Sometimes, a characteristic of the snakes is referred to for emphasis. Thus the arrows look like enraged snakes (bhujagaiḥ kopitair iva 6.96.41; cf. 6.68.22; 88.3; 114.58). The sword shines like a shining snake (jvalantam iva pannagam 6.78.33; cf. 6.75.29,45; 78.15; 96.4).

Arrows rubbed with oil shine like snakes that have just cast their skins (tailadhautā vyarājanta nirmuktabhujagopamāḥ 6.92.48). Javelins look like moving snakes (sarpāṇāṃ sarpatām iva 6.88.28). Arrows, again, look like snakes in groups with their mouths open, having a terrible appearance (vyāttānanā bhayakarā uragā iva saṃghaśaḥ 6.83.27). Spears are likened to snakes having two tongues (dvijihvair iva pannagaiḥ 1.199.33). A great spear looks like the daughter of a snake (nāgakanyopamām śubhām 6.100.29; cf. section I,12, Yama's sister). Arrows are again likened to snakes, poison, and fire (sarpaviṣāgnikalpaih 3.120.8).

Also the fellow warriors surrounding a warrior are likened to snakes (āśīviṣasamair vīrair 3.34.81). Bhīṣma on the battlefield is likened to an enraged snake (āśīviṣam iva kruddham 6.105.29; cf. 3.222.34). Warriors, when shot at, are enraged like snakes touched with the feet (pādaspṛṣṭā ivo 'ragāḥ 6.99.6). A warrior cannot bear an insult as a snake cannot bear the touch of the feet (pādasparśam ivo 'ragaḥ 1.212.30). An enraged warrior, breathing hard, is likened to a snake hissing (niḥśvasann iva pannagaḥ 6.88.2; cf. 3.253.22: 6.92.1; 102.65). Bhīṣma full of grief and anger sighs as a snake (hisses) struck by a stick (śvasamāno yathā nāgaḥ praṇunno vai śalākayā 6.94.2). Bhīma is enraged like a snake struck with a stick (daṇḍāhata ivo 'ragaḥ 6.50.67). Duryodhana could not bear Bhīma's blow as a snake cannot bear the noise caused by the palms hit together (nā 'mṛṣyata yathā nāgas tālasábdaṃ samīritam 6.69.20). The son of Sāṃyamani appearing on the battlefield looks like a snake falling from the sky (khāt patantam ivo 'ragam 6.57.26). Bhīṣma with his sharp weapons on the battlefield looks like the terrific *takṣaka*-snake (yathā ghoro mahānāgas takṣako vai viṣolbaṇaḥ 6.103.15). (Bhīma in exile), sighing heavily like a snake with terrific energy, does not sleep at night because of his wrath (viniḥśvasan sarpa ivo 'gratejā dhruvaṃ na śete vasatīr amarṣāt 3.225.13).

A snake entering an anthill or a hole symbolizes an arrow or javelin entering the surface of the earth after hitting the enemy (valmīkam iva pannagaḥ 6.91.46; 112.118; bilam sarpaśiśur yathā 6.97.47; sa śaraḥ paṇḍitaṃ hatvā vivesá dharaṇītalam / yathā naraṃ nihatyā 'śu bhujagaḥ kālacoditaḥ 6.84.24).

Arrows coming out of the pierced bodies of warriors are often compared to snakes coming out of mountains (ñagebhya iva pannagaḥ 3.221.45).

Ascetics have fled for fear of Sunda and Upasunda like snakes fearing the Garuḍa bird (vainateyād ivo 'ragaḥ 1.202.17).

A warrior, intending to restrain his enemy with his might or other devices, is compared to a snake charmer restraining snakes by means of magical chants (mantrair āśīviṣān iva 1.181.3).

A female snake living in a palm tree symbolizes heart-burning. Thus, Sītā, separated from her husband, will let her limbs languish and fade as a female snake living in a palm tree becomes emaciated in body (śoṣayiṣyāmi gātrāṇi vyālī tālagatā yathā 3.264.50). The reference is not very clear.

While she is pining for Rāma, Sītā's well-bound-up, smooth, exceedingly black hair is likened to a black female snake (dadṛśe śvasitā snigdhā kālī vyālī 'va mūrdhani 3.265.25; cf. Vālmiki, Rāmāyaṇa 4.25.9).

A boa is a standard of inaction. A warrior is advised not to sit inactive like a boa (kim āsse pīṭhasarpavat 3.36.21). So Nīlakaṇṭha interprets *pīṭhasarpa*.

The snake god Ananta with his hood symbolizes hugeness. Thus Irāvat takes on a huge form like the snake god having hoods (dadhāra sumahad rūpam ananta iva bhogavān 6.86.67).

The subterranean region full of snakes symbolizes splendor and grandeur. Thus the assembly of kings (Damayantī's *svayaṃvara*) full of elephants looks like the subterranean world full of snakes (tāṃ rājasamitiṃ pūrṇāṃ nāgair bhogavatīṃ iva 3.54.5). So the excellent city of Khāṇḍavaprastha shines with warriors and a white-cloud-like rampart, etc. (nāgair bhogavatī yathā 1.199.30,49).

The five-headed snakes are a comparison for the five-fingered hands. Thus the arms of the kings look like five-headed snakes (pañcaśīrṣā ivo 'ragāḥ 3.54.6). So do Arjuna's two hands (pañcaśīrṣāv ivo 'ragau 3.79.19). Bhīma contracts his fist that looks like a five-headed snake (pañcaśīrṣam ivo 'ragam 3.154.56). This five-headedness of a snake, in fact, presents a picture of smoothness (suślakṣṇatā) and beauty (ākāravattā) of five-fingered hands in at least the first two instances. In Bhīma's fist, however, it symbolizes terror.

Sometimes the serpent as an *upamāna* helps to illustrate moralistic or philosophical ideas.

a) yaḥ samutpatitaṃ krodhaṃ
kṣamaye 'ha nirasyati /
yatho 'ragas tvacaṃ jīrṇāṃ
sa vai puruṣa ucyate // 1.74.4.

He who by means of forbearance in this world casts off rising anger as a snake its old skin is called a real man.

b) mārayaty akṛtaprajñaṃ
bālaṃ kruddha ivo 'ragaḥ 3.206.21.

Anxiety kills an unwise fool as a wrathful snake kills a person.

c) yo 'pakartṝṃś ca kartṝṃś ca
tejasai 'vo 'pagacchati /
tasmād udvijate lokaḥ
sarpād veśmagatād iva 3.29.21.

The man who oppresses his enemies and friends (alike) with his power, people fear him as one fears a snake that has come into the house.

d) yadai 'va bhartā jānīyān
mantramūlaparāṃ striyam /
udvijeta tadai 'vā 'syāḥ
sarpād veśmagatād iva 3.222.11.

The moment a husband should come to know that his wife is interested in spells, he should fear her as one fears a snake that has come into his house.

The snake as a figure occurs at least 69 times in this corpus. *Sarpa*, *bhujaga*, *āśīviṣa*, *pannaga*, *uraga*, *vyāla*, and *nāga* are the synonyms used.

XXVI. OTHER ANIMALS

1. Monkey (Vānara)

All other women look like female monkeys in comparison with beautiful Draupadī (etāṃ dṛṣṭvā striyo me 'nyā yathā śākhāmṛgastriyaḥ 3.251.3).

2. Camel (Uṣṭra)

The Kaurava warriors get bewildered at the sight of Bhīma like camels passing through mud (pravivyathuḥ paṅkagatā ivo 'ṣṭrāḥ 6.22.13).

3. Domestic Animals (Paśu)

Bhīma ties up Kirmīra by both of his arms as one ties an animal with a rope (yoktrayām āsa bāhubhyāṃ paśuṃ raśanayā yathā 3.12.61). Bhīṣma drives before him the Pāṇḍava army as a herdsman drives the flocks (kālayām āsa balavān pālaḥ paśugaṇān iva 6.74.29; cf. 6.58.59; 105.17). *Vide* section XX.

4. Wolf (Vṛka)

As a wolf chases animals, so does Bhīma chase the Kaurava brothers (yathā vā paśumadhyastho drāvayeta paśūn vṛkaḥ / vṛkodaras tava sutāṃs tathā vyadrāvayad raṇe 6.92.34).

5. Boar (Śūkara)

A fool selects bad expressions from the good and bad words that he hears, as a boar selects excrement out of various other edible things available (aśubhaṃ vākyam ādatte purīṣam iva śūkaraḥ 1.69.9).

6. Jackal (Kroṣṭuka)

Sītā's acceptance of Rāvaṇa as her husband, giving up Rāma, would be the same as a female tiger's accepting a jackal as her mate (rāmaṃ bhartāram utsṛjya na tv ahaṃ tvāṃ kathaṃ canā / nihīnam upatiṣṭheyaṃ śārdūlī kroṣṭukaṃ yathā 3.262.39).

7. Deer (Mṛga)

Damayantī, pining for Nala, describes herself as a deer separated from the herd (yūthabhraṣṭām ivai 'kāṃ māṃ hariṇīṃ pṛthulocana 3.61.23). Jamadagni, killed by the kinsmen of Sahasrārjuna, is likened to a deer killed in the forest by arrows (vane mṛga ive 'ṣubhiḥ 3.117.1). Diseases are destroyed by competent physicians as deer are by hunters (mṛgā vyadhair iva 3.200.15). A huge army, if broken, is difficult to control like frightened herds of deer (trastā mṛgagaṇā iva 6.4.28). Sītā is, however, afraid of Rāvaṇa's threats like a helpless Rauhī deer (trastāṃ rauhīm ivā 'balām 3.265.7).

8. Dog (Śvā)

What worse calamity can there be than that one runs around asking food from strangers like a dog (yācamānaḥ parād annaṃ paridhāvemahi śvavat 1.147.17)?

9. Porcupine (Śalyaka)

As a porcupine, giving its tongue to many small greedy creatures, gets its food through deceit, so does a king gain his kingdom through deceit by giving his tongue (speech) to many small, greedy-minded persons (jihvāṃ dattvā bahūnaṃ hi kṣudrāṇāṃ lubdhacetasām / nikṛtyā labhate rājyam āhāram iva śalyakaḥ 3.34.57).

Atiratha with all his limbs broken to pieces looked like a porcupine (śakalīkṛtasarvāñgaḥ śvāvidvat samadṛśyata 6.78.55).

10. Rabbit (Śaśa)

The warriors killing each other rendered the entire earth a funeral pile as if it were the blood of rabbits (mahīṃ cakruś citāṃ sarvāṃ śaśaśoṇitasaṃnibhām 6.50.12).

11. Frog (Maṇḍūka)

Vasiṣṭha's cow's eyes are likened to those of frogs (maṇḍūkanetrāṃ svākārām 1.164.13).

12. Mouse (Indura)

Among them some snakes were like (i.e. small as) rats, others were like elephant's trunks (i.e. normal-sized), and (others were) like must-elephants, big-bodied and of great strength (i.e. enormous-sized snakes) (indurā iva tatrā 'nye hastihastā ivā 'pare / mattā iva ca mātaṅgā mahākāyā mahābalāḥ 1.47.24).

It may be noted that the reading *indura-* depends on a few manuscripts. It is not found anywhere else, and the nearest form otherwise known, *indūra-*, 'mouse, rat,' is only lexical. Hence the various changes to *lectiones faciliores*, such as *dardurā*, 'frogs,' in a number of southern manuscripts and *turagā*, 'horses,' in numerous northern manuscripts. The reading *uragā*, 'snakes,' of several manuscripts from Kashmir is of course nonsensical, but is closely related to the northern *turagā*, either as its source or as a further change. Manuscripts G_6 $M_{1,5}$ and T $G_{1,2,4,5}$, $M_{2,3}$ (inf. lin.) have the reading *indura-*.

The common literary form as attested from Suśruta and Śakuntalā 6.32.6 (Prākṛta) is, however, *undura*. Suśruta also has *unduru* (MW,PW).

13. Tortoise (Kūrma)

When one withdraws his senses from the objects of sense, as a tortoise withdraws its limbs from all sides, his mind is well established (yadā saṃharate cā 'yam kūrmo 'ngānī 'va sarvaśaḥ / indriyāṇī 'ndriyārthebhyas tasya prajñā pratiṣṭhitā 6.24.58).

14. Conch Shells (Śaṅkha)

The conch shell serves as a simile for the beauty of the neck. Thus, Bhīma and the sun god are each described as shell-necked (kambugrīvo 3.157.28; 290.8).

In one passage, heaps of corpses are likened to heaps of conch shells (ākīrṇair ācitā bhūmiḥ śaṅkhānām iva rāśibhiḥ 3.100.9).

15. Female Crab (Karkaṭakī)

The female crab is a figure of self-destruction. Thus, Draupadī remarks that Jayadratha attempting to kidnap her is digging his own grave like a female crab conceiving for her own destruction (ādāsyase karkaṭakī 'va garbham 3.252.9; *vide* the commentaries quoted on 6.114.60 to the effect that young crabs, being born, eat their way out of their mother's body).

XXVII. BIRDS (PAKṢIN)

1. Birds in General

Birds in general stand for freedom of movement and swiftness. Thus, Brāhmaṇas, who depend on no one, are likened to free-moving birds (kāmagāḥ pakṣiṇo yathā 1.148.11). Sudeva, flying like a bird, went across rivers, mountains, forests, and lakes swiftly (acireṇā 'ticakrāma khecaraḥ khe carann iva 3.70.11). Excellent horses fly like birds (hayottamān utpatato dvijān iva 3.70.37). Arrows fly like flocks of birds (khagamānāṃ vrajā iva 6.82.7). A banner is likened to a bird in the sky (ākāśaga ivā 'kāśe 6.46.43; cf. 3.22.27; 158.31; 252.18).

Birds in a cage or those without wings symbolize helplessness. Thus, the Gandharvas confined within a network of arrows look like birds in a cage (śakuntā iva pañjare 3.234.12; cf. 3.273.2). The Pāṇḍavas, after Arjuna has left, look like birds without wings (chinnapakṣā iva dvijāḥ 3.79.5).

The bird tied with a string symbolizes dependence and subordination. Thus, everyone is restrained, powerless, dependent on the will of God and no one else, not lord of himself, like a bird tied with a string (śakunis tantubaddho vā niyato 'yam anīśvaraḥ / īśvarasya vaśe tiṣṭhan nā 'nyeṣāṃ nā 'tmanaḥ prabhuḥ 3.31.24).

The birds seeking for meat thrown on the ground symbolize libertines and greedy persons. Thus, as birds seek for meat thrown on the ground, so all men run after a woman deprived of her husband (utsṛṣṭaṃ āmiṣaṃ bhūmau prārthayanti yathā khagāḥ / prārthayanti janāḥ sarve vīrahīnāṃ tathā striyam 1.146.12). As meat is eaten by birds in the sky (by beasts of prey on the ground, and by fish in the water), so a wealthy person (is devoured) by all (yathā hy āmiṣam ākāśe pakṣibhiḥ śvāpadair bhuvi / bhakṣyate salile matsyais tathā sarveṇa vittavān 3.2.39).

The arrows shot by Suśarman entered the body of Arjuna as birds enter among the branches of a tree having fruit of good taste, bent down with a burden of fruit (te śarāḥ prāpya kaunteyaṃ samastā viviśuḥ prabho / phalabhāranataṃ yadvat svāduvṛkṣaṃ vihaṃgamāḥ 6.98.12). This presents in one sentence pictures of the swiftness of arrows, Arjuna's predicament, and the skill of the archer in shooting numerous arrows simultaneously.

Thirst-tormented Yuvanāśva's voice is inaudible like the cry of a bird (śakuner iva vāśitam 3.126.13).

The loud neighing noise of Kubera's horses is compared with the sound of birds flying (pakṣiṇām iva nirghoṣaḥ 3.159.31).

Of specific birds appearing in figures, Garuḍa, swans, ospreys, peacocks, cuckoos, eagles, curlews, cranes, *cakravākas*, crows, and partridges deserve special mention. Some are mentioned more than once: Garuḍa, swans, ospreys, peacocks, cuckoos, eagles, curlews.

Taken in all, the bird as an *upamāna* occurs in at least 57 passages in this corpus. *Pakṣin, khecara, dvija, khaga, khagama, ākāśaga, śakuni, pataṅga, śakunta* and *vihaṃgama* are the synomyns used.

2. Garuḍa

Garuḍa, the king of birds, primarily symbolizes the speedy attack on the enemy, Garuḍa's enemies being snakes. Thus, Bhīma intends to fall upon his enemy like Garuḍa, the best among the birds (vainateyo yathā pakṣī garuḍaḥ patatāṃ varaḥ 3.13.82; cf. 3.17.7; 146.37; 153.19: 6.89.5). Bhīma rushes towards Maṇimat speedily as Garuḍa rushes towards a snake (garutmān iva pannagam 3.157.66; cf. 1.96.36).

Sometimes, fast-moving horses and their sounds are likened to Garuḍa and the noise of his motion (e.g., garutmadbhir ivā 'have 6.101.12; śuśruve dāruṇaḥ śabdaḥ suparṇapatane yathā 6.86.18).

A fast-moving arrow also is compared with speedy Garuḍa (garutmān iva vegavān 6.79.50).

Garuḍa, *vainateya, patagendra, pakṣirāj, garutmat*, and *suparṇa* are the synonyms used.

3. Swan (Haṃsa)

Whiteness and speed are the primary *upamānadharmas* of swans. Thus (white) horses are described as flying like swans (e.g., haṃsair iva mahāvegair 6.44.22). Swans flying towards the ocean (e.g., haṃsā iva mahodadhau 6.86.16), or a lake (e.g., haṃsair iva mahat sarah 6.101.15) render this picture of speed more effective.

Arrows enter the body of Duhśāsana as swans enter a pond (yathā haṃsā mahārāja taḍāgaṃ prāpya bhārata 6.106.42). The arrows shot by Arjuna and Suśarman shine in the sky like swans flying in the sky in the autumn (haṃsā iva mahārāja śaratkāle nabhastale 6.98.11).

The white palaces look like swans (haṃsācchavarṇair bahubhir 1.76.21). The Gaṅgā, flowing, going towards the ocean in three streams, with water agitated by heaps of foam, looks like three rows of swans (sā babhūva visarpantī tridhā rājan samudragā / phenapuñjākulajalā haṃsānām iva paṅktayaḥ 3.108.10).

The swan's voice symbolizes sweetness. Ṛṣyaśṛṅga, the ascetic (brahmacārin), describes the sound of the bark garments (in fact, anklets) of the visiting ascetic (in fact, a harlot) as sweet like that of intoxicated swans singing in a lake (viceṣṭamānasya ca tasya tāni kūjanti haṃsāḥ sarasī 'va mattāh / cīrāṇi tasyā 'dbhutadarśanāni ne 'māni tadvan mama rūpavanti 3.112.6).

A swan's famed ability to separate milk from water (nīrakṣīraviveka) is referred to once: a wise person, having heard the good and bad words of persons speaking, accepts the good ones as a swan extracts milk from water in which it has been mixed (prājñas tu jalpatāṃ puṃsāṃ śrutvā vācaḥ śubhāśubhāḥ / guṇavad vākyam ādatte haṃsaḥ kṣīram ivā 'mbhasaḥ 1.69.10).

4. Osprey (Kurarī)

The crying osprey is the figure of a woman's grief and lamentation. Damayantī, being separated from Nala, cries like a female osprey (kurarīm iva vāśatīm 3.60.19). So Pulomā cries, being carried off by a demon (krośantīṃ kurarīm iva 1.6.11). The expressions *kurarīṇām ivā 'rtānām* (3.128.4) and *kurarya iva duḥkhitāḥ* (3.170.56) occur respectively in connection with the affliction of mothers whose sons are being snatched away from them and that of wives whose husbands have been slain in battle.

5. Peacock (Mayūra)

The peacock in two instances symbolizes the variegated color or the mane of horses (mayūrasadṛśān hayān 3.169.23; mayūrasamaromabhiḥ 3.165.12).

Sahadeva brings down warriors from the backs of elephants with his iron shafts, as one brings down peacocks from trees (pātayām āsa nārācair drumebhya iva barhiṇaḥ 3.255.11).

Mayūra and *barhin* are the only synonyms used.

6. Cuckoo (Puṃskokila)

The cuckoo has always been a figure of melody. The visiting ascetic's (really the harlot's) voice is thus like that of a male cuckoo (puṃskokilasye 'va ca tasya vāṇī 3.112.7).

A clear contrast between a coarse and a melodious sound is shown by bringing a crow's voice into connection with a cuckoo's voice, e.g., the Mahābhārata having been heard, nothing else seems to be worth hearing, just as the voice of the male cuckoo having been heard, the coarse voice of a crow (does not seem to be) worth hearing (śrutvā tv idam upākhyānaṃ srāvyam anyan na rocate / puṃskokilarutaṃ śrutvā rūkṣā dhvāṅkṣasya vāg iva 1.2.236).

7. Eagle (Śyena)

The eagle is the standard of fight and speedy attack right from the time of the Ṛgveda. Bhīma and Śikhaṇḍin wander about in the battlefield, enraged like an eagle (śyenavad vyacarad bhīmo 6.50.40; śyenavad vyacarat kruddhaḥ 6.78.28). The Pāṇḍavas rush towards Jayadratha's army as an eagle rushes towards meat (śyenā yathai 'vā 'miṣasamprayuktā(ḥ) 3.253.24). The Pāṇḍavas and the Kauravas fight like two eagles fighting for meat (śyenayor āmiṣe yathā 6.111.42).

8. Curlew (Krauñca)

As contrasted with the osprey, the curlew symbolizes a loud cry. Thus, elephants trumpet like curlews (krauñcavad vyanadan bhītāḥ 6.85.29; krauñcavad ninadaṃ muktvā 6.44.10).

9. Crane (Baka)

Everybody enjoys the fruit of his own action as the crane (gets the fish as a result of his own acts) in water (paśyāmi svaṃ samutthānam upajīvanti jantavaḥ / api dhātā vidhātā ca yathā 'yam udake bakaḥ 3.33.7).

10. Cakravāka

A couple are attached to each other like *cakravāka* birds (ekaikam anuraktaṃ ca cakravākasamaṃ vibho 6.8.9). Thus, the *cakravāka* is a figure of conjugal love.

11. Crow (Kāka)

The Brāhmaṇas, distressed by robbers, will flee in terror like crows (dasyuprapīḍitā rājan kākā iva dvijottamāḥ 3.188.61). *Vide* 6, Cuckoo, above and chapter 9,A,II,5,6.

12. Partridge (Tittiri)

Horses of variegated color are likened to partridges (tittirikalmāṣān 3.79.24; cf. 5, Peacock, above).

XXVIII. INSECTS

1. Moth (Śalabha)

The moth primarily symbolizes a multitude. Multitudinous arrows are thus compared to moths (bahutvāc chalabhā iva 3.168.23; cf. 3.21.27: 6.54.4).

The well-known relationship of the moth and the flame is referred to in at least nine passages as a figure of self-destruction. As moths rush towards kindled fire for destruction only, so Yudhiṣṭhira's warriors all rush towards Bhīṣma for (self)-destruction (yathā 'nalaṃ prjvalitaṃ pataṃgāḥ samabhidrutāḥ / vināśāyai 'va gacchanti tathā me sainiko janaḥ 6.46.11; cf. 6.33.29; 55.27; 70.32; 96.10; 103.20; 112.110). Arjuna burns the army of the Kauravas as fire burns the moths (pataṃgān iva pāvakaḥ 6.112.112). A greedy person falls into the fire of greed as a moth falls into the flame owing to greed for light (viddhaḥ patati lobhāgnau jyotirlobhāt pataṃgavat 3.2.65).

Synonyms: *śalabha*, *pataṃga*.

2. Bee (Bhramara)

Like the moth, the bee primarily stands for a multitude. Thus, Abhimanyu's sharp, yellow arrows issue forth on the battlefield, like swarms of bees issuing forth from a forest full of blossoming trees (śarāś ca niśitāḥ pītā niścaranti sma saṃyuge / vanāt phulladrumād rājan bhramarāṇām iva vrajāḥ 6.96.13; cf. 3.167.22).

The bee often symbolizes unity. Even a strong enemy can be conquered by the weak, provided they are united in all ways, as the collector of honey is killed by the united bees (sarvathā saṃhatair eva durbalair balavān api / amitraḥ śakyate hantuṃ madhuhā bhramarair iva 3.34.68).

XXIX. FOREST (VANA)

The following four examples of the forest in figures are found in different contexts:

a) ubhe citre vanarājiprakāśe 6.20.3.

Both the armies shine with variegated colors like the defiles of the woods.

b) yathā vanaṃ mādhavamāsi madhye
samīritaṃ śvasanenā 'bhivāti /
tathā sa vaty uttamapuṇyagandhī
niṣevyamāṇaḥ pavanena tāta 3.112.8.

As a forest smells being agitated by the wind in the middle of spring, so he (the pretended visiting ascetic, really a harlot), with a most excellent fragrance, emits perfume being served by the wind.

c) śuṣkavṛkṣam ivā 'raṇyam
adṛśyam abhavat puram 3.170.59.

(The city of the demons, after the death of the demons) did not look beautiful, like a forest with its trees dried up.

d) asurair vadhyamānaṃ tat
pāvakair iva kānanam /
apatad dagdhabhūyiṣṭhaṃ
mahādrumavanaṃ yathā 3.221.37.

The army of the gods, being destroyed by the demons like a forest being destroyed by fire, fell like a forest of great trees with its greater part burnt.

Vana, *aranya*, and *kānana* are the synonyms found in these passages.

XXX. TREES AND PLANTS

1. The Tree in General

The central *upamānadharma* of figures based on the tree is not easily predictable. Duryodhana is described as a great tree of anger (duryodhano manyumayo mahādrumaḥ 1.1.65; cf. chapter 2); the universe is described as an upside-down tree (the *aśvattha* 6.37.1; cf. chapter 2). These metaphors seem to suggest hugeness and extensiveness as the probable central imagery. As Emeneau has shown, the picture in the *aśvattha* metaphor "is based on an epiphytic stage of the *aśvattha*. It is rooted above, on another tree, and thence lets roots down to the ground. Its branches grow in all directions from the lodging place on the host tree, both up and down."[10] Cf. RV 1.24.7; Kaṭhopaniṣad 6.1; Taittirīya Āraṇyaka 1.11.5 (referred to by Emeneau).

The significance of trees in similes, however, is different in different contexts.

Thus, a tree broken by a thunderbolt or the wind, etc., is a symbol of death. Bhīṣma lies sighing on the ground like a tree broken by the wind (sa śete niṣṭanan bhūmau vātarugṇa iva drumaḥ 6.14.13; cf. 3.17.20; 270.4: 6.15.15). Parīkṣit bitten by the *takṣaka*-serpent dies like a tree hit by a thunderbolt (pañcatvam agamad rājā vajrāhata iva drumaḥ 1.3.187; cf. 3.271.17: 6.70.24; 103.91). The hunter, coveting Damayantī, fell down on the ground like a tree burnt by fire (vyasuḥ papāta medinyāṃ agnidagdha iva drumaḥ 3.61.38). Jayadratha's soldier, with his chest broken, vomiting blood from his mouth, fell down in front of Arjuna like a tree severed from its root (sa bhinnahṛdayo vīro vaktrāc choṇitam udvaman / papātā 'bhimukhaḥ pārthaṃ chinnamūla iva drumaḥ 3.255.14; cf. 3.17.20; 252.23: 6.86.62).

A tree fallen from the bank into the river current is a figure of dependence and subordination. Thus, a man is not at his own command, even for a while, like a tree fallen from the bank approaching the middle of the stream (nā 'tmādhīno manuṣyo 'yaṃ kālaṃ bhavati kaṃ cana / srotaso madhyam āpannaḥ kūlād vṛkṣa iva cyutaḥ 3.31.26).

[10] Emeneau, "The Strangling Figs in Sanskrit Literature," *University of California Publications in Classical Philology*, XIII (1949), 367. Discussion on pp. 365–367.

In one passage, a tree shaken by the wind symbolizes the charm of dancing. Thus, the pretended visiting ascetic (really a harlot), having hit the ball, turns about with agitated motion (i.e., dances) like a tree shaken by the wind (tac cā 'pi hatvā parivartate 'sau vāterito vṛkṣa ivā 'vaghūrṇaḥ 3.112.9).

A burning tree emitting flames is the standard of anger. Thus, the flames of brilliance (i.e., anger) came out of the apertures of the body of Rāvaṇa as the flames come out of the apertures of a burning tree in the night (ity evaṃ bruvatas tasya srotobhyas tejaso 'rciṣaḥ / niścerur dahyato rātrau vṛkṣasye 'va svarandhrataḥ 3.261.59).

The solitary tree of a village symbolizes happy living. Thus, one whose kinsmen are not wicked nor disgracing the family lives happily like a solitary tree in a village (jñātayo yasya nai 'va syur viṣamāḥ kulapāṃsanāḥ / sa jivet susukham loke grāme druma ivai 'kajaḥ 1.138.24).

The trees in the forest stand for coöperation and interdependence. Powerful persons with their wealth increased, pleasing to their friends and kinsmen, live depending upon each other like trees in the forest (balavantaḥ samṛddhārthā mitrabāndhavanandanāḥ / jīvanty anyonyam āśritya drumāḥ kānanajā iva 1.138.27).

We find the *kalpavṛkṣa* (the divine tree that fulfills all desires) and the *śmaśānacaitya* (the *aśvattha* tree in a cemetery), both in one passage, used as figures of grace and terror respectively:

Rāvaṇa approaching Sītā in his garden, even though carefully decorated so as to look like the *kalpavṛkṣa*, looks frightful in spite of decoration as the *aśvattha* tree of a cemetery (though well decorated, looks frightful).

sa kalpavṛkṣasadṛśo
yatnād api vibhūṣitaḥ /
śmaśānacaityadrumavad
bhūṣito 'pi bhayaṃkaraḥ 3.265.5.

Of the various species of trees, each of the following occurs a number of times: *Butea frondosa* (kiṃśuka), palmyra palm (tāla), the sal tree (śāla, *Shorea robusta*), bamboo (vaṃśa), the *aśoka* tree, and the plantain tree (kadalī). Several others occur once each: the mango tree (āmra), the silk-cotton tree (śālmali), and the *aśvattha* tree (religious fig).

2. *Butea frondosa* (Kiṃśuka)

In spite of its charming red blossoms, the *kiṃśuka* tree has been traditionally used as a symbol either of a frightful scene of bloodshed or of ineffectiveness. In both the epics it seems to occur only in the former sense.

Thus, in this corpus in all its seven occurrences (puṣpitā iva kiṃśukāḥ 3.103.11: 6.44.43; puṣpitāv iva kiṃśukau 3.264.32: 6.43.13, 49.23; kiṃśukaḥ puṣpavān iva 6.106.34; sapuṣpa iva kiṃśukaḥ 6.48.50), the blossoming *kiṃśuka* is an *upamāna* of wounded warriors. An example of the complete imagery is 3.103.11:

te hemaniṣkābharaṇāḥ
kuṇḍalāñgadadhāriṇaḥ /
nihatya bahv aśobhanta
puṣpitā iva kiṃśukāḥ //

They (the warriors) with golden necklaces, wearing earrings and armlets, having been killed, looked like blossoming *kiṃśuka* trees. Cf. Vālmīki, Rāmāyaṇa 6.67.30.

PW quotes two specimens in which the *kiṃśuka* is a symbol of ineffectiveness.

a) avijñāya phalaṃ yo hi
karma tv evā 'nudhāvati /
sa śocet phalavelāyāṃ
yathā kiṃśukasevakaḥ //[11]

One who without considering the result, just follows (a course of) action, he would repent at the time of the result (lit. fruition), as one attending upon a *kiṃśuka* tree (would repent, finding that howsoever charming the flowers might be, they bear no fruits at all).

b) rūpayauvanasaṃpannā
viśālakulasaṃbhavāḥ /
vidyāhīna na śobhante .
nirgandhā iva kiṃśukāḥ //[12]

Persons, even though endowed with beauty and youth and coming of a high family, do not look brilliant if they are devoid of learning, as the odorless *kiṃśuka* trees (though charming to look at, do not attract us).

3. Palmyra Palm (Tāla)

The Palmyra palm primarily stands for height. Thus, Bhīma and Karṇa are each tall like a golden palm tree (prāṃśuh kanakatālābhaḥ 1.126.5: 3.146.30). Plantain trees are equal in height to many palm trees together (bahutālasamucchrayān 3.146.44). So is the summit of a mountain (bahutālocchrayaṃ śṛñgam 3.157.33).

Sometimes, it symbolizes just hugeness; e.g., bows are huge like palm trees (tālamātrāṇi cāpāni 6.89.3).

[11] Rāmāyaṇa 2.63.8.
[12] Cāṇakya. 7; Hitopadeśa, Pr. 39.

The trees with their tops lopped off symbolize chariots without charioteers; e.g., Bhīṣma rendered the host of chariots like lopped palm trees (muṇḍatālavanānī 'va cakāra sa rathavrajān 6.102.12, 112.68).

The heads (of those slain in the battle between the gods and the demons) falling from the sky are likened to the palm fruits falling from the stalk (śirobhiḥ prapatadbhiś ca antarikṣān mahītalam / tālair iva mahīpāla vṛntād bhraṣṭair adṛśyata 3.99.5).

4. Sal Tree, *Shorea robusta* (Śāla)

The sal tree is on a par with the palmyra palm as a standard of height. The only difference between these two figures lies in the vocabulary of the *upamānadharma*. The palmyra palm uses *prāṃśu-* and *samucchraya-* mostly, while the sal tree has *udgata-*. Moreover, the trunk of the sal tree is often mentioned as a figure of height.

Thus, it seems strange how a child has become tall like the trunk of a sal tree (katham alpena kālena śālaskandha ivo 'dgatah 1.68.78). Bhīma is also *śālaskandha(m) ivo 'dgata(m)* 1.139.13. Abhimanyu is tall like a big sal tree (mahāśāla ivo 'dgataḥ 6.108.38). Nakula is likewise *bṛhacchāla ivo 'dgataḥ* 3.297.66. Bhīma's tallness is likened to that of a young sal tree (śālapota ivo 'dgataḥ 3.157.27) and a lofty sal tree (mahābhujaṃ śālam iva pravṛddham 3.254.9).

Sometimes the sal tree symbolizes the strength (so Roy's translation) of human thighs; e.g., Pratīpa's wife sat on his sal-like right thigh (dakṣiṇaṃ śālasaṃkāśam ūruṃ bheje śubhānanā 1.92.3).

The sal tree is also the figure of outstanding merit, e.g., Yudhiṣṭhira cannot remain unrecognized any more than a big sal tree in a well-watered place, endowed with branches, flowers and leaves, or a white elephant (bṛhacchāla ivā 'nūpe śākhāpuṣpapalāśavān / hastī śveta ivā 'jñātaḥ kathaṃ jiṣṇuś cariṣyati 3.36.24; cf. 1.214.30). Cf. section XXII.

5. Bamboo (Vaṃśa)

The bamboo, when it cracks or burns, produces a loud splintering or cracking noise. Bamboo is found in two situations symbolizing noise in this corpus.

Through the rubbing together of the arms of those two strong warriors (Bhīma and Kirmīra), then there arose a terrible noise in the battle, like that of the splintering of a bamboo (tayor bhujaviniṣpeṣād ubhayor balinos tadā / śabdaḥ samabhavad ghoro veṇusphoṭasamo yudhi 3.12.58).

The exceedingly great noise of the hoofs of horses was heard then like that of a great bamboo grove burning on a mountain (khuraśabdaś ca sumahān vājinām śuśruve tadā / mahāvaṃśavanasye 'va dahyamānasya parvate 6.101.13; cf. 6.88.26; 89.24).

Veṇu and *vaṃśa* are the only two synonyms used.

6. Aśoka Tree

As the following examples show, the *aśoka* tree (= *raktāśoka* = red-flowering *aśoka* tree in this corpus) by its blossoms symbolizes extreme redness.

a) kesarotkarasaṃmiśram
aśokānām ivo 'tkaram 3.146.69.

God Hanumat covered with his reddish mane, (looks) like a heap of *aśoka* flowers.

b). bahudhā dāritaś cai 'va
viṣāṇais tatra dantibhiḥ /
phullāśokanibhaḥ pārthaḥ
śuśubhe raṇamūrdhani 6.98.34.

Bhīma, wounded much by the elephants with their tusks, there shone like a blossoming *aśoka* in the van of the battle.

c) vasante puṣpaśabalo
raktāśoka ivā 'babhau 6.99.10.

Bhīṣma, pierced by arrows, looked like a red-flowering *aśoka* tree covered with flowers in the spring.

7. Plantain Tree (Kadalī)

The tapering shape of the plantain stem stands for that of the thigh. Thus, *rambhoru* ('O one having plantain-stem-like thighs') is the common form of address for beautiful girls (e.g., 1.67.4; 160.34; cf. also the thigh compared with the elephant's trunk, section XXII).

The felled banana tree symbolizes the sudden fall of a woman; e.g., Sītā, having heard those frightening words, trembling, suddenly fell down like a felled plantain tree (tataḥ sā sahasā bālā tac chrutvā dāruṇaṃ vacaḥ / papāta devī vyathitā nikṛttā kadalī yathā 3.275.14; cf. 3.144.4).

Rambhā and *kadalī* are the synonyms used.

8. Mango (Cūta)

vasante puṣpaśabalāś
cūtāḥ prapatitā iva 6.92.27.

The warriors falling look like the falling mango trees variegated with flowers in the spring.

9. Silk-cotton Tree (Śālmali)

na jñāyate kāyavṛddhyā vivṛddhir
yathā 'sṭhīlā śālmaleḥ sampravṛddhā /
hrasvo 'lpakāyaḥ phalito vivṛddho
yaś cā 'phalas tasya na vṛddhabhāvaḥ 3.133.9.

Development is not known by the development of the body as (is the case with) the well-developed knot of the silk-cotton tree (Nīlakaṇṭha: sa hi kevalatūlamayatvān niḥsāraḥ; ato dehavṛddhir vyarthā, "the knot, being full of cotton only, is fruitless, so the development of the body is useless"). One is developed, in spite of having a small body, if he has fruitful ends. One having no fruitful objectives, is not developed (though he may have a bigger shape).

10. Pipal Tree, *Ficus religiosa* (Aśvattha)

. . . devarājaḥ pravepamāno . . .
. . . anilene 'va nunnam
aśvatthapatram girirājamūrdhani 1.189.22.

Indra trembled like an *aśvattha* leaf disturbed by the wind on the top of the Himālayas.

Note that the leaves of the *aśvattha* are always in motion, like those of the aspen.

11. Reed, *Amphidonax karka* (Nala)

yathā ca veṇuḥ kadalī nalo vā
phalaty abhāvāya na bhūtaye 'tmanaḥ /
tathai 'va māṃ taiḥ parirakṣyamāṇām
ādāsyase karkaṭakī 'va garbham 3.252.9.

(Draupadī's rebuff to Jayadratha) As the bamboo, the plantain, or the reed bears fruit only to perish and not to grow large, so you will lay hands upon me, who am protected by the Pāṇḍavas, as a crab conceives (for her own destruction).

Cf. sections XXVI,15, and 5 and 7 above.[13]

12. Creeper (Latā)

A creeper symbolizes slimness, generally that of young women. So, a broken creeper symbolizes a young woman bending or falling down.

Thus, the harlot playing with a ball at the feet of Ṛṣyaśṛṅga is compared to a creeper with fruits, broken by the weight of the fruits (sā kandukenā 'ramatā 'sya mūle vibhajyamānā phalitā late 'va 3.111.15).

[13] *Vide* Emeneau, "A Dravidian Etymology of the Sanskrit Proper Name Nala," *University of California Publications in Classical Philology*, XII (1943), 255–262.

Kuntī overcome by bewilderment falls on the bed like a broken creeper (tasmin puṇye śayanīye papāta mohāviṣṭā bhajyamānā late 'va 3.297.27).

Sometimes, a creeper is a figure for the need for help, as it needs the support of a tree or the like for its growth. Thus, Nakula supports Draupadī who is falling down and clinging to him like a creeper (tāṃ patantīṃ varārohāṃ sajjamānāṃ latām *iva* 3.144.5). Hiḍimbā approaches Bhīma like a bashful creeper (vilajjamāne 'va latā 1.139.18).

13. Soma and Pūtīka

Soma and *pūtīka* (*Guilandina bounducella*) occur as a figure in just one passage. The *pūtīka* already appears in the Taittirīya Saṃhitā 2.5.35 as a prescribed substitute for the *soma* plant in the Vedic ritual. So, *pūtīka* as a substitute for *soma* (pūtīkān iva somasya) symbolizes a substitute for something better which is not available.

Thus, Bhīma, tired of exile, suggests to Yudhiṣṭhira that sometimes a month equals a year and so the proposed thirteen years of exile are replaceable by thirteen months, just as the *soma* plant is replaceable by the *pūtīka* plant (asti māsaḥ pratinidhir yathā prāhur manīṣiṇaḥ / pūtīkān iva somasya tathe 'daṃ kriyatām iti 3.36.32).

14. Flowers (Puṣpa)

Like the red-flowering *kiṃśuka*, flowers in general symbolize bright color as of blood, etc.

Thus, Bhīma with his weapons made the earth to be covered (with cut-off heads, etc.), as one does with bright-colored flowers (sa cakre vasudhāṃ kīrṇāṃ śabalaiḥ kusumair iva 6.50.55). Again, the earth covered (with broken chariots, heads accompanied by earrings, etc., of slain kings) looked like the earth decorated with flowers in the spring (saṃchannā vasudhā bhāti vasante kusumair iva 6.85.34).

The flower of the flax (atasī; *Linum usitatissimum*), however, symbolizes blue color. At the time of the deluge, the boy, who is Viṣṇu, is described as having a complexion blue as the flax flower (atasīpuṣpavarṇābhaḥ 3.186.86).

15. Fruit (Phala)

The fruit (phala) represents the last stage of a plant product when it falls automatically or is made to fall from its stalk. Thus, rightly enough, it primarily symbolizes falling or making to fall; e.g., Jaṭāsura's head falls like a fruit falling from its stalk (phalaṃ vṛntād iva cyutam 3.154.60). Again, the horsemen cut off (and made to fall) the heads of the warriors, as one makes the fruit fall from a tall tree (acchinann uttamāṅgāni phalānī 'va mahādrumāt 6.101.21). Bhīṣma makes the heads of charioteers fall on the battlefield as a skillful person (makes to fall with stones, etc.) the ripe fruit from the palm trees (śirāṃsi rathināṃ bhīṣmaḥ pātayām āsa saṃyuge / tālebhya iva pakvāni phalāni kuśalo naraḥ 6.82.21).

The bitter fruit of the *kiṃpāka* (a cucurbitaceous plant, *Trichosanthes palmata*), however, symbolizes a repugnant consequence of actions, e.g., the exceedingly serious, terrible outcome (of those actions) is at hand, like the *kiṃpāka* fruit (saṃprāptaṃ sumahad ghoraṃ phalaṃ kiṃpākasaṃnibham 6.61.20).

16. *Sesamum indicum* (Tila)

The stalk of *Sesamum indicum* (tilakāṇḍa) carries the same figure as fruit in general, i.e., falling or causing to fall. Thus, Bhīmasena cuts a spear with three arrows, as one causes to fall the stalk of *Sesamum indicum* by a sickle, etc. (paṭṭiśaṃ ca tribhir bāṇaiś ciccheda tilakāṇḍavat 6.109.37). The hand of Kabandha falls, cut off like the stalk of *Sesamum indicum* (nikṛttas tilakāṇḍavat 3.263.33).

17. Black Gram (Māṣa)

The black gram (māṣa) is one of the pulses, botanically *Phaseolus radiatus*, which is a variant of *Phaseolus mungo*.

In the following passage, a heap of black gram (māṣarāśi) symbolizes extreme blackness and resultant terror. Thus, the rampart in Laṅkā was again and again made devoid of monkeys by the demons of terrible appearance, who looked like a heap of black gram (sa māṣarāśisadṛśair babhūva kṣaṇadācaraiḥ / kṛto nirvānaro bhūyaḥ prākāro bhīmadarśanaiḥ 3.268.34).

18. Rice (Śāli)

A field of rice is a symbol of reddish-brown color, particularly the rice field at sunrise: prababhau harisainyaṃ tac chālatālaśilāyudham / sumahac chālibhavanaṃ yathā sūryodayaṃ prati 3.267.18. That army of monkeys armed with sal trees, palm trees, and stones, looked like a huge ricefield facing the sun at dawn.

In another passage, the reddish-brown color of rice flowers is combined with parallel figures based on the color of *śirīṣa* blossoms, the *śara* reed, and the rising sun:

śāliprasūnasadṛśaiḥ
śirīṣakusumaprabhaiḥ /
taruṇādityasadṛśaiḥ

śaragaurais ca vānaraiḥ
prākāraṃ dadṛśus te tu
samantāt kapilīkṛtam 3.268.27–28.

They saw the city wall colored reddish-brown on all sides because covered by monkeys, which were like the flowers of rice, like *śirīṣa* flowers, like the rising sun, which were reddish-brown like the *śara* reed.

Cf. section V.

19. Turmeric (Haridrā)

Turmeric symbolizes yellow color. Thus, the *ajagara*-snake is described as having a skin-color like the color of turmeric (haridrāsadṛśacchavim 3.175.13).

20. Cotton (Tūla)

Cotton being burnt by fire or being dispersed by the wind symbolizes defeat of the enemy (cf. sections IV and XIV). In isolation, however, it is a standard of softness. Thus Vasiṣṭha's head falls on a stone as on a heap of cotton; i.e., the stone becomes as soft as a heap of cotton for Vasiṣṭha's head (śiras tasya śilāyāṃ ca tūlarāśāv ivā 'patat 1.166.41).

21. A Tuft of Reeds (Śaratūla)[14]

In the following passage, a tuft of reeds symbolizes destruction of a weapon:

tatas tad astram astreṇa
vidhūtaṃ śaratūlavat 3.21.37.

One missile was destroyed by another missile, as a tuft of reeds is easily destroyed.

22. Plants as Elucidative of Philosophical or Ethical Ideas

A few miscellaneous passages show application of various phases of plant life to philosophical and moralistic ideas:

a) arthatyāgo hi kāryaḥ syād
arthaṃ śreyāṃsam icchatā /
bījaupamyena . . . 3.34.63.

By one desirous of better wealth, wealth would have to be sacrificed according to the likeness of seeds (i.e., just as one has to sow seeds before he can expect a harvest).

b) kālaṃ pratīkṣasva sukhodayāya
paktiṃ phalānām iva bījavāpaḥ 3.35.18.

Await the proper time of the rise of prosperity as the sower of seeds awaits the ripening of fruits.

---

[14] See also 11 above.

c) adharmā dharmarūpeṇa
tṛṇaiḥ kūpā ivā 'vṛtāḥ 3.198.54.

Sinful men are covered with apparent virtue as wells are covered with grass.

d) sukham āpatitaṃ seved
duḥkham āpatitaṃ sahet /
kālaprāptam upāsīta
śasyānām iva karṣakaḥ 3.245.15.

One should accept prosperity (or pleasure) that has befallen one; one should tolerate pain that has befallen one; one should wait for what arrives in its season, like a cultivator of crops.

e) rājan sarṣapamātrāṇi
paracchidrāṇi paśyasi /
atmano bilvamātrāṇi
paśyann api na paśyasi 1.69.1.

(Śakuntalā rebuffs Duḥṣanta) O King, you see the faults of others even though they are small as a mustard seed; but you do not notice your own which are big as a *bilva* fruit, even though you see them.

XXXI. LOTUS (KAMALA)

1. Day-blooming Lotus

The lotus is a favorite *upamāna* for anything that is charming. Thus, Draupadī's face looks like a lotus (mukhaṃ ca kamalaprabham 3.144.11). Sudeva noticed an excellent lotus-like natural mole between the eye brows of the young lady (Damayantī), but later it became hidden (asyāś cai 'va bhruvor madhye sahajaḥ piplur uttamaḥ / śyāmāyāḥ padmasaṃkāśo lakṣito 'ntarhito mayā 3.66.5). The hands placed together in salutation (añjali) are compared to red lotus petals (padmapatranibhaḥ 1.113.29); the comparison is because of the red color of the fingers and palms (raktāṅgulitalaḥ) and also the shape.

The lotus as a comparison for male or female eyes is more common in compounded epithets, as follows:

(*a*) (kanyāḥ) kamalalocanā(ḥ), 'lotus-eyed girls'; 1.60.11; 68.13: 3.12.16. (*b*) kamalapatrākṣ(a), 'lotus-petal-eyed'; 1.1.7; 61.67; 93.27; 113.10: 3.147.24; 186.12; 275.3: 6.33.2; cf. 3.61.1; 104.17; 249.6. (*c*) kamalekṣaṇ(a), 'lotus-eyed'; 1.113.23: 3.292.23. (*d*) puṇḍarīkākṣa, 'lotus-eyed'; for Kṛṣṇa, 1.213.22: 3.13.42; 19.27: 6.102.59; for Rāma, 3.264.49; for Arjuna, 3.79.14; for Viṣṇu, pundarikanibhekṣaṇā 3.192.24. (*e*) puṣkarekṣaṇa, 'lotus-eyed'; 1.112.24; 211.16; 213.45. (*f*) rājīvalocanā(ḥ), 'lotus-eyed'; 1.46.34; 55.33; 89.6; 112.2; 116.7: 3.16.23; 44.38; 83.112; 128.17; 185.17; 277.23: 6.102.63; cf. 1.77.27: 3.182.6. (*g*) vanajapatrākṣ(īm), 'lotus-petal-eyed'; 1.160.40. (*h*) padmāyatākṣ(ī), 'having long eyes like a lotus'; 1.61.96; 180.20; cf. 1.175.7: 3.44.31; 65.11; 186.87; 187.50; 194.16; 292.19. (*i*) śatapatrāyatekṣaṇām, 'having long eyes like a lotus'; 3.65.20.

It would appear that *puṣkara, rājīva,* and *vanaja,* which have dark blue flowers, are used because of the color resembling that of the eyes. But *padma* and *kamala,* which have red flowers, and *puṇḍarīka* (white) argue against this. In all probability, the comparison is based on the shape and beauty of the lotus rather than on its color. As passages such as 1.61.96 and 3.65.20 clearly show, the shape of the lotus (its petals?) is to be regarded as the *tertium comparationis* in this context.

It is interesting to note that *puṇḍarīkākṣa* is an epithet of Kṛṣṇa (at least four times), Rāma (once), Viṣṇu (once), and Arjuna (once)—all related to Viṣṇu and His incarnations or to His devotee. Does it show that this term found more favor with the Vaiṣṇavas? In fact, Amarasiṃha lists it as one of the synonyms for Viṣṇu. *Puṇḍarīka* as a synonym for a lotus occurs as early as RV 10.142.7.

Ruru's wife Pramadvarā is described as having splendor like that of a lotus (padmavarcasam 1.8.19) and also as having luster like that of the filament of a lotus (padmakiñjalkasaprabhām 1.9.18). Śantanu sees a beautiful damsel wearing delicate garments, having splendor like that of the interior part of the lotus (sūkṣmāmbaradharām ekāṃ padmodarasamaprabhām 1.92.27). So Arjuna's mother Kuntī has splendor like that of the interior part of a lotus (puṇḍarikāntaraprabhām 1.138.17; cf. 1.161.8). Even a child has splendor like that of a lotus (putraṃ kamalagarbhābham 3.293.10). Sudeva sees Damayantī, who is in distress, looking like a lotus fiber, just drawn up from the water and burnt with heat (dahyamānām ivo 'ṣṇena mṛṇālīm aciroddhṛtām 3.65.15).

Draupadī's body exhales fragrance like that of a blue lotus, even from a distance of a *krośa,* i.e., about two miles (nīlotpalasamo gandho yasyāḥ krośāt pravāyati 1.155.43).

Karṇa's head stooping with shame on account of an insulting question put to him looks like a lotus sinking down, wet with rain water (evam uktasya karṇasya vrīḍāvanatam ānanam / babhau varṣāmbubhiḥ klinnaṃ padmam āgalitaṃ yathā 1.126.33).

Karṇa as a baby is described as having palms bright like a red lotus or copper, i.e., 'with palms bright as red lotuses' (padmatāmratalojjvalam 3.292.19; cf. tāmratalau caraṇau 3.186.119).

Iravat's head cut off and lying on the ground has splendor like that of a lotus or the moon (padmendusadṛśaprabham 6.86.70).

Apart from human beings or human forms and limbs, tips of elephants' trunks (puṣkaraiḥ padmasaṃkāśair 6.13.36), a banner (dhvajam indīvaraśyāmam 3.43.8, i.e., 'the banner blue like a blue lotus'), and elephants (caturviṣāṇāḥ padmābhāḥ 3.155.77, i.e., 'four-tusked lotus-like elephants') are compared to lotuses in various ways. Weapons are likened to the blue lotus, because they are made of dark iron or steel. Thus, there arose the blue lotus-like splendor of spears with bright points, of javelins being hurled, and of well-tempered swords (śaktīnāṃ vimalāgrāṇāṃ tomarāṇāṃ tathā 'syatām / nistriṃśānāṃ ca pītānāṃ nīlotpalanibhāḥ prabhāḥ 6.68.17).

The following descriptions of clouds, though including several other *upamānas*, contain three involving the lotus and one the night lotus (kumuda):

ke cin nīlotpalaśyāmāḥ
ke cit kumudasaṃnibhāḥ /
ke cit kiñjalkasaṃkāśāḥ
ke cit pītāḥ payodharāḥ //
ke cid dharidrāsaṃkāśāḥ
kākāṇḍakanibhās tathā /
ke cit kamalapatrākṣāḥ
ke cid dhingulakaprabhāḥ 3.186.66–7.

Some clouds are blue like a blue lotus, some white like the *kumuda* water lily, some like the filament of a lotus, some yellow. Some are like turmeric and like the tree *Diospyros tomentosa;* some are like the leaves of a red lotus; some look like vermilion.

All the aspects of the beauty of the people of Airāvatavarṣa are compared to red lotuses, as follows:

padmaprabhāḥ padmavarṇāḥ
padmapatranibhekṣaṇāḥ /
padmapatrasugandhāś ca
jāyante tatra mānavāḥ 6.9.12.

Men are born there (in Airāvatavarṣa) with red-lotus-like splendor, red-lotus-like complexion, red-lotus-petal-like eyes, and red-lotus-petal-like fragrance.

Sometimes, a lotus transferred from one pond to another symbolizes a bride leaving her parent's home to go to an equally happy home. Thus Draupadī living with the Pāṇḍavas is likened to a lotus transferred from one pond to another (padminī 'va sute 'yaṃ te hradād anyaṃ hradaṃ gatā 1.187.10; cf. 3.287.25).

A lotus also symbolizes growth. Thus, all those children (the Kauravas and the Pāṇḍavas) grew in a short time like lotuses in water (sarve vavṛdhur alpena kālenā 'pasv iva nīrajāḥ 1.115.28).

Lotus leaves repel water, which stands on them in drops. Hence similes for (i) inattentiveness (Vidura's advice produces no effect on Dhṛtarāṣṭra as water dropped on the leaf of a lotus does not stick to it: yathā parṇe puṣkarasye 'va siktaṃ jalaṃ na tiṣṭhet pathyam uktaṃ tathā 'smin 3.6.16) and (ii) detachment (To those endowed with knowledge, eminent ones, knowers of scriptures, with their spirit disciplined, attachment does not fix itself, as water does not fix itself to lotus leaves: jñānānviteṣu mukhyeṣu śāstrajñeṣu kṛtātmasu / na teṣu sajjate snehaḥ padmapatreṣv ivo 'dakam 3.2.32; one who works, having surrendered actions to Brahman and relinquished attachment, is not adhered to by sin, as a lotus leaf is not adhered to by water: brahmaṇy ādhāya karmāṇi saṅgaṃ tyaktvā karoti yaḥ / lipyate na sa pāpena padmapatram ivā 'mbhasā 6.27.10).

The day-blooming lotus as an *upamāna* occurs in at least 74 passages in this corpus. *Kamala*, *padma*, *puṣkara*, *puṇḍarīka*, *utpala*, *rājīva*, *vanaja*, and *śatapatra* are the synonyms used. In some of its occurrences, its color (red, blue, or white) is identifiable, as shown above. Otherwise, the shape of the lotus symbolizes beauty and charm.

2. Night-blooming Lotus (Kumuda)

The night-blooming lotus (kumuda) is white and so symbolizes the beauty of white-complexioned women; the women living in the region towards the east of Mt. Meru are likened to night-blooming lotuses in complexion, beautiful and charming (striyaḥ kumudavarṇāś ca sundaryaḥ priyadarśanāḥ 6.8.15).[15]

XXXII. METAL

Gold, silver, and copper are the three metals that appear as *upamānas* in this corpus.

1. Gold (Svarṇa)

Gold symbolizes brightness. Thus, Lord Śiva's splendor is likened to that of gold (kāñcanaprabhaḥ 3.40.17; cf. 3.40.18; 71.11; 213.47; 219.24; 249.6: 6.41.96). A Brāhmaṇa is described as having splendor like that of gold purified by heat (prataptakanakaprabhaḥ 1.214.30). People of Ketumāla and Jambūṣaṇḍa are born with the effulgence of gold purified

[15] *Vide* Richard Schmidt, "Beitrage zur Flora Sanscritica III: Der Lotus in der Sanskrit-Literatur," *Zeitschrift der deutschen morgenländischen Gesellschaft*, LXVII (1913), 462–470.

by heat—free from any disease, devoid of anxiety, always cheerful in mind (anāmayā vītaśokā nityaṃ muditamānasāḥ / jāyante mānavās tatra niṣṭaptakanakaprabhāḥ 6.7.31).

The sun god is described as having splendor like that of excellent gold and fire (varakanakahutāśanaprabham 3.3.31). Yudhiṣṭhira is bright like pure gold (jāmbūnadaśuddhagauraḥ 3.254.7).

Sāvitrī is likened to a golden statue (pratimāṃ kāñcanīm iva 3.277.26). A warrior's arms look like golden pillars (stambhāv iva hiraṇmayau 3.44.24), or appear as if made of gold (hairaṇyau bhavato bāhū 3.36.9). The tableland of the mountain in which Tapatī was staying became, with its trees, bushes, and creepers, as if gold-colored (giriprasthe tu sā yasmin sthitā svasitalocanā / sa savṛkṣakṣupalato hiranmaya ivā 'bhavat 1.160.26). Gold-like men are born on the top of Mt. Mālyavat (mahārajatasaṃkāśā jāyante tatra mānavāḥ 6.8.28).

Chariots are bright-colored like gold and the lotus (ime rathāḥ kāñcanapadmacitrāḥ 1.186.2).

Gold even though not purified is charming. Damayantī's body shines though covered with dirt and unadorned; her beauty does not perish in any circumstances (na cā 'syā naśyate rūpaṃ vapur malasamācitam / asaṃskṛtam api vyaktaṃ bhāti kāñcanasaṃnibham 3.66.7; cf. ABHS 1.19).

Thus, gold as an *upamāna* occurs in at least 24 passages. *Kanaka*, *cāmīkara*, *jāmbūnada*, *tapanīya*, *heman*, *hiraṇya*, *kāñcana*, *jātarūpa*, and *mahārajata* are the synonyms used; cf. 1.15.5; 142.7: 3.119.12; 184.7: 6.66.7; 93.21. It is just accidental that the synonym *suvarṇa* or *svarṇa* never occurs in this corpus as an *upamāna*.

2. Silver (Rajata)

Silver (rajata) is the symbol of white splendor. The snow mountain (the Himālayas) shines like silver (śvetaś ca rajataprabhaḥ 6.7.3).

Silver often stands as a comparison for (white) horses (e.g., aśvai rajataprakāśaiḥ 6.59.25; rajataprakhyā(n) 6.55.47; 102.38,53).

3. Copper (Tāmra)

Copper (tāmra) symbolizes red splendor. Thus, Subhadrā's (beautiful) wide, red eyes are likened to copper (vavande pṛthutāmrākṣī 1.213.18; cf. 3.42.26). Nala's eyes are, however, coppery-red through anger (roṣatāmrākṣas 3.77.17). Cf. 3.186.119; 292.19.

The following description of the Himālayas has more than one metal standing as comparisons for various aspects of its beauty:

kva cit kanakasaṃkāśaṃ
kva cid rajatasaṃnibham /
kva cid añjanapuñjābhaṃ
himavantam upāgamat 3.107.12.

Bhagīratha came to the Himālayas, which looked like gold in some places, in some places like silver, in some places having splendor like that of eye ointment.

XXXIII. JEWEL (RATNA)

Jewels primarily symbolize brightness.

1. Cat's Eye (Vaiḍūrya)

God Varuṇa and a lake are bright like the cat's eye (vaiḍūryavarṇābha- 3.42.5; 155.77; cf. 1.61.97: 3.155.61; 175.9). Rivers with many whirlpools look like blue cat's eye gems (nadīś ca bahulāvartā nīlavaiḍūryasaṃnibhāḥ 3.39.17).

2. Crystal (Sphaṭika)

The town of Kubera is decorated with crystal-like gold buildings (sphaṭikākārair 3.157.35). Lakes look transparent like spotless crystals (vimalasphaṭikābhāni 3.155.66).

3. Pearl (Maṇi)

Pearls strung on a thread symbolize philosophical unity in diversity. Thus, Lord Kṛṣṇa says that all this universe is strung on Him as many pearls are strung on a thread (mayi sarvam idaṃ protaṃ sūtre maṇigaṇā iva 6.29.7).

The Gangā River is likened to a garland of pearls (muktā*valī*):

tāṃ dadhāra haro rājan
gaṅgāṃ gaganamekhalām /
lalāṭadeśe patitāṃ
mālāṃ muktāmayīm iva 3.108.9.

Lord Śiva bore that Gaṅgā having the sky as girdle, who fell on his forehead, like a garland made of pearls. Cf. Ragh. 13.48.

4. Gem (Ratna)

In one passage, a gem symbolizes the dearest one. Draupadī, the dearest one (iṣṭatamā) to the Pāṇḍavas, is likened to an excellent gem (anuttamaṃ ratnam iva 3.253.13).

XXXIV. RELATIVES (SAṂBANDHIN)

We have already seen a kinship term used to intensify the force of a simile (mṛtyor ghorām iva śvasām 6.112.3; section I,12). The relatives occurring as primary *upamānas* in this corpus are mainly father (pitṛ) and mother (matṛ). The teacher (guru) may also be included here.

1. Father (Pitṛ)

Already in a number of passages in the Ṛgveda, the father (pitṛ) appears as a standard of affection. The vedic seer implores the fire god to be of easy access as a father is to his son (sá naḥ pité 'va sūnáve ágne sūpāyanó bhava RV 1.1.9).

In the present corpus, the father as an *upamāna* is found employed in two ways: from the point of view of paternal affection and from the point of view of filial regard; but more often it appears in the first form, usually accompanied by the son (putra, suta, or prajā).

i) *Paternal affection.*—Vyuṣitāśva protects all the castes as a father protects his own sons (apālayat sarvavarṇān pitā putrān ivau 'rasān 1.112.13; cf. 1.110.11: 3.3.5; 24.7; 47.9). Yudhiṣṭhira going into exile in the forest is described as abandoning his subjects like a father abandoning his sons (pite 'va putrān apahāya cā 'smān 3.24.9).

Sometimes, paternal affection takes the shape of advice; e.g., like a father instructing his sons, Mātali instructs the Pāṇḍavas and goes away (pite 'va putrān anuśiṣya cai 'nān 3.161.25; cf. 3.173.21).

Arjuna implores Lord Kṛṣṇa to pardon his faults as a father pardons those of a son, a friend those of a friend, a lover those of his beloved (pite 'va putrasya sakhe 'va sakhyḥ priyaḥ priyāyā 'rhasi deva soḍhum 6.33.44).

As a father lifts his fallen son, so does the minister lift the fallen king Saṃvaraṇa who is unable to bear his beloved Tapatī's sudden disappearance (taṃ samutthāpayām āsa . . . pite 'va patitaṃ sutam 1.162.5).

Bhīṣma embraces Karṇa by one arm as a father embraces his son (pite 'va putraṃ gāṅgeyaḥ pariṣvajyai 'kabāhunā 6.117.7).

Damayantī, lamenting, accuses the Himālaya of not consoling her with its voice as a father consoles his distressed daughter (girā nā 'śvāsayasy adya svāṃ sutām iva duḥkhitām 3.61.52; cf. 3.240.25).

ii) *Filial regard.*—From very childhood, Parāśara, the grandson, treats Vasiṣṭha as his father (janmaprabhṛti tasmiṃś ca pitarī 'va vyavartata 1.169.4; cf. 3.24.7: 6.110.35; 1.80.18 ananvaya).

2. Mother (Mātṛ)

The mother symbolizes nourishment. Thus, a good reputation nourishes a person in the world as a mother nourishes her child (kīrtir hi puruṣaṃ loke saṃjīvayati mātṛvat 3.284.32).

In some contexts, this figure predominantly stands for sacredness; e.g., Duḥṣanta views the Mālinī River near the hermitage, having sacred water, as a mother of all creatures (nadīm āśramasaṃśliṣṭāṃ puṇyatoyāṃ dadarśa saḥ / sarvaprāṇibhṛtāṃ tatra jananīm iva viṣṭhitām 1.64.20).

A sincere housewife who properly feeds her husband and other members of the family is also likened to a mother. Thus, Draupadī used to eat what was left of the food after feeding her husband (and other members of the family) as a mother eats the rest of the food after feeding her children (māte 'va bhojayitvā 'gre śiṣṭam āhārayat tadā 3.47.10).

3. Teacher (Guru)

The teacher (guru) is an *upamāna* as one worthy of honor; e.g., Arjuna respects his elder brother (Yudhiṣṭhira) as his teacher (guruvan mānavagurum mānayitvā manasvinam 3.25.4).

The following passages have kinsmen in general as *upamānas* for intimacy of feeling:

a) satataṃ smā 'nvatapyanta
tam eva bharatarṣabham /
paurajānapadāḥ sarve
mṛtam svam iva bāndhavam 1.119.4.

Townsmen and country people always regretted him (Pāṇḍu), the lord of the Bharatas, like their own dead kinsman.

b) ayaṃ sa puruṣavyāghraḥ
punar āyāti dharmavit /
yo naḥ svān iva dāyādān
dharmataḥ parirakṣati 1.199.17.

This tiger among men (Pāṇḍu) comes again, the knower of virtue, the one who protects us in accordance with what is right, as his own kinsmen.

c) sa samaṃ dharmakāmārthān
siṣeve bharatarṣabhaḥ /
trīn ivā 'tmasamān bandhūn
bandhumān iva mānayan 1.214.3.

He (Yudhiṣṭhira), the best among the Bharatas, devoted himself to virtue, pleasure, and profit equally, considering them like three kinsmen equal to himself, as if having them as kinsmen. Cf. Bhāravi, Kirātārjunīya 1.10.

We find the figurative use of more than one kinship term in each of the following passages:

a) keṣāṃ cid abhavad bhrātā
keṣāṃ cid abhavat sakhā /
ṛṣayas tv apare cai 'naṃ
putravat paryapālayan 1.111.3.

Pāṇḍu (while practising penance in the forest) behaved like a brother to some, like a friend to others; the sages, however, protected him like their own son.

b) guruvat pūjayām āsa
kāṃś cit kāṃś cid vayasyavat /
kāṃś cid abhyavadat premṇā
kaiś cid apy abhivāditaḥ 1.213.39.

Yudhiṣṭhira treated some as his teacher, some as his friend; he welcomed some with love and was himself respected by others.

c) putrān iva priyān jñātīn
bhrātṝn iva sahodarān /
pupoṣa kauravaśreṣṭho
dharmarājo yudhiṣṭhiraḥ 3.47.9.

The best among the Kurus, the king of virtue (Dharmarāja), Yudhiṣṭhira, maintained his kinsmen like dear sons, like own brothers.

d) snuṣā iva sa dharmātmā bhaginyā iva cā 'nujāḥ
yathā duhitaraś cai 'va pratigṛhyā 'yayau kurūn 1.96.44.

That virtuous one (Bhīṣma), having accepted them (the daughters of the king of Kāśī) as tenderly as if they were his daughters-in-law, younger sisters, or daughters, went back to the land of the Kurus.

XXXV. SAGES (ṚṢI)

The sages symbolize brilliance and virtue. Thus, the sons of Pracetas are described as having splendor like that of the great sages (maharṣisamatejasaḥ 1.70.3; cf. 1.89.54). Pāṇḍu practising penance is likened to an enlightened sage (brahmarṣisadṛśaḥ pāṇḍur 1.111.4).

The names of the sages occurring as *upamānas* are (1) Bṛhaspati, (2) Vālmīki, (3) Vasiṣṭha, (4) Kapila, (5) Dadhīca, (6) Aṅgiras, (7) Bhṛgu, (8) Atri, (9) Agastya, (10) Aurva, (11) Trita, and (12) Kākṣīvat.

1. Bṛhaspati

Bṛhaspati, the learned priest of the gods, primarily symbolizes learning; e.g., Dhaumya, enumerating the sacred places to the Pāṇḍavas, is likened to Bṛhaspati in learning (bṛhaspatisamo 'bravīt 3.85.1; cf. 3.261.10). Virtue cannot be understood even by Bṛhaspati-like (learned) men without knowledge of duty and devotion to the elders (na hi dharmam avijñāya vṛddhān anupasevya ca / dharmo vai veditum śakyo bṛhaspatisamair api 3.149.26).

Vasiṣṭha causing the Ikṣvākus to perform sacrifice is likened to Bṛhaspati causing the gods to perform sacrifice (bṛhaspatir ivā 'marān 1.164.11). Cf. section I,2.

Sometimes, Bṛhaspati symbolizes the powers of a sage, e.g., Autathya became the sage Dīrghatamas by name, like Bṛhaspati in power, through the curse of Bṛhaspati of great fame (sa vai dīrghatamā nāma śāpād ṛṣir ajāyata / bṛhaspater bṛhatkīrter bṛhaspatir ivau 'jasā 1.98.16)

2. Vālmīki

Vālmīki symbolizes patience; e.g., Janamejaya's great constancy is firm like that of Vālmīki when overrun by ants (vālmīkivat te nibhṛtaṃ sudhairyam 1.50.14).

3. Vasiṣṭha

Vasiṣṭha, who never retaliated even upon such enemies of his as Viśvāmitra and others, is the standard of the restraint of anger, as well as a standard of brilliance. Thus, Janamejaya's anger is restrained like that of Vasiṣṭha (vasiṣṭhavat te niyataś ca kopaḥ 1.50.14). Vasiṣṭha's son himself in brilliance is likened to Vasiṣṭha (ṛṣeḥ putraṃ vasiṣṭhasya vasiṣṭham iva tejasā 1.166.13).

4. Kapila

Kapila, the sage who burnt up with his eyes the sixty thousand sons of Sagara who were falsely accusing him of stealing the sacrificial horse released by Sagara, is an *upamāna* of destruction, e.g.:

> āsyād vaman pāvakaṃ sa
> saṃvartakasamaṃ tadā /
> tān sarvān nṛpateḥ putrān
> adahat svena tejasā //
> mukhajenā 'gninā kruddho
> lokān udvartayann iva /
> kṣaṇena rājaśārdūla
> pure 'va kapilaḥ prabhuḥ /

sagarasyā 'tmajān kruddhas
tad adbhutam ivā 'bhavat 3.195.24–25.

The demon Dhundhu, vomiting from his mouth fire like that of the time of the final destruction of the age, burnt up with his flames all those sons of Kuvalāśva, overwhelming as it were the whole world with his mouth-born fire as the enraged sage Kapila burnt up the sons of Sagara in times of yore, O tiger among men. This was wonderful indeed.

5. Dadhīca. 6. Añgiras

Dadhīca, the sage who gave his bones to Indra to kill Vṛtra, and Añgiras, the sage who guards the sun (cf. *Epic Myth.*, pp. 84, 180), symbolize protection, e.g.:

dadhīca iva devendraṃ
yathā cā 'py angirā ravim /
tathā rakṣasva kaunteyaṃ
rākṣasebhyo dvijottama 3.90.6.

As Dadhīca protected Indra, and also as Añgiras protected the sun god, so you (the sage Lomaśa) should protect Yudhiṣṭhira from the demons, O best one among the twice-born.

7. Bhṛgu. 8. Atri

Bhṛgu and Atri, along with Vasiṣṭha, occur as standards of brilliance; e.g., the forest of the hermits shines with the hermits, brilliant like Bhṛgu, Atri, and Vasiṣṭha (vasiṣṭhabhṛgvatrisamais tāpasair upaśobhitam 3.61.58).

9. Agastya

Agastya is the sage who digested the demon Vātāpi, whose habit it was to enter the bowel of a brāhmaṇa in the form of cooked food and to tear through the bowel subsequently. Thus, he symbolizes digestion of difficult objects; e.g., the demon Kirmīra intends to devour and digest Bhīma as Agastya digested the great demon (saṃbhakṣya jarayiṣyāmi yathā 'gastyo mahāsuram 3.82.89).

10. Aurva. 11. Trita

Aurva and Trita symbolize brightness. Janamejaya's brightness is likened to that of Aurva and Trita (aurvatritābhyām asi tulyatejāḥ 1.50.14).

12. Kākṣīvat

Kākṣīvat (= kakṣīvat) symbolizes enjoyment and delight; one who bathes in the Tapodas of Rajagṛha (modern Rajgir) rejoices like Kākṣīvat (upaspṛśya tapodeṣu kākṣīvān iva modate 3.82.89).

XXXVI. KING (RĀJAN)

The king symbolizes the giving of prosperity. Thus, this legend (the Mahābhārata) is drawn upon for sustenance by all excellent poets as a king of high birth is lived upon by the servants desirous of elevation to prosperity (idaṃ sarvaiḥ kavivarair ākhyānam upajīvyate / udaya-prepsubhir bhṛtyair abhijāta ive 'śvaraḥ 1.2.241).

The king lives luxuriously. The sage Vibhāṇḍaka, being treated as was his due by those cowherds, spent that night like a king (gopaiś ca tair vidhivat pūjyamāno rāje 'va tāṃ rātrim uvāsa tatra 3.113.16).

Duryodhana, being praised by the Brāhmaṇas with blessings for victory, is likened to a supreme king (jayāśīrbhir dvijendrais tu stūyamāno 'dhirājavat 3.240.44).

In the following passage, the king of the Dramiḍas symbolizes grace and charm:

aho batā 'yam agamaḥ
śrīmān asmin vanāntare /
āpīḍair bahubhir bhāti
śrīmān dramiḍarāḍ iva 3.61.98.

This beautiful *aśoka* tree shines with many chaplets of flowers in the heart of the forest like a beautiful king of the Dramiḍas.

Names of kings occur as *upamānas* for specific regal qualities. Brilliance and fame are, however, the highest common denominators.

The names that occur are: (1) Yayāti, (2) Purūravas, (3) Pūru, (4) Śibi, (5) Manu, (6) Ikṣvāku, (7) Bhagīratha, (8) Rantideva, son of Saṃkṛti, (9) Māndhātṛ, (10) Pṛthu, (11) Dambhodbhava, (12) Khaṭvāṅga, (13) Nābhāga, (14) Dilīpa, (15) Sahasrārjuna, (16) Rāma, (17) Kṛṣṇa, (18) Arjuna, (19) Bhīṣma, (20) Ajamīḍha, (21) Śaśabindu, (22) Gaya, and (23) Nṛga.

1. Yayāti

Yayāti, the son of king Nahuṣa, the celebrated founder of the Yādava and Paurava lines of the lunar race of kings, is referred to as an *upamāna* in various ways.

Thus, Nala performs the horse-sacrifice like Yayāti, the son of Nahuṣa (īje cā 'py aśvamedhena yayātir iva nāhuṣaḥ 3.54.36). It may be interesting to note that Yayāti already appears as an author of RV 9.101.4–6, and as a sacrificer in RV 1.31.17; 10.63.1. Yudhiṣṭhira shines with virtue like Yayāti, the virtuous one (yathā yayātir dharmātmā 3.83.108; cf. 1.50.13: 3.90.13). Karṇa wishes that the Pāṇḍavas would treat Duryodhana like Yayāti, the son of Nahuṣa (pāṇḍavās tvā 'bhivīkṣantāṃ yayātim iva nāhuṣam 3.226.15).

Yayāti's fall from heaven and his subsequent rescue by his daughter's sons are referred to. The form of Vasudeva falling from heaven is likened to that of Yayāti with his virtue consumed, falling from heaven to the surface of the earth (yayāteḥ kṣīṇapuṇyasya svargād iva mahītalam 3.22.23). Sātyaki does not want to wait for Yudhiṣṭhira's request for help; he wants to defeat Duryodhana and hand over the entire kingodm to Yudhiṣṭhira of his own initiative. Thus, he speaks to Balarāma: Those in the world who have helpers do not undertake a work of themselves; they have helpers in their works as Yayāti had Śibi and others (ye nāthavanto hi bhavanti loke te nā 'tmanā karma samārabhante / teṣāṃ tu kāryeṣu bhavanti nāthāḥ śaibyadayo rāma yathā yayāteḥ 3.120.2). The Brāhmaṇa-disciple, as a mark of gratitude for the immense knowledge he has gained from the hunter, speaks to the latter: As king Yayāti, fallen from heaven, was rescued by his noble daughter's sons, so I have been rescued by you, O tiger among men (rājā yayatir dauhitraiḥ patitas tārito yathā / sadbhiḥ puruṣaśārdūla tathā 'ham bhavatā tv iha 3.205.17). Cf. Ādiparvan, chapters 82–88. Note especially evaṃ rājā sa mahātmā hy atīva svair dauhitrais tārito 'mitrasāhaḥ 1.88.26, "thus was the exceedingly great-souled king, the conqueror of enemies, rescued by his own daughter's sons." The epithet *amitrasāha*, 'a conqueror of enemies,' also appears as a synonym for Indra in Atharvaveda 1.20.4, śāsá itthá mahā́ṅ asy amitrasāhó astṛtáh, "you are verily a great ruler, a conqueror of enemies, unsubdued." Cf. *Epic Myth.*, p. 104.

In ABHS 4.82, Yayāti paired with Śarmiṣṭhā appears as a standard of conjugal love.

2. Purūravas

Purūravas, the great-grandfather of Yayāti and the son of Budha (Mercury) and Ilā, stands as an *upamāna* for both a lover who has attained his beloved, and a virtuous person.

Thus, Janamejaya, the powerful one, the best among the kings, with pleased mind enjoyed himself in company of his wife in lakes and flowering woods, as Purūravas did in the past on attaining Urvaśī as his wife (sarahsu phulleṣu vaneṣu cai 'va ha prasannacetā vijahāra vīryavān / tathā sa rājanyavaro vijahrivān yatho 'rvaśīṃ prāpya purā purūravāḥ 1.40.10). As Yayāti is virtuous, or as is King Purūravas, so Yudhiṣṭhira shines with his own virtue (yathā yayātir dharmātmā yathā rājā purūravāḥ / tathā tvaṃ kuruśārdūla svena dharmeṇa śobhase 3.83.108). Cf. 1, Yayāti, above.

3. Pūru

Pūru, the son of Yayāti and Śarmiṣṭhā and sixth monarch of the lunar race, is referred to as a personality of great fame. Thus, Yudhiṣṭhira's great fame is likened to Pūru's (yathā pūrur mahāyaśāḥ 3.83.110).

4. Śibi

Śibi, a king of the lunar race through Yayāti's daughter, "renowned for his liberality and unselfishness, and said to have saved Agni transformed into a dove from Indra transformed into a hawk by offering an equal quantity of his own flesh weighed in a balance" (MW), is referred to as a standard of piety, truthfulness, and courage. The famous story of his giving his own flesh is, however, not used as an *upamāna* in this corpus.

Satyavān is like Saṃkṛti's son Rantideva in bestowal of gifts according to his power; he is devoted to Brāhmaṇas and is truthful in speech like Śibi, the son of Uśīnara (saṃkṛte rantidevasya sa śaktyā dānataḥ samaḥ / brahmaṇyaḥ satyavādī ca śibir auśīnaro yathā 3.278.17); cf. 8, Rantideva, below.

Kuntī's son, Arjuna, like Sahasrārjuna, in courage like Śibi, invincible like Indra, will enhance his family's glory (kārtavīryasamaḥ kunti śibitulyaparākramaḥ / eṣa śakra ivā 'jeyo yaśas te prathayiṣyati 1.114.29).

5. Manu

Manu, the first man, possesses all good qualities. He symbolizes fame and possession of virtue. Yudhiṣṭhira is exceedingly famous (mahāyaśāḥ) like Manu (yathā manur 3.83.110). At the close of a description of Nala as possessing all virtue, he is likened to Manu (sākṣād iva manuḥ svayam 3.50.4).

6. Ikṣvāku

Ikṣvāku, a son of Manu and the first king of the solar dynasty in Ayodhyā, is also a standard of fame. Yudhiṣṭhira's fame is like Ikṣvāku's (yathe 'kṣvākur 3.83.110).

7. Bhagīratha

Bhagīratha, the son of Dilīpa and grandfather of Sagara, who brought down the Gangā River from heaven to earth, symbolizes fame and brightness. Yudhiṣṭhira is illustrious like Bhagīratha (yathā bhagīratho rājā 3.83.109; cf. 3.90.13). Janamejaya's scorching brightness is likened to Bhagīratha's (duṣprekṣaṇīyo 'si bhagīratho vā 1.50.16).

8. Rantideva

Rantideva, the son of Saṃkṛti, the benevolent ancient king (referred to in Megha. 1.45), symbolizes benevolence; cf. 4, Śibi, above, 3.278.17.

9. Māndhātṛ

King Māndhātṛ, the son of Yuvanāśva, author of RV 10.134, is referred to as a standard of brilliance. Arjuna shines as Māndhātṛ shone in times of yore (vyarocata yathā pūrvaṃ māndhātā pārthivottamaḥ 3.43.37; cf. 1.50.13).

10. Pṛthu

King Pṛthu, son of king Vena, is famous as a brilliant king. So is Yudhiṣṭhira (yathā vainyo mahātejāḥ 3.83.110).

11. Dambhodbhava

King Dambhodbhava is the *upamāna* of might. Janamejaya is like Dambhodbhava in might (dambhodbhavenā 'si samo balena 1.50.16).

12. Khatvāṅga. 13. Nābhāga. 14. Dilīpa

Janamejaya is brilliant like Khatvāṅga, Nābhāga, Dilīpa, Yayāti and Māndhātṛ (khatvāṅganābhāgadilīpakalpo yayātimāndhātṛsamaprabhāvaḥ 1.50.13; cf. 1 and 9 above).

15. Sahasrārjuna

Sahasrārjuna is a prince of the Haihayas, referred to in the passages in which he is the *upamāna* by his other name, Kārtavīrya. He symbolizes valor and fame through virtue. King Bhoja is likened to Kārtavīrya on the battlefield (kārtavīryasamo yudhi 3.13.30; cf. 1.114.29: 3.79.12). Nārada predicts that, like Sahasrārjuna, Yudhiṣṭhira will attain fame through virtue (khyātiṃ yāsyasi dharmeṇa kārtavīryārjuno yathā 3.83.112).

16. Rāma

Rāma symbolizes knowledge of the secrets of missiles (cf. rāmah śastrabhṛtām aham 6.32.31), protection, pursuit of virtue and truth, and fame.

Janamejaya knows both *śastra* and *astra* (various kinds of missiles) like Rāma (rāmo yathā śastravid astravic ca 1.50.16).

In truth and in virtue, Bhīṣma and Droṇa are not inferior to Rāma, the son of Daśaratha, and to Gaya himself (dharme cā 'navamau rājan satyatāyāṃ ca bhārata / rāmād dāśarātheś cai 'va gayāc cai 'va na saṃśayaḥ 1.197.6). Yudhiṣṭhira's fame is likened to that of Rāma (yathā rāmaś ca viśrutaḥ 3.83.109).

17. Kṛṣṇa

Kṛṣṇa, son of Vasudeva, appears as a standard of might and powers. Abhimanyu is likened to Kṛṣṇa in might and strength (sadṛśo vāsudevasya vikrameṇa balena ca 6.97.31; cf. 3.84.3; 142.19: 6.51.16; 91.4; 117.14).

18. Arjuna

Like Rāma, Arjuna symbolizes a thorough knowledge of missiles, although his figurative value is doubtful in the passage we have. Thus, Bhīṣma describes Karṇa as equal to Arjuna (Phalguna) and great-souled Kṛṣṇa in his bow, on aiming a multitude of arrows (i.e., in shooting arrows in rapid succession), in dexterity, and also in the strength of his weapons (iṣvastre bhārasaṃdhāne lāghave 'strabale tathā / sadṛśaḥ phalgunenā 'si kṛṣṇena ca mahātmanā 6.117.14).

19. Bhīṣma

Bhīṣma, son of king Śantanu and grandfather of the Pāṇḍavas and Kauravas, symbolizes brilliance and strictness in observing vows (owing to his famous vow of life-long abstinence), as in Janamejaya's comparison with him (bhīṣmo yathā bhrājasi suvratas tvam 1.50.13).

20. Ajamīḍha. 21. Śaśabindu. 22. Gaya. 23. Nṛga

The names of Ajamīḍha, Śaśabindu, Gaya, and Nṛga are referred to in 1.50.1–7 in a long list of kings who performed celebrated sacrifices in the past and as such serve as *upamānas* for Janamejaya performing the snake-sacrifice. Gaya also appears in 1.197.6 and 3.90.13 as a standard of virtuous acts and brilliance respectively; cf. 16 and 7 above.

It seems that the epic has a special regard for the kings of the lunar line in connection with the *upamānas* for regal qualities. A comparison of the similar *upamānas* of the whole Mahābhārata (depicting primarily the life of the kings of the lunar line) with those of the Rāmāyaṇa (dealing primarily with the life of Rāma and his immediate predecessors of the solar line) may result in some conclusive evidence in this connection.

XXXVII. OTHER PERSONAL NAMES

1. Paraśurāma

Paraśurāma, the son of Jamadagni, Brāhmaṇa-warrior, is a standard of might, destruction of the warrior class, and respect for parents.

Arjuna, like Paraśurāma and Viṣṇu in valor, the best one among the powerful, will be invincible (jāmadagnyasamaḥ kunti viṣṇutulyaparākramaḥ / eṣa vīryavatāṃ śreṣṭho bhaviṣyaty aparājitaḥ 1.114.34; cf. 3.142.19).

Droṇa, being a skillful archer, meant for the destruction of the warrior class, is likened to Paraśurāma (kṣatrocchedāya vihito jāmadagnya ivā 'sthitaḥ 1.155.26).

The parents admire the services of their son, the hunter: As his old parents were honored by Paraśurāma, so everything has been done by you—rather even better than by him, O dear son (jāmadagnyena rāmeṇa yathā vṛddhau supūjitau / tathā tvayā kṛtaṃ sarvam tadviśiṣṭaṃ ca putraka 3.204.12).

2. Hanumat

Hanumat, the monkey god, leaped over the ocean. So, if he (i.e., Bhīma) had not known that he should not do so, Bhīma would have leaped over Hanumat (lying incognito on the way) and the mountain (krameyaṃ tvāṃ giriṃ ce 'maṃ hanumān iva sāgaram 3.147.9).

3. Vālin and Sugrīva

That tree fight (between Bhīma and Kirmīra), destructive of trees, was like that in times of yore between the brothers Vālin and Sugrīva who were desirous of the kingship of Kiṣkindhā (tad vṛkṣayuddham abhavan mahīruhavināśanam / vālisugrīvayor bhrātror yathā śrīkāṅkṣiṇoḥ purā 3.12.47; cf. 3.154.49).

4. Personal Names as Standards of Conjugal Love

The following passage contains the names of the gods, kings, and sages, and their wives as standards of conjugal love:

śāntā cai 'nāṃ paryacarad yathāvat
khe rohiṇī somam ivā 'nukūlā //
arundhatī vā subhagā vasiṣṭhaṃ
lopāmudrā vā 'pi yathā hy agastyam
nalasya vā damayantī yathā 'bhūd
yathā śacī vajradharasya cai 'va //
nāḍāyanī ce 'ndrasenā yathai 'va
vaśyā nityaṃ mudgalasyā 'jamīḍha
tathā śāntā ṛṣyaśṛṅgaṃ vanasthaṃ
prītyā yuktā paryacaran narendra // 3.113.22–4.

And Śāntā duly waited upon Ṛṣyaśṛṅga as faithful Rohiṇī waits upon Soma (the moon), or as fortunate Arundhatī and Lopāmudrā (wait upon) Vasiṣṭha and Agastya respectively.

As Damayantī was an obedient wife to Nala, Śacī to Indra, Indrasenā, the descendent of Nada, to Mudgala, O descendent of Ajamīḍha, likewise Śāntā, endowed with love, waited upon Ṛṣyaśṛṅga when he was staying in the forest, O King!

Cf. sections I,2, Indra, VI, Moon, XI, Constellation and Stars. Note that Mudgalānī (Indrasenā) as Mudgala's wife occurs already in RV 10.102. Mudgala wins a chariot race through her help. It is not clear whether Mudgala has two wives, Nāḍāyanī and Indrasenā, or only one, the same Indrasenā being a descendent of Naḍa. The *Vedic Index*, *Epic Mythology*, and the available dictionaries are all silent about Nāḍāyanī.

This much is clear, however: according to available evidence, Mudgala has only one wife. Thus, presumably Nāḍāyanī is an epithet denoting Indrasenā's descent.

5. Sāvitrī

Sāvitrī saved her husband Satyavān from death. So Draupadī will save all her husbands from destruction (tārayiṣyati vaḥ sarvān sāvitrī 'va kulāṅganā 3.283.15).

XXXVIII. VARIOUS PHASES OF HUMAN LIFE

The following are examples of the various phases of human life employed as *upamānas*.

1. Witness (Sākṣin)

The fire god (Agni) always pervades the hearts of all creatures, like a witness of their merits and sins, and as such he is asked to tell the real fact (tvam agne sarvabhūtānām antaś carasi nityadā / sākṣivat puṇya-pāpeṣu satyaṃ brūhi kave vacaḥ 1.5.23; cf. 3.75.9).

2. Ordinary, Common Folk (Prākṛta)

Nakula and Sahadeva, who are like the Aśvins among the gods by virtue of their high degree of beauty, now sleep in the forest on the ground like common folk (aśvināv iva devānāṃ yāv imau rūpasampadā / tau prākṛtavad adye 'mau prasuptau dharaṇītale 1.138.23; cf. 1.138.21,22).

Duryodhana and Duḥśāsana, when in a state of affliction, are described by Karṇa as yielding to sorrow like ordinary men through folly (viṣīdataḥ kiṃ kauravyau bāliśyāt prākṛtāv iva 3.238.34; cf. 3.238.37: 6.99.23).

3. Helpless or Unprotected Person (Anātha)

The term *anāthavat*, 'like one who is helpless or unprotected,' occurs in five passages in this corpus. In 3.116.26, it is an *upamāna* for Jamadagni, who, being ruthlessly killed by the enemy, cried "Rāma, Rāma" again and again like a helpless person (asakṛd rāma rāme 'ti vikrośantam anāthavat 3.116.26). Otherwise it is used in connection with helpless women; e.g., Damayantī being swallowed by the *ajagara*-snake or weeping is likened to a helpless person (grasyamānām anāthavat 3.60.22; vilapantīm anāthavat 3.61.22); cf. 1.165.26, in which a cow refers to herself with the words krandantīṃ mām anāthavat. Nala is, moreover, worried about the fact that Damayantī, his beloved, whom neither the wind nor the sun ever saw, now sleeps on the ground in a public place like a helpless person (yāṃ na vāyur na cā 'dityaḥ purā paśyati me priyām / se 'yam adya sabhāmadhye śete bhūmāv anāthavat 3.59.19).

4. Intoxicated Person (Matta)

The River Gaṅgā, in places going crooked because of her windings, in various places tumbling (over rapids), covered over with her own foam as clothing, sometimes uttering a loud sound with the sounds of water, moved like an intoxicated wanton woman (kvacid ābhogakuṭilā praskhalantī kvacit kvacit / svaphenapaṭasaṃvītā matte 'va pramadā 'vrajat / kvacit sā toyaninadair nadanti nādam uttamam 3.108.11).

The boat in the ocean at the time of the deluge, tossed about by stormy winds, moved to and fro like a wanton drunken woman (kṣobhyamāṇā mahāvātaiḥ sā naus tasmin mahodadhau / ghūrṇate capale 'va strī mattā parapuraṃjaya 3.185.40).

The Kaurava army is not able to resist like a woman on the road who is in the stupor of intoxication (na saṃhārayituṃ śaktā tava senā janādhipa / madamūrchānvitā 'tmānaṃ pramade 'vā 'dhvani sthitā 6.73.57; cf. 6.96.18).

An intoxicated woman, rather than a man, is an *upamāna* of reeling movement in all the three passages given above; however, the *upameya* in each case is of the feminine gender, and lack of a masculine in this corpus may be accidental.

Mattakāśini, 'O (you) who look like an intoxicated person,' is a form of address to a bewitching woman; cf. Saṃvaraṇa's address to Tapatī in 1.160.37; 161.7.

5. A Diseased Person (Vyādhikliṣṭa)

Warriors smitten by Droṇa, writhing on the ground, seem like persons afflicted with disease (viveṣṭantaḥ sma dṛśyante vyādhikliṣṭā narā iva 6.85.22).

Vidura's advice was not liked by Dhṛtarāṣṭra as wholesome food is not liked by a sick person (yathā 'turasye 'va hi pathyam annam na rocate smā 'sya tad ucyamānam 3.6.14).

The terrible fight of Abhimanyu with Vikarṇa and others took place like that of the body with the three humors—wind (vāta), bile (pitta), and phlegm (kapha) (abhimanyos tatas tais tu ghoraṃ yuddham avartata / śarīrasya yathā rājan vātapittakaphais tribhiḥ 6.80.39).

A creature in a new rebirth accumulates again much other new *karma* and is tormented by it again, as a patient having eaten unwholesome food is later troubled by it (tataḥ karma samādatte punar anyan navaṃ bahu / pacyate tu punas tena bhuktvā 'pathyam ivā 'turaḥ 3.200.36). Cf. section XXXIX,1, Soul.

6. Dumb Person (Jaḍamūka)

Nakula, Sahadeva, and Kuntī, longing for Yudhiṣṭhira's welfare but sitting quiet, are likened to an apathetic, dumb person (tavai 'va priyam icchanta āsate jaḍamūkavat 3.36.14).

7. Lame Persons, Persons with Crippled Arm (Kuṇi-paṅgu), Blind Person

The man whose arms are crippled and the lame man symbolize weakness and helplessness. Bhīma reproaches Yudhiṣṭhira for the latter's pacific policy, due to which the Pāṇḍavas' fortune has been snatched away by the Kauravas, as the *bilva* fruits of the man with a crippled arm and the cows of the lame man are enjoyed by others (kuṇīnām iva bilvāni paṅgūnām iva dhenavaḥ hṛtam / aiśvaryam asmākaṃ jivatām bhavataḥ kṛte 3.34.7). Blind person, *vide* section V.

8. A Disordered, Frantic Person (Unmatta)

Disorder in actions or frantic actions (madness) is the figure of bewilderment. Thus, Nala, leaving Damayantī sleeping alone in the forest, visualizes her feelings after she should wake: How she will be like a frantic person, after waking (unmatte 'va varārohā kathaṃ buddhvā bhaviṣyati 3.59.20). Again, Damayantī, weeping, afflicted with grief, and going alone in the forest is likened to a frantic person (unmattavad bhīmasutā vilapantī tatas tataḥ 3.60.18; unmattarūpā śokārtā 3.61.110; unmattām iva gacchantīm 3.62.19).

Nala is distressed like a frantic person (unmattam iva vihvalam 3.62.29; cf. 3.246.12; 282.5).

The battle between the Pāṇḍavas and the Kauravas was interesting to look at for a moment; but very soon it became too complicated in its actions like a frantic person, and nothing could be made out (muhūrtam iva tad yuddham āsīn madhuradarśanam / tata unmattavad rājan na prājñāyata kiṃ cana 6.43.78).

One may compare the description of the winds as persons of frantic actions (. . . prāvartanto 'nmattā matariśvānaḥ) in Bāṇabhaṭṭa's Harṣacarita.[16]

9. One Insane Owing to Demoniac Seizure (Āviṣṭa)

The Pāṇḍavas fought with the Kauravas, as if possessed by demons (āviṣṭā iva yudhyante pāṇḍavāḥ kurubhiḥ saha 6.44.3; cf. 6.86.85). Cf. Caraka, Cikitsā 9.20 (16) and Suśruta, Uttar. 60.14.

[16] Bāṇabhaṭṭa's Harṣacarita, ed. A. A. Fuhrer (Bombay, 1909), Ucch. II, p. 81.

10. Eunuch (Klība)

Though primarily a figure of timidity and weakness (cf. Kṛṣṇa's accusation against Arjuna of eunuch-like cowardice in klaibyam mā sma gamaḥ pārtha 6.24.3), eunuch-like behavior towards other men's wives by a faithful husband is a standard of nobility. Damayantī is proud of her husband Nala, who being a faithful husband with respect to acts of privacy, behaves like a eunuch towards other women (raho 'nīcānuvartī ca klībavan mama naiṣadhaḥ 3.71.14).

11. The Virtuous (Sukṛtin)

The best ones among the Bharatas, the Pāṇḍavas, entered that beautiful forest, as the virtuous enter heaven (tad vanaṃ bharataśreṣṭhāḥ svargaṃ sukṛtino yathā 3.244.16; cf. 1.213.53: 3.43.18). *Vide* section I,2, Indra's heaven.

12. The Enemy (Amitra)

Śeṣa complains to Brahmā about the behavior of his brothers: they always envy one another like enemies (abhyasūyanti satataṃ parasparam amitravat 1.32.9).

13. An Unchaste Woman (Puṃścalī)

Duḥṣanta sarcastically says to Śakuntalā, who appeared in his court to be accepted as his wife: Being a child of the divine harlot (apsaras) Menakā and the sage Viśvāmitra, how will you speak like an unchaste woman? (tayor apatyaṃ kasmāt tvam puṃścalī 'vā bhidhasyasi 1.68.75; cf. 3.6.15). This, in fact, is a specimen of *kākuvakrokti* (cf. SD 10.643), where something else is meant than what is uttered, and is indicated by means of intonation. In the above passage, Duḥṣanta means that Śakuntalā, being a harlot's daughter, is definitely speaking like an unchaste woman.

Vidura is disappointed to note that Dhṛtarāṣṭra cannot be led to a virtuous path, like an unchaste wife of one well versed in the Vedas; he does not appeal to Dhṛtarāṣṭra, as a sixty-year-old husband does not appeal to a girl (na śreyase nīyate 'jātaśatro stri śrotriyasye 'va gṛhe praduṣṭā / bruvan na rucyai bharatarṣabhasya patiḥ kumāryā iva ṣaṣṭivarṣaḥ 3.6.15; cf. section XXXIV).

14. Impure Person (Aśuci)

Anu, rejecting his father Yayāti's request that they should exchange their ages, says: An old man takes his food like a child, like an impure person, at the wrong time, and he does not offer oblation to the fire at the right time; therefore I do not desire that old age (jīrṇaḥ śiśuvad ādatte 'kāle 'nnam aśucir yathā / na juhoti ca kāle 'gniṃ tāṃ jarāṃ nā 'bhikāmaye 1.79.21).

15. A Wicked Person (Nṛśaṃsa)

The Brāhmaṇa, who must send a member of his family as food for the demon, wants to go himself instead of, like a wicked person, giving up another member of his family while he himself is alive (svayaṃ jīvan nṛśaṃsavat 1.145.30).

16. A Distressed Person (Ārta)

Having heard of the death of Kirmīra, Dhṛtarāṣṭra sighed heavily like a distressed person (niśaśvāsā 'rtavat tadā 3.12.75).

17. A Coward (Kāpuruṣa)

Pradyumna, who while lying senseless on his chariot has been brought back from the battlefield by the charioteer, is, after coming to his senses, unhappy about his going away and leaving the battlefield like a coward (apayātaṃ raṇam hitvā yathā kāpuruṣaṃ tathā 3.19.32).

18. Hungry Persons

The noise of persons moaning, shrieking, and groaning on the battlefield was heard unceasingly, resembling that of persons afflicted with hunger (kūjatāṃ krandatāṃ cai 'va stanatām cai 'va saṃyuge / aniśam śrūyate śabdaḥ kṣutkṛśānāṃ nṛṇām iva 6.85.23).

19. Persons Afflicted with Heat

As one afflicted with heat receives showers of rain, so Bhīṣma received the showers of arrows of Śikhaṇḍin (uṣṇārto hi naro yadvaj jaladhārāḥ pratīcchati / tathā jagrāha gāṅgeyaḥ śaradhārāḥ śikhaṇḍinaḥ 6.112.100).

20. Base Men (Nīca)

Saṃjaya says that the atrocities perpetrated by the Kauravas are like those done by base men (nīcair iva yathā naraiḥ 6.61.18).

21. Spectators

All the other kings saw the terrible battle as spectators witness a spectacle (prekṣakā iva bhārata 6.42.23).

22. Neutral (Udāsīna)

Lord Kṛṣṇa describes Himself as sitting like a neutral king (udāsīnavad āsīnam 6.31.9). Likewise, a wise person unaffected by the qualities (guṇas) of Nature is likened to a neutral king (udāsīnavad āsīno 6.36.23).

23. Caste (Varṇa)

The Mahābhārata is as excellent as a Brāhmaṇa among human beings (dvipadāṃ brāhmaṇo yathā 1.1.201). After the Pāṇḍavas and Kauravas are united, Vidura thinks, all the kings would at once humbly approach them like merchants (tato rājan pārthivāḥ sarva eva vaiśyā ivā 'smān upatiṣṭhantu sadyaḥ 3.5.13). Duryodhana, as if jumping in (to the pool) through a mistake, was derided by Bhīma, like a person of low descent, in the presence of Kṛṣṇa (yatrā 'vahasitaś cā 'sīt praskandann iva saṃbhramāt / pratyakṣaṃ vāsudevasya bhīmenā 'nabhijātavat 1.1.90). The conduct of the Kauravas in the assembly (where Draupadī was insulted) was like that of Dasyus, i.e., robbers (dasyūnām iva yad vṛttam sabhāyāṃ kurunandana 3.11.7).

The wrathful one (Duryodhana), being himself unable to defeat the Pāṇḍavas in the battlefield and being devoid of courage, proposed an unfair game of dice with the help of the king of Gāndhāra, in order to gain the kingly fortune in unkṣatriya-like fashion (amarṣitaḥ svayaṃ jetum aśaktaḥ pāṇḍavān raṇe / nirutsāhaś ca samprāptuṃ śriyam akṣatriyo yathā / gāndhārarājasahitaś chadmadyūtam amantrayat 1.1.100).

24. Age (Vayas)

Janamejaya remarks about the learned benediction of Āstīka: (though) a child, he speaks like an old (and wise) person (bālo vākyam sthavira iva prabhāṣate 1.51.1).

25. A Corpse

The *niṣādha*-woman with her five sons slept in the Vāraṇāvata palace, unconscious as if a corpse (suṣvāpa vigatajñānā mṛtakalpā narādhipa 1.136.8).

26. Falsehood (Anṛta)

How could such an (unfortunate) occurrence afflict Draupadī conversant with virtue, virtuous-acting, any more than a false accusation of theft an honest man? (kathaṃ hi patnīm asmākaṃ dharmajñāṃ dharmacāriṇīm / saṃspṛśed īdṛśo bhāvaḥ śuciṃ stainyam ivā 'nṛtam 3.257.5).

27. Phases of Human Life as Elucidative of Philosophical or Ethical Ideas

a)
saṃprayojya viyojyā 'yaṃ
kāmakārakaraḥ prabhuḥ /
krīḍate bhagavān bhūtair
bālaḥ krīḍanakair iva 3.31.36.

Draupadī says: This Lord, acting at his own will, the powerful one, plays with the creatures, (sometimes) uniting, (sometimes) separating them, as a child plays with his toys.

b) na mātṛpitṛvad rājan
dhātā bhūteṣu vartate /
roṣād iva pravṛtto 'yam
yathā 'yam itaro janaḥ 3.31.37.

(Draupadī): O King (Yudhiṣṭhira), God does not act like a mother or a father in relation to creatures; he acts as if from anger like this other (ordinary) person.

c) tathai 'va haṭhabuddhir yaḥ
śaktaḥ karmaṇy akarmakṛt /
āsīta na ciraṃ jīved
anātha iva durbalaḥ 3.33.13.

Likewise, one who, thinking that all is absolutely determined, should sit, capable of action but doing no action—he would not live long, like a weak person without a protector.

d) ativelaṃ hi yo 'rthārthī
ne 'tarāv anutiṣṭhati /
sa vadhyaḥ sarvabhūtānāṃ
brahmahe 'va jugupsitaḥ 3.34.25.

The one who, extremely desirous of wealth, does not practise the other two (virtue and desire), deserves to be destroyed by all creatures, as a contemptible killer of a Brāhmaṇa deserves to be killed by all.

e) yasya cā 'rthārtham evā 'rthaḥ
sa ca nā 'rthasya kovidaḥ /
rakṣate bhṛtako 'raṇyaṃ
yathā syāt tādṛg eva saḥ 3.34.24.

And he whose wealth is only for wealth's sake, but he is not conversant with wealth, he would be like that hired laborer who guards the forest (not for his own use but for the use of his master).

f) lakṣaṇaṃ tu prasādasya
yathā tṛptaḥ sukhaṃ svapet /
nivāte vā yathā dīpo
dīpyet kuśaladīpitaḥ 3.203.36.

The characteristic of spiritual peace is: as a person in contentment could sleep at ease, or as a lamp in a windless place could shine when lighted by an expert (cf. 6.28.19).

g) saktāḥ karmaṇy avidvāṃso
yathā kurvanti bhārata /
kuryād vidvāṃs tathā 'saktaś
cikīrṣur lokasaṃgraham 6.25.25.

As the unwise persons act being attached to action, O descendent of the Bharatas, so should a wise person act (though seemingly attached to action, yet in fact) detached, desirous to effect the guidance of the world.

A good *virodha*, which actually negates the *upamā!* A very complicated figure indeed. Cf. chapter 6,II.

XXXIX. PHILOSOPHICAL TERMS

1. Soul (Ātman)

Like the soul among things that are to be known and the life among things that are dear, this Itihāsa (the Mahābhārata) with its excellent contents is the best among all scriptures (ātme 'va veditavyeṣu priyeṣv iva ca jīvitam / itihāsaḥ pradhānārthaḥ śreṣṭhaḥ sarvāgameṣv ayam 1.2.31).

This kind of emotion (i.e., affliction owing to Sītā's separation) ought not to touch you, O Rāma, O bestower of honors, as disease cannot touch a person who is self-possessed, having the nature of an old man (na tvām evaṃvidho bhāvaḥ spraṣṭum arhati mānada / ātmavantam iva vyādhiḥ puruṣaṃ vṛddhaśīlinam 3.264.4; cf. XXXVIII, 5 and 24).

2. Indifference to Things of the World (Vairāgya)

The Mahābhārata is approached for aid by learned men as indifference to the things of the world is by those desirous of salvation (abhipannaṃ naraiḥ prājñair vairāgyam iva mokṣibhiḥ 1.2.30).

3. Virtue (Dharma)

Nobody could see any difference between Arjuna and Bhīṣma in battle, as nobody finds sin anywhere in one established in virtue (na tayor vivaraṃ kaś cid raṇe paśyati bhārata / dharme sthitasya hi yathā na kaś cid vṛjinaṃ kva cit 6.48.60).

Arjuna practising penance is likened to virtue incarnate (dharmo vigrahavān iva 3.78.21; cf. 1.45.7).

4. The *Vedas* (Veda)

As the expounders of the Vedas obtained the Vedas through penance, so Śaradvat endowed with penance obtained all his weapons (adhijagmur yathā vedāṃs tapasā brahmavādinaḥ / tathā sa tapaso 'petaḥ sarvāṇy astrāṇy avāpa ha 1.120.4).

Sītā, like the vedic revelation (at the beginning of creation), was recovered from Laṅkā (punaḥ pratyāhṛtā bhāryā naṣṭā vedaśrutir yathā 3.147.36).

The weak-spirited one, by whom virtue or the words of the sages are doubted, would be debarred from that world which is devoid of old age and death, as a *śūdra* would be from the Vedas (dharmo yasyā 'ti śaṅkyaḥ syād ārṣaṃ vā durbalātmanaḥ / vedāc chūdra ivā 'peyāt sa lokād ajarāmarāt 3.32.7; cf. 1.146.16).

Like milk put in a dog hide bag, a Vedic hymn in a Vṛṣala (a kind of *śūdra*), truth in a thief, and might in a woman, so is the sovereignty (if placed) in Duryodhana (śvadṛtau kṣīram āsaktaṃ brahma vā vṛṣale yathā / satyaṃ stene balam nāryāṃ rājyam duryodhane tathā 3.34.78; cf. 3.198.45; section XL,15, Leather Bag).

5. Elements of Speech

The best knowledge is included in this excellent work on history (the Mahābhārata), as all of worldly and Vedic speech is included in the vowels and consonants (itihāsottame hy asminn arpitā buddhir uttamā / svaravyañjanayoḥ kṛtsnā lokavedāśraye 'va vāk 1.2.32).

6. Five Elements (Pañca-mahābhūta)

From this Mahābhārata, the best among the Itihāsas, emanate the ideas of poets as the arrangements of the three worlds emanate from the five elements (itihāsottamād asmāj jāyante kavibuddhayaḥ / pañcabhya iva bhūtebhyo lokasaṃvidhayas trayaḥ 1.2.237).[17]

7. Sense Organs (Indriyas)

The five Pāṇḍavas took hold (to support her) of Draupadī, who was greatly confused through fear of Kirmīra, as the sense organs, attached to the sense objects, take hold of the pleasure of love (momuhyamānāṃ tāṃ tatra jagṛhuḥ pañca pāṇḍavāḥ / indriyāṇi prasaktāni viṣayeṣu yathā ratim 3.12.18).

Kirmīra is the great unknown enemy of the five Pāṇḍavas as an incomparable pressure of grief is an enemy to the five sense organs (pañcānāṃ pāṇḍuputrāṇām avijñāto mahāripuḥ / pañcānām indriyāṇām tu śokavega ivā 'tulaḥ 3.12.14).

Of all the qualities of action,[18] this Mabābhārata is the support, as

[17] *Vide* Emeneau, "Signed Verses by Sanskrit Poets," *Indian Linguistics* (Chatterji Jubilee Volume), XVI (1955), 51.

[18] Ray translates this "all acts, ceremonials, and moral qualities" [1.2.239].

the diverse activities of the mind serve as a support of all the sense organs (kriyāguṇānāṃ sarveṣām idam ākhyānam āśrayaḥ / indriyāṇāṃ samastānāṃ citrā iva manaḥkriyāḥ 1.2.239).

8. Mind (Manas)

In a number of passages, mind appears jointly with the wind as a standard of velocity (cf. section XIV). In isolation it occurs mostly in the compound epithet *manojava-*, 'having velocity like that of the mind'; 1.16.36; 25.6; 26.27; 27.14; 86.16; 143.18,27: 6.75.47,53. Flying birds, horses, warriors, and demons are the subjects of comparison in this connection. Arjuna rapidly moving towards Mt. Indrakīla has movement like the velocity of the mind (manojavagatir 3.38.28).

The gods, when they are rapidly proceeding towards heaven, have speed like that of passion and the mind (kāmamanojavaḥ 3.42.41).

9. Life (Prāṇa)

Ruru's wife is as dear to him as his life itself (mama prāṇasamā bhāryā 1.10.1).

10. Body (Deha)

The whole world lived happily, having taken shelter with Yudhiṣṭhira, as a soul lives happily after taking shelter in its own body which has virtuous marks and acts (āśritya dharmarājānaṃ sarvaloko 'vasat sukham / puṇyalakṣaṇakarmāṇaṃ svadeham iva dehinaḥ 1.214.2); cf. Īśvarakṛṣṇa, Sāṃkhyakārikā 41.

XL. MATERIAL CULTURE

1. Cart (Śakaṭa) and Its Parts

The snake Takṣaka, being brought down from heaven to the sacrificial altar in connection with the snake-sacrifice of Janamejaya, is halted by his savior Āstīka in mid air and stands with heart distressed (with fear), as if somebody were to stand between the ox and the wheel of a cart (vitasthe so 'ntarikṣe 'tha hṛdayena vidūyatā / yathā tiṣṭheta vai kaś cid gocakrasyā 'ntarā naraḥ 1.53.6).

Aṣṭāvakra says about the royal bandin of Janaka: He has not had discussions with persons like me. Therefore, behaving like a lion, he speaks fearlessly. After he meets me (in debate) today, he will lie struck down like a cart with weak axle, lying broken on the road (vivādito 'sau na hi mādṛśair hi siṃhīkṛtas tena vadaty abhītaḥ / sametya māṃ nihataḥ śeṣyate 'dya mārge bhagnam śakaṭam ivā 'balākṣam 3.133.20).

The wheel is used as a figure of philosophical ideas. Always afflicted by pain (but) not feeling distressed and conceived (or conceiving himself) to have enjoyment, then on account of his bondage not being removed and due to the rising of new actions suffering many miseries, the soul goes around in its transmigrations like a wheel (ajasram eva duḥkhārto 'duḥkhitaḥ sukhasamjñitaḥ / tato 'nivṛttabandhatvāt karmaṇām udayād api / parikrāmati saṃsāre cakravad bahuvedanaḥ 3.200.37; cf. 3.2.67). Pain after pleasure, pleasure after pain, approach man in succession as the spokes do the rim (sukhasyā 'nantaraṃ duḥkhaṃ duḥkhasyā 'nantaraṃ sukham / paryāyeṇo 'pavartante naraṃ nemim arā iva 3.247.45; cf. 12.170.4; Bhāsa, Svapnavāsavadattam 1.4; Megha. 2.48).

2. Ship (Nau) or Raft (Plava)

The Pāṇḍava army trembled exceedingly at Bhīṣma's attack like a ship hit with the force of the storm (saṃtrastā pāṇḍavī senā vātavegahate 'va nauḥ 6.45.48).

Draupadī warns Jayadratha that he will see his army thrown into confusion with all the warriors killed by the sons of Pāṇḍu like a ship filled with gems shattered on the ocean on the back of a sea monster (viśīryantīṃ nāvam ivā 'rṇavānte ratnābhipūrṇāṃ makarasya pṛṣṭhe / senāṃ tave 'māṃ hatasarvayodhāṃ vikṣobhitāṃ drakṣyasi pāṇḍuputraiḥ 3.254.19).

As the wind destroys the ship on the ocean, so the mind succumbing to the unrestrained sense organs destroys the wisdom of a man (indriyāṇāṃ hi caratāṃ yan mano 'nuvidhīyate / tad asya harati prajñāṃ vāyur nāvam ivā 'mbhasi 6.24.67; cf. 3.202.24; section XIV).

The Pāṇḍava army being destroyed by the Kauravas obtained no savior, like a ship sinking in the water (trātāraṃ nā 'dhyagacchanta majjamāne 'va naur jale 6.113.6).

Kuntī, the irreproachable one, is requested by Pāṇḍu to rescue Mādrī by the bestowal of a child as if by a raft (or boat), and to attain thereby the most splendid glory (sā tvaṃ mādrīṃ plavene 'va tāraye 'mām anindite / apatyasaṃvibhāgena parāṃ kīrtim avāpnuhi 1.115.14; cf. 1.147.4).

3. Swing (Dolā)

As Nala was forced by Kali to leave Damayantī behind alone in the traveler's lodging in the forest and at the same time was drawn back to the sleeping Damayantī by the force of his love, he was afflicted and his heart became rent in two as it were; like a swing it came and went to the traveler's lodging again and again (dvidhe 'va hṛdayaṃ tasya duḥkhitasyā 'bhavat tadā / dole 'va muhur āyāti yāti cai 'va sabhāṃ muhuḥ 3.59.23). Cf. ABHS 1.33.

4. Iron (Loha)

Then there was born a piece of flesh compact and hard like a ball of iron (i.e., Gāndhārī after two years' gestation bore this aborted piece of flesh) (tato jajñe māṃsapeśī lohāṣṭhīle 'va saṃhatā 1.107.12). Cf. 7, Wood, below.

5. Saw (Krakaca)

Kṛṣṇa's discus cut open the town of Saubha through the middle as a saw cuts open tall timber (madhyena pātayām āsa krakaco dārv ivo 'cchritam 3.23.33).

6. Weapons (Śastra) and Machine (Yantra)

Horses run fast like arrows desirous of reaching their goal (tariṣyanta ivā 'śugāḥ 3.158.25). Rivers with great noise are likened to the whistling arrows (mahāghoṣāḥ śvasamānā ivā 'śugāḥ 3.179.6).

The brawny arms of kings or warriors (3.54.6; 79.18; 116.24: 6.66.18), warriors themselves (3.194.4), and weapons (6.19.32; 114.59) are compared to iron bars (parigha); e.g., tatra sma pīnā dṛśyante bāhavaḥ parighopamāḥ 3.54.6.

Some of the demon Mada's teeth were ten *yojanas* (approximately eighty miles) long, having rampart-like forms, looking like the points of impaling stakes (itare tv asya daśanā babhūvur daśayojanāḥ / prākārasadṛśākārāḥ śūlāgrasamadarśanāḥ 3.124.21).

Arrows strike with the force of clubs, piercing the vitals of Bhīṣma (muśalānī 'va me ghnanti 6.114.56).

While Karṇa still had not completed his challenging statement addressed to Arjuna, people on all sides quickly stood up to see Karṇa's performance in archery as if raised (or shot up) by a machine (asamāpte tatas tasya vacane vadatāṃ vara / yantrotkṣipta iva kṣipram uttasthau sarvato janaḥ 1.126.10).

The discharge of Rāma's bow to kill Vālin seemed like that of a machine (visphāras tasya dhanuṣo yantrasye 'va tadā babhau 3.264.36).

7. Wood (Kāṣṭha)

Sāvitrī, thinking that Satyavān would die tomorrow, standing quiet, looked like one who had turned into a block of wood (tiṣṭhantī cā 'pi Sāvitrī kāṣṭhabhūte 'va lakṣyate 3.280.8).

As one might break wood with wood or stone with stone or iron with iron, (all) inert and insensate, likewise that illustrious God, self-born, the great-grandfather, destroys the creatures with creatures, having created delusion (yathā kāṣṭhena vā kāṣṭham aśmānaṃ cā 'śmanā punaḥ / ayasā cā 'py ayaś chindyān nirviceṣṭam acetanam / evaṃ sa bhagavān devaḥ svayaṃbhūḥ prapitāmahaḥ / hinasti bhūtair bhutāni chadma kṛtvā yudhiṣṭhira 3.31.34).

8. Mirror (Ādarśa)

(God is) that which the best ones among ascetics, disciplined and endowed with the power of meditation, see in their own selves like a reflection in a mirror (yat tad yativarā yuktā dhyānayogabalānvitāh / pratibimbam ivā 'darśe paśyanty ātmany avasthitam 1.1.197).

Seeing the son born of the wife, his own face in the mirror as it were, the father is happy, like a virtuous one attaining heaven (bhāryāyāṃ janitaṃ putram ādarśe svam ivā 'nanam / hlādate janitā prekṣya svargaṃ prāpye 'va puṇyakṛt 1.68.48; cf. 1.68.64: 6.6.15; section I,2).

The pleasure groves of the Pāṇḍavas were endowed with dwelling places, spotlessly clean like mirrors (gṛhair ādarśavimalaiḥ 1.199.44).

The color that had appeared in Sītā's face because of her joy (on meeting her husband Rāma after a long separation), was again marred in a moment (on hearing the news of the proposed fire ordeal she would have to undergo), as the beauty of a shining mirror is marred by breathing (yo hy asyā harṣasaṃbhūto mukharāgas tadā 'bhavat / kṣaṇena sa punar bhraṣṭo niḥśvāsād iva darpaṇe 3.275.15; cf. 6.25.38).

9. Clothes (Vastra)

As a person leaving aside worn-out clothes puts on other new ones, so the soul leaving aside worn-out bodies attains other new ones (vāsāṃsi jīrṇāni yathā vihāya navāni gṛhṇāti naro 'parāṇi / tathā śarīrāṇi vihāya jīrṇāny anyāni saṃyāti navāni dehī 6.24.22).

Broken to pieces like rushes, many trees there in the great forest looked like scattered tatters (in the scene of the fighting of Bhīma and Kirmīra) (muñjavaj jarjarībhūtā bahavas tatra pādapāḥ / cīrāṇī 'va vyudastāni rejus tatra mahāvane 3.12.49).

He who having faith and not being envious, conceals the weak points of the good, as he would the holes of a garment, would do what is good (cikīrṣed eva kalyāṇam śraddadhāno 'nasūyakaḥ / vasanasye 'va chidrāṇi sādhūnaṃ vivṛṇoti yaḥ 3.198.51–2; cf. Tulasī, Rāmacaritamānasa 1.2.3, . . . jo sahi dukha para chidra durāvā . . ., 'A virtuous person is like cotton that itself bears troubles but conceals the holes of other . . .'). *Vivṛṇoti* should have its normal meaning, 'discloses.' But it does not make sense in the present context. This is what seems to have bothered the copyists (S_1 K $D_{1.2}$) who wrote *saṃvṛṇoti*, 'conceals,' and PW, which for this passage only gives the meaning 'conceal' for $\sqrt{vṛ}$ +

vi, adducing Nīlakaṇṭha who apparently says *viśeṣataḥ pidadhāti*. PW further says "apparently a mistake for *pivṛṇoti*, i.e., *apivṛ°*." But note that $\sqrt{vṛ}$ + *pi* occurs nowhere, and $\sqrt{vṛ}$ + *api* is only RV and not common there except in the past participle *apīvṛta-*.

Great virtue consisting of intelligence and disciplined activity, when accumulated in due course, would be a good thing in a man of virtuous conduct, like red color in a white garment (krameṇa saṃcito dharmo buddhiyogamayo mahān / śiṣṭācāre bhavet sādhū rāgaḥ śukle 'va vāsasi 3.198.68).

10. Painting (Citra)

Those two armies of the Kurus and the Pāṇḍavas, thronged with elephants, horses, and chariots, looked exceedingly beautiful on the battlefield as if represented in a painting on a canvas (kurupāṇḍavasene te hastyaśvarathasaṃkule / śuśubhāte raṇe 'tī 'va paṭe citragate iva 6.42.25).

11. Garland (Mālā)

Fame to a dead man is like a garland to a moribund person (mṛtasya kīrtir martyasya yathā mālā gatāyuṣaḥ 3.285.6; cf. dīpanirvāṇagandhaṃ ca suhṛdvākyam arundhatīm / na jighranti na śṛṇvanti na paśyanti gatāyuṣaḥ, Hitopadeśa 1.69).[19]

With cushions, elephants' housings, and precious blankets (scattered here and there on the battlefield), the earth shines as if she were decorated with garland wreaths (paristomaiḥ kuthābhiś ca kambalaiś ca mahādhanaiḥ / bhūr bhāti bharataśreṣṭha sragdāmair iva citritā 6.53.20) Note that *bhūs* is feminine, a woman! Cf. 6.92.65,12 below.

12. Ornaments (Alaṃkāra)

The earth, (strewn with the debris of battle and) with elephants lying trunkless, shone like a woman adorned with ornaments of various kinds (srastahastaiś ca mātaṅgaiḥ śayānair vibabhau mahī / nānārūpair alaṃkāraiḥ pramade 'vā 'bhyalaṃkṛtā 6.92.65).

The Pāṇḍavas saw on the summits of mountains *karṇikāra* trees (*Pterospermum acerifolium*) covered with golden flowers, appearing as if they wore flower ornaments of excellent make on their ears (suvarṇakusumākīrṇān girīṇāṃ śikhareṣu ca / karṇikārān viracitān karṇapūrān ivo 'ttamān 3.155.57–58).

---

[19] *Vide* Otto Böhtlingk, *Indische Sprüche, Sanskrit und deutsch* (St. Petersburg, 1870–1873), 2815, "Moribund persons do not smell the odor of the extinction of the lamp, do not listen to the words of friends, do not see the star Arundhati."

13. Mark on the Forehead (Tilaka)

Likewise, the Pāṇḍavas saw lofty *tilaka* trees (*Clerodendrum phlomoides*) shining like (graceful) marks of sandal paste made on the forehead of the aisles of the forest (tathai 'va vanarājīnām udārān racitān iva / virājamānāṃs te 'paśyaṃs tilakāṃs tilakān iva 3.155.59).

14. Kettledrum (Dundubhi)

Hiḍimba, being killed by Bhīma, uttered a great roar, filling the entire forest, like a large kettledrum that has been wetted with water (sa māryamāṇo bhīmena nanāda vipulaṃ svanam / pūrayaṃs tad vanaṃ sarvaṃ jalārdra iva dundubhiḥ 1.142.29).

15. A Leather Bag (Dṛti)

An evil man is like a great leather bag that has been blown up. The utterances of proud fools are valueless (mahādṛtir ivā 'dhmātaḥ pāpo bhavati nityadā / mūḍhānām avaliptānām asāraṃ bhāṣitaṃ bhavet 3.198.45; cf. 3.34.78; RV 7.103.2.

16. Leather (Carman)

The great Pāṇḍava army, being thrown into confusion by Bhagadatta, contracted like leather placed on the fire (tena saṃloḍyamānaṃ tu pāṇḍūnāṃ tad balaṃ mahat / saṃcukoca mahārāja carme 'vā 'gnau samāhitam 6.91.54).

17. Needle (Sūcī)

How could he wait, whose life grows less with every moment, like the quantity of collyrium powder (that grows less each time a grain is removed) by the needle? (Bhīma's argument to Yudhiṣṭhira for immediate attack on the Kauravas) (nimeṣād api kaunteya yasyā 'yur apacīyate / sūcye 'vā 'ñjanacūrṇasya kimiti pratipālayet 3.36.3).

18. Pot (Ghaṭa)

One who, waiting for fate without making an effort, should sleep comfortably, he, a great fool, would perish like an unbaked pot in water (yo hi diṣṭam upāsīno nirviceṣṭaḥ sukhaṃ svapet / avasīdet sudurbuddhir āmo ghaṭa ivā 'mbhasi 3.33.12; cf. 3.239.3). *Vide* Emeneau's "Notes on Śrīharṣa's Naiṣadhacarita,"[20] especially the quotations as follows:

> yathā ghaṭaṃ mrṇmayam āmam āśrito
> naras titīrṣet kṣubhitaṃ mahārṇavam
> samucchrayaṃ tadvad asāram udvahan
> balam vyavasyed viṣayārtham udyataḥ

[20] Emeneau, "Notes on Śrīharṣa's Naiṣadhacarita," pp. 95–96.

> śarīram āmād api mṛṇmayād ghaṭād
> idaṃ tu niḥsāratamaṃ mataṃ mama /
> ciraṃ hi tiṣṭhed vidhivad dhṛto ghaṭah
> samucchrayo 'yaṃ sudhṛto 'pi bhidyate
> [Aśvaghoṣa, Saundarananda 9.10,11]

As would be a man who should attempt to cross the tossing ocean, supporting himself (or, depending) on a clay pot that is not fired, so would be one who, possessing (only) the frail bodily complex, should consider it strong, being eager for the objects of the senses.

But this body, I hold, is more fragile even than an unfired clay pot. For the pot kept carefully would last a long time; this bodily complex breaks up, however well tended.

> pratikṣaṇam ayaṃ kāyaḥ
> kṣīyamāṇo na lakṣyate /
> āmakumbha ivā 'mbhastho
> viśīrṇaḥ san vibhāvyate
> [Hitopadeśa, Book 4, vs.70]

It is not noticed how this body wastes away every moment. When it has dissolved, one is aware of that, as is the case with an unfired jar standing in water.

By mental agony the body is troubled, as by a heated iron ball water in a pot is heated (mānasena hi duḥkhena śarīram upatapyate / ayaḥpiṇḍena taptena kumbhasaṃstham ivo 'dakam 3.2.24).

19. Banner (Dhvaja)

Hanumat was splendid with his tail, its forepart a little bent, bristling with long hair, standing straight up like a banner (kiṃcic cā 'bhugnaśīrṣeṇa dīrgharomāñcitena ca / lāṅgūleno 'rdhvagatinā dhvajene 'va virājitam 3.146.67).

The Himālaya Mountain looks as if it were a raised banner of the great forest (asyā 'raṇyasya mahataḥ ketubhūtam ivo 'cchritam 3.61.36). Cf. 1.64.14.

20. Puppet (Dārumayī yoṣā)

As a puppet fixed (on a string) is caused to move its body by the puppeteer, so (the creator, Dhātṛ) causes these creatures to move their limbs (yathā dārumayī yoṣā naravīra samāhitā / īrayaty āngam aṅgāni tathā rājann imāḥ prajāḥ 3.31.22). The *yathā* clause with nominative and *īrayaty aṅgam* presents some syntactical difficulty. This seems to have bothered almost all the Southern manuscripts, which try to ease the contradiction with *dārumayīṃ yoṣām.*

Cf. 5.32.12; 39.1, both of which have as *pāda* b, . . . puruṣo . . . sūtraprotā dārumayī 'va yoṣā, "a man is like a wooden puppet strung on a string (or wire)." This is the *triṣṭubh* equivalent of the *śloka* unit *yathā d° y°. Sūtraprotā* is the equivalent of *samāhitā.*

21. Medicine (Auṣadha)

Even though restrained by Saṃjaya again and again, Dhṛtarāṣṭra does not take his beneficial and salutary advice, as a moribund person does not take salutary medicine (tathā mayā cā 'py asakṛd vāryamāṇo na gṛhṇasi / vākyaṃ hitaṃ ca pathyaṃ ca martyaḥ pathyam ivau 'ṣadham 6.61.22). Cf. 6.85.11.

22. Pillow (Upadhāna)

Draupadī slept on the ground along with the sons of Pāṇḍu (at their feet) as if she had been made their foot-pillow (aśeta bhūmau saha pāṇḍuputraiḥ / pādopadhāne 'va kṛtā kuśeṣu 1.184.10).

23. Trap (Vāgurā)

The forests of Devadāru trees look as if they were the traps of clouds (vanāni devadārūṇāṃ meghānām iva vāgurāḥ 3.175.10).

XLI. SUPERNATURAL APPEARANCES

1. Golden Trees

As a moribund person sees all trees as golden, so ambitious Duryodhana sees things contrary to what they actually are (mumūrṣur hi naraḥ sarvān vṛkṣān paśyati kāñcanān / tathā tvam api gāndhāre viparītāni paśyasi 6.94.12).

2. An Imaginary Town in the Sky (Gandharvanagara)

The inhabitants of Hastināpura, seeing the group of sages and *siddhas* disappearing just there, like a city of the Gandharvas (an imaginary town in the sky), were exceedingly astonished (gandharvanagarākāraṃ tatrai 'vā 'ntarhitaṃ punaḥ / ṛṣisiddhagaṇaṃ dṛṣṭvā vismayaṃ paramaṃ yayuḥ 1.117.33). Cf. *Epic Myth.*, p. 157, for Gandharvanagara as *upamāna* for evanescent phenomena (with a number of epic references).

Seeing that might of the princes (the Pāṇḍavas), armed with arrows and bows, appearing like the city of the Gandharvas, people were astonished (tat kumārabalaṃ tatra gṛhītaśarakārmukam / gandharvanagarākāraṃ prekṣya te vismitā 'bhavan 1.124.25).

The chariots moving like the wind appear like the cities of the Gandharvas (vātāyamānā dṛśyante gandharvanagaropamāḥ 6.99.20).

The Gandharvanagara ("die *Stadt der* Gandharva, eine mythische Stadt, die der under dem Namen *Fata Morgana* bekannten Lufterscheinung ihren Ursprung verdankt," PW) has been described by Varāhamihira (Br. sam. 36) as an aerial city indicative of various auspicious or inauspicious events depending on the direction where it is visible.

In all the above examples, however, the Gandharvanagara symbolizes wonder—wonderful sudden disappearance, wonderful might, and wonderful movement.

3. Celestial car (Vimāna)

Duryodhana saw the assembly hall like a celestial car (or palace) elegantly constructed by Maya, which had been given to the Pāṇḍavas (vimānapratimāṃ cā 'pi mayena sukṛtāṃ sabhām / pāṇḍavānām upahṛtām 1.1.89).

XLII. MISCELLANEOUS

1. Nectar (Amṛta)

Nectar symbolizes sweetness and extreme contentment; sweet fruits (3.155.44), water (3.152.22: 6.116.23), an interesting story (1.90.5), and a consoling word (1.147.24; 149.19: 3.79.17) are all likened to nectar; e.g.:

na tṛpyāmi kathāṃ śṛṇvann
amṛtasvādasaṃmitām 1.90.5.

I am not satiated with listening to the story, which is provided with the taste of nectar.

2. Poison (Viṣa)

The sage's son of hot temperament is likened to poison (viṣakalpa ṛṣeḥ sutaḥ 1.36.23).

Yudhiṣṭhira is very much pained to remember the insult to Draupadī in the assembly; this painful insult is likened to the essence of poison (dūye viṣasye 'va rasaṃ viditvā 3.35.17).

That great army of Dhṛtarāṣṭra, while being destroyed in the battlefield, displayed violent paroxysms like a man after having drunk poison (sā vadhyamanā samare dhārtarāṣṭrī mahācamūḥ / vegān bahuvidhāṃś cakre viṣaṃ pītve 'va mānavaḥ 6.79.23).

The following two verses contain a good contrast between nectar and poison:

yat tad agre viṣam iva
pariṇāme 'mṛtopamam /
tat sukhaṃ sāttvikaṃ proktam
ātmabuddhiprasādajam 6.40.37.

That which is initially like poison (but) like nectar in maturity, that is called the *Sāttvika* happiness, born of serenity of soul and mind (śaṅkara, 'born of serenity of one's own intelligence, or born of clarity of knowledge of the self').

viṣayendriyasaṃyogād
yat tad agre 'mṛtopamam /
pariṇāme viṣam iva
tat sukhaṃ rājasaṃ smṛtam 6.40.38.

That which is initially like nectar owing to contact of the objects of sense and the sense organs, but like poison in maturity, that is known as *Rājasa* happiness. Cf. chapter 9,A,III,*m*.

3. Seasons (Ṛtu)

At the commencement of the ages (yugas) all the things reappear, just as the seasonal fruits of various types appear in due order in season (yatha 'rtāv ṛtuliṅgāni nānārūpāṇi paryaye / dṛśyante tāni tāny eva tathā bhāvā yugādiṣu 1.1.37).

4. Spring (Vasanta)

Rāvaṇa, wearing divine garments, beautiful, with earrings of well-polished gems, having a diadem and garland of variegated color, looked like spring incarnate (divyāmbaradharaḥ śrīmān sumṛṣṭamaṇikuṇḍalaḥ / vicitramālyamukuṭo vasanta iva mūrtimān 3.265.4).

5. Food (Āhāra)

Not depending upon this legend (the Mahābhārata), there is no story on the earth as there is no sustaining of the body without depending upon food (anāśrityai 'tad ākhyānaṃ kathā bhuvi na vidyate / āhāram anapāśritya śarīrasye 'va dhāraṇam 1.2.240).

A sin committed does not, like a cow, bear fruit soon; one sees it in sons or grandsons, if not in oneself; a sin necessarily bears consequences like a heavy (indigestible) meal in the belly (nā 'dharmaś carito rājan sadyaḥ phalati gaur iva / putreṣu vā naptṛṣu vā na ced ātmani paśyati / phalaty eva dhruvaṃ pāpaṃ gurubhuktam ivo 'dare 1.75.2).

6. Perfume (Gandha)

As the perfume of flowers (in contact with them) scents clothing, water, sesamum seeds, or the ground, so qualities are born from contact (with the good or the evil) (vastram āpas tilān bhūmiṃ gandho vāsayate yathā / puṣpāṇām adhivāsena tathā saṃsargajā guṇāḥ 3.1.22).

7. A Post (Sthāṇu)

Śakuntalā, the fair-hipped, intelligent woman, having been spoken to thus (by Duḥṣanta), stood abashed as it were, as if bereft of her senses through grief, immovable as a post (sai 'vam uktā varārohā vrīḍite 'va manasvinī / visaṃjñe 'va ca duḥkhena tasthau sthāṇur ivā 'calā 1.68.20; cf. 1.37.7; 45.25; 189.16).

8. Shadow (Chāyā)

Damayantī never goes away from Nala as a shadow never goes away from a person (bhartāram api taṃ vīraṃ chāye 'vā 'napagā sadā 3.62.27; cf. 1.112.23: 3.31.8). One's own act done in past life always follows one like a shadow and bears fruits accordingly (chāye 'vā 'nugataṃ sadā 3.181.25; cf. Ragh. 2.6).

Courage is the foundation of wealth; everything else is false and is not effective any more than the shadow of a tree in winter (sattvaṃ hi mūlam arthasya vitathaṃ yad ato 'nyathā / na tu prasaktaṃ bhavati vṛkṣacchāye 'va haimanī 3:34.62).

9. Pilgrimage Centers

Decorated with the Mālinī River, with an island and with charming banks, Kaṇva's hermitage looked like the place of Nara and Nārāyaṇa (Badarikāśrama) beautified by the Gaṅgā River (alaṃkṛtam dvīpavatyā mālinyā ramyatīrayā / naranārāyanasthānaṃ gaṅgaye 'vo 'paśobhitam 1.64.24).

The Mahābhārata issuing from the lips of Vyāsa, unfathomable, auspicious, purifying, a destroyer of sin, and propitious—one who receives it when it is being recited, what need has he for the sprinkling of the water of Puṣkarakṣetra? (dvaipāyanoṣṭhapuṭaniḥsṛtam aprameyam / puṇyam pavitram atha pāpaharaṃ śivaṃ ca / yo bhārataṃ samadhigacchati vācyamānaṃ / kiṃ tasya puṣkarajalair abhiṣecanena 1.2.242).

This in fact is an example of *pratīpa;* cf. chapter 8,II.

10. Fog (Nīhāra)

Yudhiṣṭhira wants Draupadī's doubt about his nonaggressive policy towards the Kauravas to disappear after his explanation as fog disappears after sunrise (tasmāt te saṃśayaḥ kṛṣṇe nīhāra iva naśyatu 3.32.38).

11. Anthill (Valmīka)

Kṛṣṇa being struck with a shower of rocks on all sides, became covered over with the rocks (and grew) like an anthill (so 'haṃ parvatavarṣeṇa vadhyamānaḥ samantataḥ / valmīka iva rājendra parvatopacito 'bhavam 3.23.11).

12. Snow (Hima)

Then there came out ashes, white as snow, from the wound of Śiva (tato bhasma kṣatād rājan nirgataṃ himasaṃnibham 3.81.107; cf. 1.199.30). In 3.175.9, coolness of water is likened to that of snow (himasaṃsparśaiḥ).

13. Success (Siddhi)

Vyāsa imparts to Yudhiṣṭhira a knowledge called *pratismṛti*, which was like success incarnate (gṛhāṇe 'māṃ mayā proktāṃ siddhiṃ mūrtimayīm iva 3.37.27).

XLIII. MĀLOPAMĀ

The following are some examples of *mālopamā*, a kind of simile in which a subject of comparison has more than one object of comparison in the same passage.

a)

navanītaṃ yathā dadhno
dvipadāṃ brāhmaṇo yathā /
hradānām udadhiḥ śreṣṭho
gaur variṣṭhā catuṣpadām //
yathai 'tāni variṣṭhāni
tathā bhāratam ucyate 1.1.201–2.

As fresh butter is among coagulated milk (ready to churn), a Brāhmaṇa among two-footed creatures, as the sea is the best among bodies of water, the cow among the quadrupeds, as these are the most excellent ones, so is said to be the Bhārata. Cf. sections XV; XX; XXXVIII,23.

b)

sikatā vā yathā loke
yathā vā divi tārakāḥ
yathā vā varṣato dhārā
asaṃkhyeyāś ca kena cit /
tathai 'va tad asaṃkhyeyaṃ
dhanaṃ yat pradadau gayaḥ
sadasyebhyo mahārāja
teṣu yajñeṣu saptasu 3.121.9.

As grains of sand in the world, or the stars in the sky, or as showers of rain cannot be counted by anybody, so immeasurable was that wealth which Gaya gave to the priests in those seven sacrifices. Cf. sections VIII,XII.

c)

vivasvān iva tejasvī
bṛhaspatisamo matau /
mahendra iva śūraś ca
vasudhe 'va kṣamānvitaḥ 3.278.15.

Satyavān was brilliant like the sun, in intellect like Bṛhaspati, brave like Indra, enduring like the earth. Cf. sections I,2; V; X; XXXV.

d) atiṣṭhan manujendrāṇāṃ
mūrdhni devapatir yathā /
upary upari sarveṣām
āditya iva tejasā 3.50.2.

Nala stood at the head of the kings of men like Indra, above all creatures, like the sun because of his brilliance. Cf. sections I,2; V.

e) mahendrasadṛśaḥ śaurye
sthairye ca himavān iva /
samudra iva gāmbhīrye
sahiṣṇutve dharāsamaḥ 6.14.8.

Bhīṣma was like Indra in valor, like the Himālayas in stability, like the sea in depth, like the earth in endurance. Cf. sections I,2; XV; XIX.

f) kas tvaṃ yuvā vāsavatulyarūpaḥ
svatejasā dīpyamāno yathā 'gniḥ /
patasy udīrṇāmbudharāndhakārāt
khāt khecarāṇāṃ pravaro yathā 'rkaḥ 1.83.7.

Who are you, a youth like Indra in beauty, shining with your own brilliance like fire, and looking like the sun, the principal of all bodies that move in the sky, as you fall from the sky, which is dark with lofty clouds (through which the sun breaks)? Cf. sections I,2; IV; V.

g) yathā karma śubhaṃ kṛtvā
svargopagamanaṃ dhruvam /
yathā cā 'yur dhruvaṃ satye
tvayi dharmas tathā dhruvaḥ 1.97.4.

As going to heaven rests firmly in the performance of virtuous acts, and as longevity rests firmly in truth, so virtue rests firmly in you (Bhīṣma). Cf. section XXXIX.

h) rudrair iva yamo rājā
marudbhir iva vāsavaḥ /
kurubhis tvaṃ vṛto rājan
bhāsi nakṣatrarāḍ iva 3.226.10.

You shine, O king (Duryodhana), surrounded by the Kurus, as King Yama (god of death) is surrounded by the Rudras, Indra by the Maruts, and the lord of the stars (i.e., the moon) surrounded by the stars. Cf. sections I,2,12; VI.

i) arāgadveṣasaṃyuktaḥ
somavat priyadarśanaḥ
tejasā sūryasaṃkāśo

vāyuvegasamo jave
antakapratimaḥ kope
kṣamayā pṛthivīsamaḥ 1.94.12.

Śantanu was devoid of passion and hatred, of charming appearance like the moon, in brilliance like the sun, in speed like the wind, in anger like the god of death, in endurance like the earth. Cf. sections I,2; V; VI; X; XVI.

j) maṇiḥ sūtra iva proto
nasyota iva govṛṣaḥ /
dhātur ādeśam anveti
tanmayo hi tadarpaṇaḥ 3.31.25.

Like a pearl strung on a thread, like a bull tied by a nose rope, man follows the command of God, made of Him, dedicated to Him. Cf. sections XX; XXXIII,3.

2. METAPHOR (RŪPAKA)

THE TYPE OF SYMBOLISM we have been discussing so far in the sphere of similes is simple enough to produce immediately the desired effect of comparison on the mind of the audience or readers. This simplicity is accomplished by force of the particles (iva, yathā, etc.)—explicit or implicit—indicating relationship between the subject and object of comparison, and/or some suggestive expression indicating the *tertium comparationis* (upamānadharma).

The symbolism of the metaphor (rūpaka) is often more complicated: sometimes it involves a complete statement of the details of the objects of comparison. For a simile, it may be enough to say that the universe is as wide-spreading as a big banyan tree; but when, metaphorically speaking, the universe becomes a big *aśvattha* tree, various statements about its roots, its branches, its leaves, etc., sometimes seem necessary. To put it in another way, like a successful actor on the stage, the universe has to act as a tree in its totality. Of course, it is not always so. We have as well such comparatively simple metaphoric phrases as *puruṣavyāghra-*, 'a tiger among men,' *puruṣarṣabha-*, 'a bull among men,' *rājakuñjara-*, 'an elephant among kings.'

As Jayadeva defines it, a metaphor is that figure of speech in which the wall of the subject of comparison is completely painted with the picture of the object of comparison (yatro 'pamānacitreṇa sarvathā 'py uparajyate / upameyamayī bhittir yat tad rūpakam iṣyate // Candrāloka); cf. also viṣayyabhedatādrūpyarañjanaṃ viṣayasya yat / rūpakaṃ tat . . . // kuvalayānanda, 17.

Some specimens of metaphor of the complex type follow.

I. COMPLEX METAPHOR

1. Tree

duryodhano manyumayo mahādrumaḥ
skandhaḥ karṇaḥ śakunis tasya śākhāḥ /
duḥśāsanaḥ puṣpaphale samṛddhe
mūlaṃ rājā dhṛtarāṣṭro 'manīṣī //
yudhiṣṭhiro dharmamayo mahādrumaḥ
skandho 'rjuno bhīmaseno 'sya śākhāḥ /
mādrīsutau puṣpaphale samṛddhe
mūlaṃ kṛṣṇo brahma ca brāhmaṇāś ca // 1.1.65–6.

Duryodhana is the great tree of furious temper; Karṇa is the trunk; Śakuni the branches; Duḥśāsana is the full-grown flowers and fruits; and Dhṛtarāṣṭra, the unwise one, is the root.

Yudhiṣṭhira is the great tree of virtue; Arjuna is the trunk; Bhīmasena the branches; the twin sons of Mādrī the full-grown flowers and fruits; and its roots are Kṛṣṇa, Brahman, and the Brāhmaṇas.

ūrdhvamūlam adhaḥśākham aśvatthaṃ prāhur avyayam /
chandāṃsi yasya parṇāni yas taṃ veda sa vedavit //
adhaś co 'rdhvaṃ prasṛtās tasya śākhā
guṇapravṛddhā viṣayapravālāḥ /
adhaś ca mūlāny anusaṃtatāni
karmānubandhīni manuṣyaloke // 6.37.1–2.

(This is the description of the material universe of the Saṃsāra) They describe it as an above-rooted, below-branched, indestructible *aśvattha* tree, whose leaves are the vedic hymns. One who knows it is the knower of the Vedas.

Downwards and upwards are stretched its branches, nourished by the *guṇas*, with the objects of the sense organs as its sprouts; its roots are extended downwards, resulting in actions in the world of men.

2. Butter and Razor

nāvanītaṃ hṛdayaṃ brāhmaṇasya
vāci kṣuro nihitas tīkṣṇadhāraḥ /
viparītam etad ubhayaṃ kṣatriyasya
vāñ nāvanītī hṛdayaṃ tīkṣṇadhāram 1.3.132.

The heart of a Brāhmaṇa is fresh butter; but in his speech is placed a razor with a sharp edge. (This pair is reversed in a *kṣatriya;* his speech is fresh butter, his heart is (a razor) with a sharp edge.)

3. Boat on a River

kāmalobhagrahākīrṇāṃ pañcendriyajalāṃ nadīm /
nāvaṃ dhṛtimayīṃ kṛtvā janmadurgāṇi saṃtara 3.198.67.

Pass safely across the dangers of rebirths—the river full of crocodiles of passion and greed, with the five sense organs as water, by making the boat of resolution. (Cf. 3.32.22: 6.26.36.)

4. River

sa mahādhanaratnaugho vastrakambalaphenavān /
mahāgajamahāgrāhaḥ patākāśaivalākulaḥ //
pāṇḍusāgaram āviddhaḥ praviveśa mahānadaḥ /
pūrṇam āpūrayaṃs teṣāṃ dviṣacchokāvaho 'bhavat // 1.213.50–1.

That great river (of gifts bestowed upon the Pāṇḍavas by the Vṛṣṇis), with the huge amount of wealth and gems as its stream, with clothes and blankets as its foam, with great elephants as its great crocodiles, filled with flags as its duckweed, entered the ocean of the Pāṇḍavas, pouring into it and filling it completely, and brought despair to the enemy.

prāvartata mahāvegā nadī rudhiravāhinī /
mātaṅgāṅgaśilāraudrā māṃsaśoṇitakardamā //
varāśvanaranāgānāṃ śarīraprabhavā tadā /
paralokārṇavamukhī gṛdhragomāyumodinī // 6.55.11–2.

There arose a river, the stream of blood, having an impetuous current, terrible with rocks of the limbs of elephants, miry with flesh and blood, issuing out of the bodies of good steeds, men, and elephants, and proceeding towards the ocean of the next world, gladdening vultures and jackals. (Cf. 6.55.121–5; 82.42; 85.25; 89.25; 99.33–7; 112.124.)

5. Ocean

iṣvastrasāgaraṃ ghoraṃ bāṇagrāhaṃ durāsadam /
kārmukormiṇam akṣayyam advīpaṃ samare 'plavam //
gadāsimakarāvartaṃ hayagrāhaṃ gajākulam /
hayān gajān padātāṃs' ca rathāṃs' ca tarasā bahūn //
nimajjayantaṃ samare paravīrāpahāriṇam /
vele 'va makarāvāsaṃ ke vīrāḥ paryavārayan // 6.15.26–8.

Who were the heroes who resisted, as the shore does the abode of sea monsters, Bhīṣma, who was a terrible ocean of arrows and weapons, dangerous to approach because of his arrows as crocodiles, with bows as waves, inexhaustible, without islands or a boat (as refuge) in the battle, with maces and swords as sea monsters and whirlpools, with horses as crocodiles, full of elephants, with might causing many horses, elephants, foot-soldiers, and chariots to plunge beneath the surface of the battle, carrying away the heroes of the enemy, burning with anger and brilliance,[1] destroyer of the enemy? (Cf. 1.148.16; 6.73.21; 74.32; 103.18.)

agādhe majjatas tasya dvīpo bhīṣmo 'bhavat tadā 6.106.43.

For Duḥśāsana, plunging into the unfathomable (ocean of the battlefield), Bhīṣma became an island (of refuge). (Cf. 6.15.26; 103.34; also Dhammapada 2.25.)

6. Fire

so 'śvavegānilabalaḥ śarārcistalanisvanaḥ /
rajodhūmo 'strasaṃtāpo dhārtarāṣṭrāniloddhataḥ //
nisṛṣṭa iva kālena yugāntajvalano yathā /
mama sainyamayaṃ kaksaṃ pradhakṣyati na saṃśayaḥ // 3.84.9–10.

[1] Roy interprets this as suggesting the *vāḍava*—fire in the ocean.

Karṇa will undoubtedly burn up the Pāṇḍavas' army camp, which is a forest, having the speed of his horses as the power of the wind (fanning the flames), having the sound of his arrows as the sound of the sheet of flames, having the dust of battle as smoke and weapons as heat, excited by the wind of the Kauravas, as if he were the fire of the destruction of the world-age, kindled by the god of death. (Cf. 1.105.13; 125.17: 3.95.4; 120.15; 242.14: 6.25.39; 26.24; 102.10; 112.65; 114.5–6.)

7. Cloud

tam sa kṛṣṇāniloddhūto divyāstrajalado mahān /
śvetavājibalākābhṛd gāṇḍīvendrāyudhojjvalaḥ //
satataṃ śaradhārābhiḥ pradīptaṃ karṇapāvakam /
udīrṇo 'rjunamegho 'yaṃ śamayiṣyati saṃyuge // 3.84.11–2.

This rising Arjuna-cloud, excited by Draupadī-wind, with divine missile as rain cloud, great, having the white horse as cranes, bright with the bow Gāṇḍīva as rainbow, will always extinguish the kindled Karṇa-fire with the showers of arrows in the battlefield. (Cf. 6.111.38.)

8. Gambling

tāvakānāṃ raṇe bhīṣmo glaha āsīd viśāṃ pate /
tatra hi dyūtam āyātaṃ vijayāye 'tarāya vā // 6.110.43.

Bhīṣma was the stake on which depended the victory of the Kauravas in the battle. For there had arisen a gamble for victory on the reverse.

yac charīrair upastīrṇaṃ naravāraṇavājinām /
śaraśaktigadākhadgatomarākṣaṃ bhayāvaham //
prāviśan kitavā mandāḥ sabhāṃ yudhi durāsadām /
prāṇadyūte pratibhaye ke 'dīvyanta nararṣabhāḥ 6.15.66–7.

(Dhṛtarāṣṭra seeks information about the Mahābhārata war from Saṃjaya): Who were those bulls among men, the wretched gamblers who gambled there in the terrible battle which was a gamble for life, entering the gambling hall which was strewn with the bodies of men, elephants, and horses, which had for dice arrows, javelins, maces, swords, and darts, which caused fear and was dangerous to approach?

9. Palace

prajñāprāsādam āruhya muhyato mahato janān/
prekṣanto lokavṛttāni vividhāni dvijottama /
atipuṇyāni pāpāni tāni dvijavarottama // 3.198.93.

(Virtuous persons perform noble acts) having climbed (to the roof of) the palace of wisdom, and viewing (below) many persons who are going astray and those various worldly activities, exceedingly virtuous or evil, O Brāhmaṇa. (Cf. Dhammapada 2.8, paññāpāsādam āruyha.)

10. Gateway of Heaven

yadṛcchayā co 'papannaṃ svargadvāram apāvṛtam /
sukhinaḥ kṣatriyāḥ pārtha labhante yuddham īdṛśam // 6.24.32.

Arrived of itself, an open gate to heaven, blessed are the warriors who get such a combat, O Arjuna.

11. The City of Nine Gates

sarvakarmāṇi manasā saṃnyasyā 'ste sukhaṃ vaśī /
navadvāre pure dehī nai 'va kurvan na kārayan // 6.27.13.

Having renounced all actions with his mind, the soul with control sits happily in the city of nine gates (i.e., the body), neither acting nor causing others to act.

12. Chariot

rathaḥ śarīraṃ puruṣasya dṛṣṭam
ātmā niyante 'ndriyāṇy āhur aśvān /
tair apramattaḥ kuśalī sadaśvair
dāntaiḥ sukhaṃ yāti rathī 'va dhīraḥ // 3.202.21.

Man's visible (i.e., corporeal) body is a chariot, his soul is the charioteer, the sense organs, they say, are the horses; with those good horses, well-broken, he, attentive and dextrous, goes comfortably like the resolute (or skillful) master of the chariot.

13. Ornament

bhartā nāma paraṃ nāryā bhūṣaṇaṃ bhūṣaṇair vinā /
eṣā virahitā tena śobhanā 'pi na śobhate // 3.65.18.

The husband, in fact, is the best ornament of a woman, even if she have no ornaments; she without him, though beautiful, does not look beautiful. (Cf. chapter 6,I,*n*.)

14. Lamp

pradīptene 'va dīpena manodīpena paśyati 3.203.38.

One sees the Soul with the lamp of the mind as if with a lighted lamp.

15. Lotus

sudarśanaṃ cā 'sya rarāja śaures
tac cakrapadmaṃ subhujorunālam /
yathā 'dipadmaṃ taruṇārkavarṇaṃ
rarāja nārāyaṇanābhijātam // 6.55.89.

And Kṛṣṇa's discus, Sudarśana, that discus-lotus, having the brawny arms of Kṛṣṇa as its thick stalk, shone as the First Lotus born of Viṣṇu's navel, with the color of the rising sun, shone (in times of yore).

16. Lake

vidarbhasarasas tasmād daivadoṣād ivo 'ddhṛtām /
malapaṅkānuliptāṅgīṃ mṛṇālīm iva tāṃ bhṛśam 3.65.12.

Sudeva saw Damayantī appearing like a lotus fiber pulled up as if through evil fate from that Vidarbha-lake, with its parts much smeared with dirt and mud.

17. Lion

śaradaṃṣṭro dhanurvaktraḥ khaḍgajihvo durāsadaḥ /
narasiṃhaḥ pitā te 'dya pāñcālyena nipātitaḥ 6.14.9.

(Saṃjaya says to Dhṛtarāṣṭra): Your father (i.e., Bhīṣma), a man like a lion, with his arrows for its teeth, with his bow for its mouth, with his sword for its tongue, dangerous to approach, has been killed by the prince of the Pāñcālas.

18. The Old Sage

eko 'ham asmī 'ti ca manyase tvaṃ
na hṛcchayaṃ vetsi muniṃ purāṇam /
yo veditā karmaṇaḥ pāpakasya
yasyā 'ntike tvaṃ vrjinaṃ karoṣi // 1.68.27.

And you think, "I am alone"; you do not know the old sage dwelling in your heart, who knows all your wretched sinful acts, in whose presence you commit your sin.

II. SIMPLE METAPHOR

The sages have the wealth of penance (tapodhana- 1.64.42). The earth has the Himālayas or Mt. Meru as its crest (śailarājāvataṃsakām 1.69.27; cf. 1.159.20), the sea as its rim (samudranemim 1.32.22) or as its girdle (sāgaramekhalām 3.266.23) or as the outer corner of the eyes (sāgarāpāṅgām 1.58.11) or as its garment (sagarāmbarām 1.89.23). The forest is the garland of the Sarasvatī River (vanamālinī 3.88.2). Lotus-lakes have lotus-buds as their hands joined in salutation (kṛtapadmāñjalipuṭā 3.150.23). Anger is fire (krodhāgni 3.197.25). A wise person has the eyes of knowledge (prajñācakṣur nara iti 3.200.48). Draupadī is the outer heart of the Pāṇḍavas (bahiścaraṃ hṛdayaṃ pāṇḍavānām 3.253.13). The ascetics have poison in their speech (vāgviṣa 1.27.32). So, Yudhiṣṭhira has the poison of anger (kopaviṣam 3.245.5). A wicked person distresses people with the thorns of his speech and carries (personified) calamity held fast in his mouth (vākkaṇṭakair vitudantaṃ manuṣyān . . . mukhe nibaddhāṃ nirṛtiṃ vahantam 1.82.9; cf. daggers of speech 6.94.1 ff.); he has also the arrows of speech, pierced by which one is aggrieved day and night (vāksāyakā . . . yair āhataḥ śocati rātryahāni 1.82.11; cf. 3.35.1). Death and the round of transmigration are an ocean (mṛtyusaṃsārasāgarāt 6.34.7). Knowledge is one's sword that destroys doubt (jñānāsinā 'tmanaḥ 6.26.42). Passion is a great serpent that swallows a person (kāmamahāhinā 1.161.9). A king or a high personage is a lion, a tiger, a bull, or an elephant; these are so commonplace that only a few of the many need to be listed and references are almost unnecessary (e.g., rājasiṃha 1.85.18; narasiṃha 3.39.3; narendrasiṃha 1.87.9; naravyāghra 6.15.36; puruṣavyāghra 6.112.83; nṛpatiśārdūla 1.69.20; puruṣarṣabha 6.24.15; nararṣabha 6.15.67; bharatarṣabha 3.18.1; kurūṇām ṛṣabho 1.160.12; dvijarṣabha etc., etc., etc.; kṣatriyapuṃgava 1.112.20; rājakuñjara 3.240.25). The story of the Mahābhārata is born of the ocean of the mind of the great sage (manaḥsāgarasaṃbhūtām 1.53.24). Children without and with worldly experience are said to be unfledged (ajātapakṣāḥ śiśavaḥ 1.194.3) and full-fledged (jātapakṣā 1.194.4) respectively. Anything (even enmity) well developed or wide spread is said to be with flowers or fruits or both (e.g., vairaṃ sapuṣpam saphalaṃ viditvā 6.24.42; yām imāṃ puṣpitāṃ vācam 6.24.42). The fragrance of oblation has smoke as the outer corner of its eyes (havirgandhaṃ . . . dhūmāpāñgam 1.84.21). Bhīṣma slain is the felled boundary-tree of the Kurus (sīmāvṛkṣe nipatite kurūṇām 6.115.9). Bhīma, going away from his family for a while, has the word of Draupadī as the provision for his journey (draupadīvākyapātheyo 3.150.24; cf. Bhāravi, Kirātārjunīya 3.37).

3. POETICAL FANCY (UTPREKṢĀ)

MAMMAṬA DESCRIBES *utprekṣā* as a figure of speech in which a possible (or even probable) identity of the object under description with another object similar to it is imagined (saṃbhāvanam atho 'tprekṣā prakṛtasya samena yat, Kāvy. Pr. 10.6). For example, when Mt. Āmrakūṭa covered with mango trees that are laden with yellowish fruits and occupied by a black cloud in the center looks as if it were the breast of the earth (with yellowish circle and blackness in the center), this is a case of *utprekṣā* (*vide* Megha. 18). In an *upamā* (simile), the mountain would simply be likened to a heroine's breast; there would be no imagining that it was identical with the object of comparison. Thus, *utprekṣā* differs from the simile in the sense that it "employs rather the imaginative skill of the poet than conventional sets of objects of comparison" such as the ones already noted.

According to Viśvanātha, *utprekṣā* is of 32 kinds, as follows (*vide* SD 10.689):

utprekṣā

vācyā (expressed) — pratīyamānā (suggested)

jāti (group) — guṇa (quality) — kriyā (verb) — dravya (substance)

bhāva (positive) — abhāva (negative)

guṇasvarūpā (where quality is predominant) — kriyāsvarūpā (where action is predominant)

The present corpus has only examples of *vācyā utprekṣā*, where the imagination of the possible identity is expressed by means of such particles as *iva*, *yathā*, *nūnam*, *manye*, etc., as opposed to *pratīyamānā*, where no particles are used.

Without going into details about the varieties of *utprekṣā*, we may classify our examples according as they relate to verbs or nouns and adjectives.

I. UTPREKṢĀ OF VERBS

Charming Bhīma is as if displaying for sale a novel and unexpected type of beauty (navāvatāraṃ rūpasya vikrīṇann iva pāṇḍavaḥ 3.146.33). Bhīma is again described as being invited (to proceed), as it were, by the trees in the forest, with branches bowing down with flowers, delicate with coppery shoots, trembling with the breezes (kusumānataśākhaiś ca tāmrapallavakomalaiḥ / yācyamāna ivā raṇye drumair mārutakampitaiḥ 3.150.22). Kubera's horses, flying through the sky, are as if dragging clouds and drinking the wind (prakarṣanta ivā 'bhrāṇi pibanta iva mārutam 3.159.32; cf. utpatadbhir ivā 'kāśam 3.18.2). Having seen the girl, King Śantanu, startled with the perfection of her beauty, is surprised, with the hair of his body thrilling with delight; and drinking her beauty as it were with his eyes, he never becomes satiated (tāṃ dṛṣṭvā hṛṣṭaromā 'bhūd vismito rūpasaṃpadā / pibann iva ca netrābhyāṃ nā 'tṛpyata narādhipaḥ 1.92.28). Pleasantly cool, fragrant, carrying the pollen of flowers, the wind, as it wanders about in the forest, comes as it were to the trees for enjoyment (sukhaśītaḥ sugandhī ca puṣpareṇuvaho 'nilaḥ / parikrāman vane vṛkṣān upaitī 'va riraṃsayā 1.64.13). The sky is as if formed into one mass with clouds exceedingly wonderful (saṃghātitam ivā 'kāśaṃ jaladaiḥ sumahādbhutaiḥ 1.22.3). Khagama is as if burning with anger (nirdahann iva kopena 1.11.3). The demon comes as if tearing the earth (dārayann iva medinīm 1.151.4). The sky is dancing, as it were, with myriad waves of rain (saṃpranṛttam ivā 'kāśaṃ dhārormibhir anekaśaḥ 1.22.4). The sea is as if dancing, with the trembling hands of waves on all sides (vīcihastaiḥ pracalitair nṛtyantam iva sarvaśaḥ 1.19.9). Mt. Gandhamādana, with clouds clinging to its sides, seemed as if dancing with outspread wings; with the streaming waters of cascades it seemed as if decked with pearl necklaces (sapakṣam iva nṛtyantaṃ pārśvalagnaiḥ payodharaiḥ / muktāhārair iva citaṃ cyutaiḥ prasravaṇodakaiḥ 3.146.25). The hunter hits the boar causing, as it were, the mind of Arjuna to tremble (kampayann iva me manaḥ 3.163.21). The caves of the mountain also roar, as it were, with the noise of Bhīma's conch shell and shouting (nardantī 'va girer guhāḥ 3.146.56). The lake, undisturbed, is being fanned, as it were, by the soft breezes spreading on the other shore (kāñcanaiḥ kadalīṣaṇḍair mandamārutakampitaiḥ / vījyamānam ivā 'kṣobhyaṃ tīrāntaravisarpibhiḥ 3.146.53). Menakā, the fair-complexioned nymph, hurriedly comes to the earth following her garment (which is being carried off by the wind), as if smiling at the wind with shame (sā 'gacchat tvaritā bhūmiṃ vāsas tad abhiliṅgatī / utsmayantī 'va savrīḍaṃ mārutaṃ varavarṇinī 1.66.4). Loss of consciousness, pervaded with darkness, seems to enter into Dhṛtarāṣṭra while he is pained to see the circumstances of the coming war (tamasā tv abhyavastīrṇo moha āviśatī 'va mām 1.1.159). Pāṇḍu, endowed with the auspicious marks, shines, as it were, with beauty (pāṇḍuṃ lakṣaṇasaṃpannaṃ dīpyamānam iva śriyā 1.100.21).

II. UTPREKṢĀ OF NOUNS AND ADJECTIVES

Uttañka remarks that Janamejaya does one thing when something else should be done, as if through childishness (anyasmin karaṇīye tvaṃ kārye pārthivasattama / bālyād ivā 'nyad eva tvaṃ kuruṣe nṛpasattama 1.3.181). Bhīma sees the river crowded with intoxicated *kāraṇḍava*-ducks, decorated with *cakravāka*-birds, a garland as it were of bright lotuses put on by the mountain (mattakāraṇḍavayutāṃ cakravākopaśobhitām / racitām iva tasyā 'drer mālāṃ vimalapañkajām 3.150.26). Mt. Gandhamādana, with the undisturbed water of the mountain stream falling down, looks as if its clothes are getting loosened (srastāṃśukam ivā 'kṣobhyair nimnagāniḥsṛtair jalaiḥ 3.146.27; cf. Megha. 41). People see the snake Takṣaka coming from heaven, as if forming the parting of hair of the sky, having a lotus-like splendor (sīmantam iva kurvāṇaṃ nabhasaḥ padmavarcasam 1.40.3). The mountain seems to have finger smears, which are formed by rough cuts on its slopes, of various pure minerals (like streaks of unguents), golden, black, and silver (viṣamacchedaracitair anuliptam ivā 'ñgulaiḥ / vimalair dhātuvicchedaiḥ kāñcanāñjanarājataiḥ 3.146.24; cf. Megha. 1.19;[1] in all probability, Kālidāsa's phraseology shows reminiscences of that in 3.146.24,27). The Pāṇḍavas felt themselves (when joined by Dhaumya as their guru) to have gained a protector (nāthavantam ivā 'tmānaṃ menire bharatarṣabhāḥ 1.174.9). The hermitage of Dadhīca resounds with the noise of the humming of bees as if with the singers of the vedic chant (ṣaṭpadodgītaninadair vighuṣṭaṃ sāmagair iva 3.98.13). King Parīkṣit obtained a girl as if he had obtained the lordship of the three worlds (lokatrayaiśvaryam ivo 'palabhyā 3.190.41). Yudhiṣṭhira views the lake as if it were constructed by Viśvakarman (visvakarmakṛtaṃ yathā 3.296.42). The mountain, bright with minerals, trees, deer, and birds, which have various colors, looks as if it were the raised arm of the earth, filled with all ornaments (nānāvarṇadharaiś citraṃ dhātudrumamṛgāṇḍajaiḥ / sarvabhūṣaṇasaṃpūrṇaṃ bhūmer bhujam ivo 'cchritam 3.146.8; cf. Megha. 18). Probably that beauty of Tapatī has been made manifest by the creator only after having created by churning the world with the gods, the demons, and men (asyā nūnaṃ viśālākṣyāḥ sadevasuramānuṣam / lokaṃ nirmathya dhātre 'daṃ rūpam āviṣkṛtaṃ kṛtam 1.160.20). The three pursuits, virtue, prosperity, and love, seemed to be personified on earth, equally divided, and King Yudhiṣṭhira seemed

[1] Revāṃ drakṣasy upalaviṣamām vindhyapāde viśīrṇam / bhakticchedair iva viracitāṃ bhūtim añge gajasya // (You will see the Narmada River rough with stones, flowing at the foot of Mt. Vindhya, looking like a decoration made of streaks on the body of an elephant).

to be a fourth among them (teṣāṃ samavibhaktānāṃ kṣitau dehavatām iva / babhau dharmārthakāmānāṃ cathurtha iva pārthivaḥ 1.214.4). The sages, Vasiṣṭha and the rest, considered Parāśara, who blazed to heaven with his brilliance, as a second sun (taṃ vasiṣṭhādayaḥ sarve munayas tatra menire / tejasā divi dīpyantaṃ dvitīyam iva bhāskaram 1.172.7). Doing what was pleasing to each other, speaking what was pleasing to each other, of one character and conduct, they (Sunda and Upasunda) were the one made two-fold as it were (anyonyasya priyakarāv anyonyasya priyaṃvadau / ekaśīlasamācārau dvidhai 'vai 'kaṃ yathā kṛtau 1.201.4). Being impressed by Abhimanyu's prowess, warriors felt as if the world had two Arjunas (dviphalgunam imaṃ lokaṃ menire tasya karmabhiḥ 6.96.17).

Some of the examples of *utprekṣā* have already been listed in the respective sections on simile (upamā) for convenience; e.g., Śantanu's wife Gaṅgā is described as another Śrī herself, as it were (sākṣāc chriyam ivā 'parām 1.57.38); *vide* chapter 1,II,2. The use of the terms '*sākṣat*' and '*aparām*' entitles this pasage to be listed under *utprekṣā*.

In fact, the demarcating line between *upamā* and *utprekṣā* is so uncertain that sometimes even rhetoricians find it difficult to decide to which class of figure a particular passage belongs (cf. Daṇḍin, Kāvyādarśa 2.226–33). Moreover, *utprekṣā* is nothing more than *upamā* intensified; it is a variety of *upamā*, '*upamāprapañca*,' in broader terms.

4. HYPERBOLE (ATIŚAYOKTI)

THE FOLLOWING ARE EXAMPLES of hyperbole (atiśayokti), classified as to whether the hyperbolic statement relates to (I) understating the qualities of the objects of comparison, with a view to overstating the qualities of the subjects of comparison, (II) presenting something non-existent or incongruous, or (III) some fanciful overstatement with *api* ('even') or a *yadi* ('if') clause.[1]

I. UNDERSTATEMENT OF THE QUALITIES OF OBJECTS OF COMPARISON

Even the Law (dharma) can deviate from the path of morality, but the one who firmly adheres to his vows (i.e., Kaṇva) can never deviate from the path of morality (caled dhi vṛttād dharmo 'pi na calet saṃśitavrataḥ 1.65.16). The earth may give up odor; water may give up taste; light likewise may give up appearance; the air may give up the quality of touch; the sun may give up light; the comet may give up heat, the ether may likewise give up sound; the moon may give up its cool rays; Indra may give up valor; the lord of virtue (Yama) may give up virtue; but I (Bhīṣma) can on no account even think of giving up the truth (i.e., the vow of maintaining life-long celibacy) (tyajec ca pṛthivī gandham āpaś ca rasam ātmanaḥ / jyotis tathā tyajed rūpaṃ vāyuḥ sparśaguṇaṃ tyajet // prabhāṃ samutsṛjed arko dhūmaketus tatho 'ṣṇatām / tyajec chabdaṃ tathā 'kāśaḥ somaḥ śītāṃśutāṃ tyajet / vikramaṃ vṛtrahā jahyād dharmaṃ jahyāc ca dharmarāṭ / na tv ahaṃ satyam utsraṣṭuṃ vyavaseyaṃ kathaṃ cana 1.97.16–18). Kṛṣṇa, assuring Draupadī of his constant help to the Pāṇḍavas, says: The sky may fall; the Himālayas may be crushed; the earth may break into pieces; the ocean may dry up O Draupadī; but my word can never be wrong (pated dyaur himavān śīryet pṛthivī śakalībhavet / śuṣyet toyanidhiḥ kṛṣṇe na me moghaṃ vaco bhavet 2.13.117). Even Yama enraged, and Indra on the battlefield, Varuṇa holding the noose, or Kubera holding the mace, can be conquered, but Bhīṣma of great brilliance, of great might, can never be conquered (śakyo jetuṃ yamaḥ kruddho vajrapāṇiś ca saṃyuge / varuṇaḥ pāśabhṛc cā 'pi kubero vā gadādharaḥ // na tu bhīṣmo mahātejāḥ śakyo jetuṃ mahābalaḥ 6.46.7–8; cf. 6.103.16–17).

[1] *Vide* Kavy. Pr. 10.14; SD 10.696.

II. PRESENTING SOMETHING UNREAL OR INCONGRUOUS

And there arose a great joyful noise of all the citizens on account of their love for the Pāṇḍavas—noise that magnified their fame and was heaven-touching (tatprītyā cai 'va sarveṣāṃ paurāṇāṃ harṣasaṃbhavaḥ / śabda āsīn mahāṃs tatra divaspṛk kīrtivardhanaḥ 1.1.78; cf. 6.52.22; 66.3).

Damayantī in a fit of grief asks the lord of the mountains whether he, with his hundreds of sky-scraping summits, has ever seen Nala in this dreadful forest (kham ullikhadbhir etair hi tvayā śṛṅgaśatair nṛpaḥ / kaccid dṛṣṭo 'calaśreṣṭha vane 'smin dāruṇe nalaḥ 3.61.50).

The huge amount of dust raised by the flying horses reached the path of the sun and covered the sun (divākarapathaṃ prāpya chādayām āsa bhāskaram 6.101.14).

Bhīṣma is so speedy and fast in shooting his arrows that none of the Pāṇḍavas can see him; they can see only many arrows loosed from Bhīṣma's bow (na cai 'naṃ pāṇḍaveyānāṃ kaścic chaknoti vīkṣitum / viśikhān eva paśyanti bhimacāpacyutān bahūn 6.55.25).

Damayantī steals the eyes and the minds of the kings with her splendor (muṣṇantī prabhayā rajñāṃ cakṣūṃṣi ca manāṃsi ca 3.54.8; *vide* chapter 8,V).

Fallen on her limbs, the eyes of those kings looking at Damayantī were fixed just here and there on her, and did not move (elsewhere) as they stared (tasyā gātreṣu patitā teṣāṃ dṛṣṭir mahātmanām / tatra tatrai 'va saktā 'bhūn na cacāla ca paśyatām 3.54.9; cf. Harṣadeva, Ratnāvalī 2.36).

The Veda fears a semilearned person lest he should harm it (bibhety alpaśrutād vedo mām ayaṃ prahariṣyati 1.1.204).

III. FANCIFUL OVERSTATEMENT WITH API ('EVEN')[1]

A mountain without human beings is described as unapproachable even mentally by others, i.e., by ordinary persons (agamyaṃ manasā 'py 'anyais 1.26.17).

The names of all the kings fighting in the Mahābhārata war cannot be enumerated even in ten thousands of years (na śakyaṃ parisaṃkhyātuṃ varṣāṇām ayutair api 1.57.106).

[1] For fanciful overstatement with a *yadi-* (if) clause, *vide* chapter 1,V, ref. 6.33.12.

5. INFERENCE FROM CIRCUMSTANCES (ARTHĀPATTI)

THE TERM *arthāpatti* is shared in common by the philosophers and the rhetoricians. To a philosopher, it is a source of knowledge (pramāṇa) where an inevitable corollary is deduced from a statement of the prevailing circumstances; e.g., if it is stated that Devadatta, though healthy, does not eat in the daytime (pīno 'yaṃ devadatto divā na bhuñkte), the inevitable corollary, considering his health and non-eating in the daytime, would be that he must be eating at night. To a rhetorician, it is a figure of speech where a statement about some circumstances automatically suggests the inevitable corollary in the present context. Thus, even iron, when heated, becomes soft; how much more such animate beings as Aja (lamenting for his deceased wife Indumatī), (Ragh. 8.43; *vide* SD 10.740).

The following are examples from our corpus:

a) satyadharmacyutāt puṃsaḥ kruddhād āśīviṣād iva /
anāstiko py udvijate janaḥ kiṃ punar āstikaḥ 1.69.15.

Of a person who has deviated from truth and virtue, who is like a furious venomous snake, even a religious unbeliever is afraid; how much more a believer!

b) kalyau svo bhagavan yoddhum api sarvaiḥ surāsuraiḥ /
kiṃ punar vajriṇai 'kena pannagārthe yuyutsunā // 1.216.27.

(Kṛṣṇa and Arjuna speak to Agni): Both of us are ready, O lord, to fight even all the gods and demons; how much Indra alone, desirous of fighting for the sake of a snake (cf. 3.13.119: 6.55.67).

c) nā 'śakaṃs tatra bhūtāni mahānty api raṇe 'rjunam /
nirīkṣitum amogheṣuṃ kariṣyanti kuto raṇam // 1.219.25.

However great the living beings were, they were not able even to look at Arjuna, whose arrows were unfailing, in the battle there; how could they fight him (cf. 1.219.29).

d) bhīmaseno gadāṃ bibhrad vajrasāramayīṃ dṛḍhām /
caran vegena mahatā samudram api śoṣayet // 6.19.13.

Bhīmasena, wielding his mace, which was strong as if made of the essence of the thunderbolt, and running with great speed, could dry up even the ocean (let alone this army)!

6. ANTITHESIS (VIRODHA)

THE REPRESENTATION OF TWO THINGS as incongruous, although there is no incongruity between them, is termed antithesis (virodhaḥ so 'virodhe 'pi viruddhatvena yad vacaḥ / Kāvy. Pr. 10.24).

I. GENERAL

The following are unambiguous cases of antithesis:

a) mṛdunā mārdavaṃ hanti mṛdunā hanti dāruṇam /
nā 'sādhyaṃ mṛdunā kiṃcit tasmāt tīkṣṇataro mṛduḥ // 3.29.30.

One vanquishes leniency by leniency; one vanquishes violence by leniency; there is nothing that cannot be accomplished by leniency; leniency is, therefore, fiercer.

b) durbalā hi balīyāṃso viprā hi brahmatejasā 1.179.12.

Although weak, the Brāhmaṇas are strong by virtue of Brāhmanic brilliance.

c) catvāri karmāṇy abhayaṃkarāṇi
bhayaṃ prayacchanty ayathākṛtāni /
mānāgnihotram uta mānamaunaṃ
mānenā 'dhītam uta mānayajñaḥ // 1.85.25.

The four acts that bring about fearlessness, when unfittingly done bring about fear: an *agnihotra* (offering oblation to fire) instituted through pride, silence observed through pride, study with pride, and a sacrifice instituted through pride.

d) sukhaṃ sukhene 'ha na jātu labhyaṃ
duḥkhena sādhvī labhate sukhāni / 3.223.4.

Happiness can never be had through pleasure; a chaste woman gets happiness through troubles.

e) bhūtabhṛn na ca bhūtastho mamā 'tmā bhūtabhāvanaḥ // 6.31.5.

Supporting the beings, yet not residing in the beings, My self causes the beings to be.

f) na sat tan nā 'sad ucyate // 6.35.12.

(Brahman) is said to be neither existent nor nonexistent (cf. 1.1.21,29; and RV 10.129.1).

g) sarvendriyaguṇābhāsaṃ sarvendriyavivarjitam /
asaktaṃ sarvabhṛc cai va nirguṇaṃ guṇabhoktṛ ca // 6.35.14.

(Brahman is) possessing the semblance of the qualities of all sense organs, but devoid of all sense organs; detached, but sustainer of all things; devoid of the *guṇas* of the material world, but experiencing the *guṇas*.

h) bahir antaś ca bhūtānām acaraṃ caram eva ca /
sūkṣmatvāt tad avijñeyaṃ dūrasthaṃ cā 'ntike ca tat // 6.35.15.

(Brahman is) without and within the entities; immovable and movable; unknowable due to subtlety; remote, yet near.

i) avibhaktaṃ ca bhūteṣu vibhaktam iva ca sthitam /
bhūtabhartṛ ca taj jñeyaṃ grasiṣṇu prabhaviṣṇu ca // 6.35.16.

(Brahman is) undistributed among the beings, yet appearing as if distributed; as the supporter of creatures it is to be known, as their destroyer and their creator (this reminds one of Brahmā, Viṣṇu, and Śiva).

j) amṛtaṃ cai 'va mṛtyuś ca sad asac cā 'ham arjuna // 6.31.19.

I (Kṛṣṇa) as immortality and death, the existent and the nonexistent, O Arjuna.

k) yā niśā sarvabhūtānāṃ tasyāṃ jāgarti saṃyamī /
yasyāṃ jāgrati bhūtāni sā niśā paśyato muneḥ // 6.24.69.

The restrained one is awake when it is night for all creatures; when other creatures are awake, it is night for the sage of vision.

l) karmaṇy abhipravṛtto 'pi nai 'va kiṃ cit karoti saḥ 6.26.20.

(The wise one) though engaged in action, does not really do anything.

m) karmaṇy akarma yaḥ paśyed akarmaṇi ca karma yaḥ /
sa buddhimān manuṣyeṣu sa yuktaḥ kṛtsnakarmakṛt // 6.26.18.

One who can see inaction in action and action in inaction, he is wise among men; he is a self-disciplined doer of all acts.

n) bhartā nāma paraṃ nāryā bhūṣaṇaṃ bhūṣaṇair vinā /
eṣā virahitā tena śobhanā 'pi na śobhate // 3.65.18.

The husband, in fact, is the best ornament of a woman without ornaments; she, devoid of him, though beautiful, does not look beautiful (cf. chapter 2,I,13).

o) pūrvasyāṃ diśi taṃ dṛṣṭvā pratīcyāṃ dadṛśur janāḥ /
udīcyaṃ cai 'nam ālokya dakṣinasyāṃ punaḥ prabho // 6.55.23–4.

(Bhīṣma was so fast moving in the battle that) seeing him in the east, people saw him in the west; seeing him in the north, people saw him in the south.

II. AMBIGUOUS ANTITHESIS

Among the examples of ambiguous antithesis, there are some in which ambiguity is due to Sandhi rules, e.g., paras tasmāt tu bhāvo 'nyo 'vyakto 'vyaktāt sanātanaḥ 6.30.20. The accepted interpretation, necessitated indeed by the context is: There is, however, another state of being unmanifest and eternal, which is higher than that unmanifest; there is apparent ambiguity as to whether the interpretation is *vyakto vyaktāt, vyakto avyaktāt, avyakto vyaktāt,* or as the context requires, *avyakto avyaktāt.* Similar, but less complex, are 6.24.41 (vyavasāyātmikā buddhir . . . buddhayo 'vyavasāynām), and 6.25.25 (saktāḥ karmaṇy . . . tathā 'saktas); note that all three are Gītā passages. In some other passages ambiguity is caused by a pun. In fact, ambiguity lies at the very root of antithesis. But in the former class, there is no verbal ambiguity. In this class of examples, however, ambiguity itself is shrouded in doubt.

Thus, in the following examples (where ambiguity is caused by pun), apparent ambiguity or antithesis is quite clear in the Sanskrit passages, but not in idiomatic translations:

a) artha eva hi keṣāṃ cid anartho bhavitā nṛṇām / 3.2.40.

Wealth itself will be profitless (lit. 'non-wealth') to some persons.

b) sarveṣām ajaghanyas tu rāma āsīj jaghanyajaḥ / 3.116.4.

Rāma, the youngest son, was superior (lit. 'not-latest-or-lowest') to all (cf. 1.60.47).

c) sā daṣṭā sahasā bhūmau patitā gatacetanā /
vyasur aprekṣaṇīyā 'pi prekṣaṇīyatamākṛtiḥ // 1.8.17.

She (Pramadvarā), bitten, suddenly fell down on the ground, unconscious, devoid of life, and although too painful to be looked at, still possessed of the most charming appearance (lit. 'with appearance to be seen').

d) asitaṃ sitakarmasthaṃ kas taṃ nā 'rcitum arhati / 1.86.15.

Who would not adore him, who, though black-colored, engages in virtuous acts (lit. 'white acts')?

Sometimes, a subtle type of antithesis occurs. Thus, by virtue of his excellence of beauty, Nala appears as the god of beauty himself standing on the ground (atha devāḥ pathi nalaṃ dadṛśur bhūtale sthitam / sākṣād iva sthitaṃ mūrtyā manmathaṃ rūpasaṃpadā 3.51.26); antithesis involves the traditional belief that a god never touches the ground. Cf. 3.54.24.

7. EXCLUSION BY SPECIFICATION (PARISAṂKHYĀ)

THE TERM *parisaṃkhyā* originally belongs to the Mimāṃsā system where it designates a type of passage that means something exclusive of what is verbally specified. Thus the words pañca pañcanakhā bhakṣyāḥ, 'five five-nailed animals should be eaten,' are taken to mean 'the animals other than the five five-nailed ones should not be eaten.'

In poetry this term, however, represents a stylistic feature where "the mention of something, with or without a query, results in the exclusion of something else similar to it" (kiṃ cit pṛṣṭam apṛṣṭaṃ vā kathitaṃ yat prakalpate / tādṛganyavyapohāya parisaṃkhyā tu sā smṛtā, Kavy. Pr. 10.33). For example, when it is said that in Rāma's administration, crookedness was confined to the dancing pose of dancers, it is taken to mean that none was ever found with a crooked, dishonest nature (*vide* Tulasī, Rāmacaritamānasa 7.22).

The following are examples from our corpus, which, however, are not of a very high order:

a) yaḥ samutpatitaṃ krodhaṃ nigṛhṇāti hayaṃ yathā /
sa yante 'ty ucyate sadbhir na yo raśmiṣu lambate // 1.74.2.

One who controls rising anger like a horse, he is called the charioteer by the virtuous, not one who clings to the reins.

b) ṣaṇṇām ātmani nityānām indriyāṇāṃ pramāthinām /
yo dhīro dhārayed raśmiṃ sa syāt paramasārathiḥ 3.202.22.

When the six senses inherent in one's self are troublesome, he who resolutely holds in the reins is the best charioteer.

c) anāśritaḥ karmaphalaṃ kāryaṃ karma karoti yaḥ /
sa saṃnyāsī ca yogī ca na niragnir na cā 'kriyaḥ 6.28.1.

One who, detached from the fruit of action, performs the required actions is the real Saṃnyāsin and Yogin, not one who has no (sacrificial) fire, nor one who does no actions.[1]

d) kiṃ svit pravasato mitraṃ
kiṃ svin mitraṃ gṛhe sataḥ /
āturasya ca kiṃ mitraṃ
kiṃ svin mitraṃ mariṣyataḥ //
sārthaḥ pravasato mitraṃ bhāryā mitraṃ gṛhe sataḥ /
āturasya bhiṣañ mitraṃ dānaṃ mitraṃ mariṣyataḥ // 3.297.44–45.

Which is the friend of one away from home? The company (of traders). Which is the friend of one who is at home? His wife. Which is the friend of one suffering from a disease? A physician. Which is the friend of a moribund person? Charity.

---

[1] Franklin Edgerton, *Bhagavadgītā, Sanskrit and English* (Cambridge, Mass., 1944), interprets *karma*, 'action,' as 'ritual acts.'

8. MISCELLANEOUS FIGURES

I. EXCELLENCE (VYATIREKA)

IN VYATIREKA, THE SUBJECT OF COMPARISON is shown as excelling the object of comparison (upamānād yad anyasya vyatirekaḥ sa eva saḥ / Kavy. Pr. 10.19). The following are examples:

a) aśvamedhasahasrād dhi satyam eva viśiṣyate 1.69.22.

Just the truth is superior to a thousand horse-sacrifices.

b) kruddhād āśīviṣāt sarpāj jvalanāt sarvatomukhāt /
durādharṣataro vipraḥ puruṣeṇa vijānatā // 1.76.22.

To a learned man, a Brāhmaṇa (when offended) is more dangerous than a furious, venomous snake, or a fire, facing all directions.

c) na vāsasāṃ na rāmāṇāṃ nā 'pāṃ sparśas tathā sukhaḥ /
śiśor āliṅgyamānasya sparśaḥ sūnor yathā sukhaḥ // 1.68.55.

The touch of garments, charming women, or water is not so pleasing as the touch of an infant son, being embraced, is pleasing.

II. CONVERSE (PRATĪPA)

paripatya yadā sūnur dharaṇīreṇuguṇṭhitaḥ /
pitur āśliṣyate 'ṅgāni kim ivā 'sty adhikaṃ tataḥ // 1.68.52.

When a son running to him, besmeared with the dust of the earth, embraces the limbs of the father, what is more pleasant than that?

III. POETICAL DOUBT (SAṂDEHA)

The following are examples of poetical doubt (*saṃdeha*):

a) aho rūpam aho kāntir aho dhairyaṃ mahātmanaḥ /
ko 'yam devo nu yakṣo nu gandharvo nu bhaviṣyati // 3.52.16.

(The women speak about Nala in Damayantī's apartment): Such wonderful beauty. Such wonderful brilliance. Such wonderfully firm composure of the great-souled man. Who is he? Might he be a god, a *yakṣa*, or a *gandharva* (divine musician)?

b) apsarā devakanyā vā māyā vā devanirmitā / 3.248.10.

Is she (referring to Draupadī) a divine harlot (apsaras), a divine maiden, or an illusion created by the gods?

c) dīryante kiṃ nu girayaḥ kiṃ svid bhūmir vidīryate /
kiṃ svid āpūryate vyoma jalabhāraghanair ghanaiḥ // 1.125.28.

(Referring to the noise of a warrior's challenge): Are the mountains being broken? Or is the earth being torn asunder? Or is the sky being filled with (thundering) clouds dense with masses of water? (Cf. 3.143.11.)

IV. MISTAKER (BHRĀNTIMĀN)

The following are examples of *bhrāntimān*, in which the subject of comparison is mistaken for an object of comparison:

a) vicitrakavacaṃ vīraṃ paramāstravidaṃ nṛpam /
devo 'yam ity amanyanta carantaṃ vanavāsinaḥ // 1.106.10.

People living in the forest mistook King Pāṇḍu for a god, having shining armor, brave, conversant with the best missiles, as he roamed about.

b) te śrutvā rathanirghoṣaṃ vāraṇāḥ śikhinas tathā /
praṇedur unmukhā rājan meghodayam ive 'kṣya ha // 3.71.7.

Having heard the sound of (Nala's) chariot, those elephants and peacocks, with their faces turned upward, trumpeted and screamed as if having seen the rising of clouds.

V. EQUAL PAIRING (TULYAYOGITĀ)

dharmarāje atiprītyā pūrṇacandra ivā 'male /
prajānāṃ remire tulyaṃ netrāṇi hṛdayāni ca 1.214.9.

In Yudhiṣṭhira, spotless like the full moon, owing to his immense affection, both the eyes and the hearts of people were equally delighted.

VI. ACCOMPANIMENT (SAHOKTI)

taṃ patantam abhiprekṣya mahātmānaṃ pitāmaham /
saha bhīṣmeṇa sarveṣāṃ prāpatan hṛdayāni naḥ // 6.114.83.

Having seen the great-souled grandfather (Bhīṣma) falling, the hearts of all of us fell down along with Bhīṣma.

VII. POETICAL REASON (KĀVYALIÑGA)

ekam āśīviṣo hanti śastreṇai 'kaś ca vadhyate /
hanti vipraḥ sarāṣṭrāṇi purāṇy api hi kopitaḥ /
durādharṣataro vipras tasmād bhīru mato mama // 1.76.24–5.

The snake kills only one man; and only one man is killed by a weapon. But a Brāhmaṇa, enraged, destroys even cities, along with their kingdoms. O timid one! that is why to me a Brāhmaṇa is more dangerous (cf. chapter 9,A,II,4,*b*).

Although the reason given does not quite sound poetical, the example represents the germ of the later highly developed *kāvyaliñga*.

VIII. DESCRIPTION OF NATURE (SVABHĀVOKTI)

A striking poetic description of the characteristics or movements of various living objects of nature is regarded as a separate figure (svabhāvoktiḥ svabhāvasya jātyādisthasya varṇanam, Kuvalayānanda 160). The following are a few of the many examples:

a) kareṇubhir vāraṇaiś ca prabhinnakaraṭāmukhaiḥ /
sarovagāḍhaiḥ krīḍadbhiḥ samantād anunāditam // 3.98.15.

(The hermitage of Dadhīca) resounds on all sides with female elephants and male elephants having the fissures of their temples flowing with must-fluid, playing, having plunged into the lake.

b) tathai 'va padmaṣaṇḍais ca maṇḍiteṣu samantataḥ /
śikhaṇḍinībhiḥ sahitāṃl latāmaṇḍapakeṣu ca //
meghatūryaravoddāmamadanākulitān bhṛśam /
kṛtvai 'va kekāmadhuraṃ saṃgītamadhurasvaram //
citrān kalāpān vistīrya savilāsān madālasān /
mayūrān dadṛśuś citrān nṛtyato vanalāsakān // 3.155.53–54.

(Yudhiṣṭhira and Draupadī saw) likewise bright peacocks accompanied by the peahens in small bowers of creepers decorated on all sides with clumps of lotuses. The forest dancers, amorous and languid with love, spread their bright tails and danced. They uttered the sweet sound of their music, their sweet peacocks' cries. They were exceedingly agitated by great passion because of the trumpeting of the clouds.

c) kāṃś cic chakunajatāṃś ca viṭapeṣū 'tkaṭān api /
kalāparacitāṭōpān vicitramukuṭān iva /
vivareṣu tarūṇāṃ ca muditān dadṛśuś ca te // 3.155.56.

And they saw some birds sitting haughtily on the branches with their tails swelled out, looking like bright diadems (of the trees, or worn by themselves?), and rejoicing in the hollows of the trees.

IX. INCONGRUITY (VIṢAMA)

The following are examples of *viṣama* in which either "a combination of two incongruous things is described" or "a production of an effect from an incongruous cause" is shown (Kāvy. Pr. 10.40–41).

a) kva maharṣiḥ sadai 'vo 'graḥ sā 'psarā kva ca menakā /
kva ca tvam evaṃ kṛpanā tāpasīveṣadhāriṇī // 1.68.77.

What have the great sage, always terrible, and the *apsaras* Menakā to do with you who are wretched like this and wearing the garb of a female ascetic? (Duhṣanta's insulting remarks about Śakuntalā).

b) yenā 'patrapate sādhur asādhus tena tuṣyati 3.2.50.

The thing a virtuous person is ashamed of, a wicked person finds contentment with.

X. MODAL METAPHOR (SAMĀSOKTI)

Samāsokti may be defined as poetic personification of nature by virtue of "paronomastic attributes only." Here, a thing at hand is described in the most naturalistic fashion; but the words are so arranged as to suggest elements of personification as well. The following is an example from Vālmīki's Rāmāyaṇa (4.30.45).

cañcaccandrakarasparśaharṣonmīlitatārakā /
aho rāgavatī saṃdhyā jahāti svayam ambaram //

The evening (beloved Saṃdhyā), red (with love), having made visible the stars through delight in contact with the rays of the trembling moon (having opened her eyes through joy in the caresses of the hands of the trembling lover Moon [trembling, '*vepathu*,' is one of the expressions of love; SD 3.166]), leaves the sky (casts off her garment) herself. Wonderful indeed!

This brevity in signifying two meanings in one set of words constitutes the essence of *samāsokti* (paroktir bhedakaiḥ śliṣṭaiḥ samāsoktiḥ / Kāvy. Pr. 10.11).

The *samāsoktis* of the Mahābhārata are not so striking as the Rāmāyaṇa's, especially with regard to the poetic complexity of details; e.g.,

a) . . . tāmrapallavabāhavaḥ /
vidūrajātāś ca latāḥ samāśliṣyanta pādapān // 3.12.12.

The creepers (personified as beloved women), having red armlike shoots (having for arms the creeper's red shoots), growing at a distance from the trees (born in a far distant land), embraced the trees (personified as lovers).

b) mahānadībhir bahvībhiḥ spardhaye 'va sahasraśaḥ /
abhisāryamāṇam aniśaṃ dadṛśāte mahārṇavam // 1.19.15.

They saw the ocean (personified as the lover) being always flowed into (approached at the rendezvous) by many great rivers (personified as beloved women) in thousands, as if in amorous rivalry.

9. IDIOMS

THE FOLLOWING ARE EXAMPLES of what we may call popular idioms as adopted in the Mahābhārata. Although most of them, as we shall see, are classifiable under illustration (nidarśanā), exemplification (dṛṣṭānta), corroboration (arthāntaranyāsa), or periphrasis (paryāyokta), they seem to form a basic unit, which in modern terms may be called idiom.

A. IDIOMS IN GENERAL

I. HUMAN BODY

Of the various fields from which the constituents of these idioms are collected, the human body is the most significant one.

1. Feet

Without Bhīma, Arjuna cannot even be equal to the feet of Karṇa (tam ṛte phalguno yuddhe rādheyasya na pādabhāk 1.193.12; cf. na pādarajasā tulyo 3.53.6.[1] Duryodhana asks Karṇa to place his feet on the heads of the enemy (durhṛdāṃ kuru sarveṣāṃ mūrdhni pādam arindama 1.126.16; cf. padaṃ śiraḥsu dviṣatāṃ·kurudhvam 1.185.17). These are examples of periphrasis (paryāyokta).

2. Hands

The hands are well known as symbols of expressions of the emotions. The present corpus has, however, only three such gestures: (*a*) rubbing one hand on the other (desperate anger), (*b*) grinding one hand with the other (vindictive attacks), (*c*) hiding one's face with one's hand (distressed weeping).

Thus, having heard from the ministers the story of the tragic death of his father, Janamejaya sighed heavily, afflicted with pain, and rubbed his one hand upon the other (paryatapyata duḥkhārtaḥ pratyapiṃṣat kare karam 1.46.33; cf. hastair hastāgram apare pratyapiṃṣann amarṣitāḥ 2.42.27 [referring to the kings on the death of Śiśupala]; PW also refers to 7.8484). Having ground his one hand with the other, biting his lips, the mighty Bhīma ran to attack Kirmīra (niṣpiṣya pāṇinā pāṇiṃ saṃdaṣṭoṣṭhapuṭo balī / tam abhyadhāvad vegena . . . 3.12.42; PW has missed this passage under *nis* + *piṣ;* 1.5922 and 4.778, which are referred to, do not occur in the critical text; 5.5596 is doubtful).

[1] Roy translates *pāda* as 'quarter,' which does not seem to be in keeping with the context.

Having told her grievances to Kṛṣṇa, Draupadī wept, hiding her face with her hand (ity uktvā prārudat kṛṣṇā mukhaṃ pracchādya pāṇinā 3.13.109).

All these three gestures may be taken as expressions (anubhāvas) of anger (krodha).

3. Lips and Teeth

Clenching the teeth and biting the lips with the teeth signify anger; e.g., Hiḍimba, with red eyes, ran to kill Hiḍimbā, clenching his teeth (evam uktvā hiḍimbāṃ sa hiḍimbo lohitekṣaṇaḥ / vadhāyā 'bhipapātai 'nāṃ dantair dantān upaspṛśan 1.140.20; cf. 3.261.46). Warriors, biting their lips with their teeth in anger, look at each other with frowning faces (nirdaśya daśanaiś cā 'pi krodhāt svadaśanacchadān / bhrukuṭīkuṭilair vaktraiḥ prekṣante ca parasparam 6.44.41; cf. 1.140.20). These also are expressions (anubhāva) of anger. *Vide* SD 3.232.

4. Eyes

Karṇa describes himself as one who is always detested and hated by Bhīṣma; the compound *akṣigata-*, 'in the eyes,' equals *dveṣya* according to the Sanskrit lexica, and PW refers also to *kāvya* passages (rādheyo 'haṃ kuruśreṣṭha nityaṃ cā 'kṣigatas tava / dveṣyo . . . 6.117.5). These are examples of *paryāyokta*.

Śakuntalā, being insulted by Duḥṣanta, with her eyes red from anger and inability to endure it, with her lips quivering, burning him up, as it were, by her glances, looked at the king sideways (saṃrambhāmarṣatāmrākṣī sphuramāṇoṣṭhasaṃpuṭā / kaṭākṣair nirdahantī 'va tiryag rājānam aikṣata 1.68.21). Here 'looking sideways' signifies anger and grievance simultaneously. (Expression [anubhāva] of anger [krodha].)

An angry person is described as one with red eyes (lohitekṣaṇaḥ 1.140.20; krodhasaṃraktalocana- 1.78.24; krodharaktekṣaṇa- 1.73.31; cf. 1.73.33; 68.21) (anubhāva of krodha).

One's eyes are wide open through surprise (vismayotphullalocanaḥ 1.122.18; cf. 1.124.26; 126.1). In one instance, however, the eyes wide open signify passionate desire. Thus, Gautama's eyes were wide open to see the divine harlot, wearing one garment, with limbs unexcelled in the world (tām ekavasanāṃ dṛṣṭvā gautamo 'psarasaṃ vane / loke 'pratimasaṃsthānām utphullanayano 'bhavat 1.120.8). The eyes of the child, playfully consoling his anxious parents with his inarticulate words, are also, naturally enough, wide open (utphullanayano bālaḥ kalam avyaktam abravīt 1.147.20). These are expressions of wonder (vismaya), love (rati), and affection (vātsalya), respectively.

The Pāṇḍavas always keep looking at Draupadī's face; i.e., they love her exceedingly (tava vaśyā hi satataṃ pāṇḍavāḥ priyadarśane / mukhaprekṣāś ca te sarve . . . 3.222.5). This is an example of *paryāyokta*. Cf. 6.44.41 above, for frowning face.

5. Corners of the Mouth

Licking the corners of the mouth occurs almost in the same context as biting the lip with the teeth. Thus, Ghaṭotkaca, having bitten his lip with his teeth, licking the corners of his mouth, poured upon Duryodhana a great shower of arrows (saṃdaśya daśanair oṣṭhaṃ sṛkkiṇī parisaṃlihan / śaravarṣeṇa mahatā duryodhanam avākirat 6.87.29-30; cf. 6.90.5; 104.42; 107.11; 114.26). This is an expression (anubhāva) of anger (krodha); cf. 3.134.3 for similar phraseology in connection with a venomous snake.

6. Back

All the mothers always attend upon Jantu, the newly-born child, having put behind them (lit. 'having made at the back') the enjoyments of life (taṃ jātaṃ mātaraḥ sarvāḥ parivārya samāsate / satataṃ pṛṣṭhataḥ kṛtvā kāmabhogān viśāṃ pate 3.127.5; cf. 1.165.43; 6.2.31). This is an example of *paryāyokta*.

7. Marrow of the Bones

Having seen Bhīmasena standing in front of them with the mace in his hand, warriors became exceedingly terrified (lit. 'the marrow of their bones perished, as it were') (sraṃsanta iva majjāno yodhānāṃ bharatarṣabha / dṛṣṭvā 'grato bhīmasenaṃ gadāpāṇim avasthitam 6.19.44). This is an example of *utprekṣā*. According to the rhetoricians, passages like this suffer from the defect of vulgarity (grāmyadosa; *vide* SD 7.576). They are, however, listed here as examples of popular idioms in earlier times; cf. 3.119.14; 137.5; 268.40.

II. ANIMAL WORLD

1. Lion

bālyāt prasuptasya mahābalasya
siṃhasya pakṣmāṇi mukhāl lunāsi /
padā samāhatya palāyamānaḥ
kruddhaṃ yadā drakṣyasi bhīmasenam // 3.252.6.

(nidarśanā)

(O Jayadratha) In your folly, you cut off the eyelashes from the face of a mighty lion, having kicked him awake when he was sleeping, but taking to flight, when you see him, Bhīmasena, in his anger (cf. 3.252.7; 261.49).

2. Tiger

sakuṇḍalaṃ sakavacaṃ divyalakṣaṇalakṣitam /
katham ādityasaṃkāśaṃ mṛgī vyāghraṃ janiṣyati // 1.127.15.
(nidarśanā)

How will a doe bear a tiger, with earrings and armor, marked with divine marks, shining like the sun? (Duryodhana's remarks about Karṇa's pedigree; cf. 3.134.3.)

3. Elephant

nāgaṃ prabhinnaṃ girikūṭakalpam upatyakāṃ haimavatīṃ carantam /
daṇḍī 'va yūthād apasedhase tvaṃ yo jetum āśaṃsasi dharmarājam
3.252.5. (nidarśanā)

You (Jayadratha) who hope to defeat Yudhiṣṭhira are trying to drive away from his herd, as if with a stick, an elephant in must, mountain-like, grazing on the slopes of the Himālayas.

4. Snake

a) kṛṣṇoragau tīkṣṇaviṣau dvijihvau
mattaḥ padā 'krāmasi pucchadeśe /
yaḥ pāṇḍavābhyāṃ puruṣottamābhyaṃ
jaghanyajābhyāṃ prayuyutsase tvam 3.252.8.
(nidarśanā)

You (Jayadratha) wantonly trample upon the tails of two cobras with virulent poison, having two tongues—you who want to fight with the two youngest Pāṇḍavas, the best among men.

b) vyāghraṃ śayānam prati mā prabodhaya
āśīviṣaṃ sṛkkiṇī lelihānam /
padāhatasye 'va śiro 'bhihatya
nā 'daṣṭo vai mokṣyase tan nibodha 3.134.3.
(nidarśanā and kāvyaliṅga)

Don't wake a sleeping tiger or a venomous snake, licking the corners of its mouth. For you will not be spared unbitten (by a snake) which is hit on its head by your foot. Know this. (This is the royal bard's challenge to Aṣṭāvakra.)

c) āśīviṣas tvāṃ saṃkruddhaś caṇḍo daśati durbhage 3.261.17.
(nidarśanā)

(Mantharā, taunting Kaikeyī, says): The venomous snake, enraged and terrible, bites you, O unfortunate lady (i.e., Daśaratha is doing injustice to you; cf. 3.261.49).

5. Crow and Jackal

brāhmaṇasya pramattasya havir dhvāṅkṣair vilupyate /
śārdūlasya guhāṃ śūnyāṃ nīcaḥ kroṣṭā 'bhimarśati 1.205.8.
(nidarśanā)

(Lament of a Brāhmaṇa whose property was stolen): The sacrificial offering of a careless Brāhmaṇa is being taken away by crows. The wicked jackal is invading the empty cave of a tiger.

6. White Crow

tathai 'va sā ca bhartāraṃ duḥkhaśīlam upācarat /
upāyaiḥ śvetakākīyaiḥ priyakāmā yaśasvinī 1.43.10
(upamā)

Jaratkāru the illustrious wife, of loving desire, waited upon Jaratkāru her husband, who was of irascible character, by white-crow-like (unusual) means.

PW, however, refers to Nīlakaṇṭha's gloss on *śvetakākīya* as follows: śvā ca etaś ca (i.e., mṛga) kākaś ca teṣām ime śvetakākīyās tair nityajāgarūkatvabhayacakitatveṅgitajñatvaiḥ / anye tu śvetakāko bakas tadīyaiḥ taṃ hi varṣāsu nīḍasthaṃ baky eva puṣṇāti / .

This occurs on the above passage and on 12.105.15 (in the text with Nīlakaṇṭha's commentary). Nīlakaṇṭha himself seems unconvinced by his first gloss, viz., the analysis into the wakefulness of a dog (śvā), the timidity of a deer (eta), and the acquaintance with signs of a crow (kāka), since he puts forward an alternative gloss of *śvetakāka*, 'crane,' which he supports by referring to a commonly believed fact that during the rainy season, the male crane, sitting in the nest, is looked after just by the female crane.

III. MISCELLANEOUS

1. Sesamum Seeds (Tila)

khādāma pātayāmai 'nāṃ tilaśaḥ pravibhajya tām 3.264.47.
(upamā)

(The demons terrifying Sītā say): Let us devour and tear her to pieces, dividing her up in pieces small as sesamum seeds (cf. 3.231.5).

2. Grass (Tṛṇa)

a) tṛṇānāṃ muṣṭinai 'kena himavantaṃ tu parvatam /
channam icchasi kaunteya yo 'smān saṃvartum icchasi // 3.36.22.
(nidarśanā)

(Bhīma's grievances uttered to Yudhiṣṭhira): By one handful of grass, you want to have the Himālayas covered, O Yudhiṣṭhira, you who want to restrain us from war.

b) ity uktā tena vaidehī parivṛtya śubhānanā /
tṛṇam antarataḥ kṛtvā tam uvāca niśācaram // 3.265.17.

Having been addressed thus by Rāvaṇa, Sītā of auspicious face turned towards him, and having placed a straw between (herself and Rāvaṇa), spoke to that demon.

This is an expression (anubhāva) of anger (krodha)—a wrathful insult or expression of indifference. Cf. Vālmiki, Rāmāyaṇa 3.56.1; 5.21.3; Adhy. Ram. 5.2.31; Tulasi, Rāmacaritamānasa 5.9.3.

3. Root

chinnaṃ mūlam anarthānāṃ mṛte tasmin bhaviṣyati 1.34.27.
(paryāyokta)

(The snakes, afraid of the consequences of the snake-sacrifice, plan to bite Janamejaya to death): He being dead, the root of the troubles will be cut off (cf. 3.5.3).

4. Thorns

kṣaṇenā 'dya kariṣye 'ham idaṃ vanam akaṇṭakam 1.141.10.
(paryāyokta)

(Bhīma's challenge to Hiḍimba): In a moment today I will render this forest free of thorns (i.e., free from Hiḍimba's atrocities; cf. 3.12.72).

5. Sacrificial Objects

(purā . . .) dadāti kasmai cid anarhate tanuṃ
varājyapūrṇām iva bhasmani srucam //
purā tuṣāgnāv iva hūyate haviḥ
purā śmaśāne srag ivā 'pavidhyate /
purā ca somo 'dhvarago 'valihyate
śunā yathā viprajane pramohite /
mahaty araṇye mṛgayāṃ caritvā
purā śṛgālo nalinīṃ vigāhate // 3.253.18–19.

(Dhātreyikā's anxiety for Draupadi, who has been kidnapped by Jayadratha): Before she gives herself to some unworthy person, like a ladleful of the best ghee poured on ashes, before the sacrificial oblation is poured on a fire of chaff, before a garland is thrown away in a cemetery, before the sacrificial *soma* is licked up by a dog while the Brāhmaṇas are bewildered, before a jackal plunges into the lotus lake, after having roamed around to hunt in the great forest (Indrasena should rescue Draupadī). (Cf. 1.184.15).

6. Fire and Javelin

a) śuśrūṣavaś cā 'pi jitendriyāś ca
jñānāgame cā 'pi gatāḥ sma niṣṭhām /
na bāla ity avamantavyam āhur
bālo 'py agnir dahati spṛśyamānaḥ // 3.133.7.
(arthāntaranyāsa and dṛṣṭānta)

(Aṣṭāvakra replies to the royal bard): We (i.e., I) are desirous of learning, and have the sense organs restrained, and have attained familiarity with the acquisition of knowledge. They say, one should not be insulted simply because he is a child. Even a small fire, being touched, burns.

b) kaḥ śūlam tīkṣṇam āsādya sarvagātrair niṣevate /
kaḥ śirasy agnim ādhāya viśvastaḥ svapate sukham 3.261.48.
(nidarśanā)

(Rāvaṇa's challenge to Rāma): Who, having got a sharp javelin, lies on it with all his limbs? Who, having placed fire near the head, confidently sleeps at ease?

7. Mountain and Mustard

a) yo vai darpāt saṃhananopapannaḥ
sudurbalaḥ parvatam āvihanti /
tasyai 'va pāṇiḥ sanakho vidīryate
na cai 'va śailasya hi dṛśyate vraṇaḥ // 3.134.4.
(dṛṣṭānta)

(The royal bard's challenge to Aṣṭāvakra): One who, endowed with strength but still very weak, strikes a mountain through vanity, it is his hand with its nails that breaks, and no wound whatsoever is seen on the mountain (cf. 3.134.3).

b) avayor antaram viddhi merusarṣapayor iva 1.69.3.
(upamā)

Śakuntalā traveling in the air, Duhṣanta only on earth, differ as widely as Mt. Meru and a mustard seed.

8. Mud

ataś ca dharmibhiḥ puṃbhir anīhārthaḥ praśasyate /
prakṣālanād dhi pāṅkasya dūrād asparśanaṃ varam // 3.2.47.
(dṛṣṭānta)

And therefore desirelessness is praised by virtuous persons. For non-contact and keeping one's distance is better than washing off the mud (i.e., prevention is better than cure).

9. Hook

baḍiśo 'yaṃ tvayā grastaḥ kālasūtreṇa lambitaḥ /
matsyo 'mbhasī 'va syūtāsyaḥ kathaṃ me 'dya gamiṣyasi // 3.154.35.
(nidarśanā, cf. 1.24.6, and upamā)

You (Jaṭāsura) have swallowed this hook fastened to the line of fate. Like a fish in water with its mouth hooked, how will you go away from me (Bhīma)?

10. River

śūrāṇāṃ ca nadīnāṃ ca prabhavā durvidāḥ kila 1.127.11.
(dīpaka)

The origins of the brave and of rivers are difficult to know.

Here the subject of comparison (the brave) and the object of comparison (the rivers) are associated with a common quality; *vide* SD 10.699.

11. Needle

rūpe ca te na paśyāmi sūcyagram api ninditam 1.77.14.
(paryāyokta)

(Yayāti to Śarmiṣṭhā): And in your beauty, I don't find even as much as the point of a needle to be found fault with.

12. Mirror

virūpo yāvad ādarśe nā 'tmanaḥ paśyate mukham /
manyate tāvad ātmānam anyebhyo rūpavattaram //
yadā tu mukham ādarśe vikṛtam so 'bhivīkṣate /
tade 'taraṃ vijānāti ātmānaṃ ne 'taraṃ janam 1.69.6,7.
(dṛṣṭānta)

(Śakuntalā's rebuke to Duḥṣanta): So long as an ugly man does not see his own face in the mirror, he considers himself more handsome than others. But when he sees his own ugly face in the mirror, then he perceives himself as inferior, not anybody else (cf. 1.69.5).

13. Poison

a) etām adya parāmṛśya striyaṃ rākṣasa mānuṣīm /
vişam etat samālodya kumbhena prāśitaṃ tvayā 3.154.18.
(nidarśanā)

(Yudhiṣṭhira's challenge to Jaṭāsura): Today, having done violence to this human female, O Demon, you have drunk this poison having shaken it up with a pot (i.e., you have invited trouble upon yourself).

b) vimokṣyanti viṣam kruddhāḥ kauraveyeṣu bhārata 3.9.3.
(paryāyokta)

The Pāṇḍavas, enraged, will let loose poison upon the Kauravas, O descendant of the Bharatas.

14. Pot

ko hi tatrai 'va bhuktvā 'nnaṃ bhājanaṃ bhettum arhati 1.212.27.
(nidarśanā)

(Baladeva talks about Arjuna's breach of trust in carrying off Subhadrā): Who having eaten food would break the plate there itself?

15. Knot

subaddhasyā 'pi bhārasya pūrvabandhaḥ ślathāyate 1.213.15.
(dṛṣṭānta)

(Draupadī's envy towards Arjuna's second wife Subhadrā): Even of a well-bound load, the previous knot becomes loose (i.e., howsoever loved Draupadī might have been before, she will now be loved less after Subhadrā's arrival).

16. Wilderness

na khalv aham idaṃ śūnye raumi kiṃ na sṛṇoṣi me 1.68.34.
(paryāyokta)

(Śakuntalā at Duḥṣanta's court): I am not crying in the wilderness. Why don't you listen to me?

17. Scraping with a Sharp Object

arthena tu samo 'nartho yatra labhyeta no 'dayaḥ /
na tatra vipaṇaḥ kāryaḥ kharakaṇḍūyitaṃ hi tat 3.34.64.
(nidarśanā)

One should not carry on business at a place where loss is equal to profit, and where prosperity cannot be attained. For that is (like) scraping with a sharp object (i.e., making an evil worse).

B. Idioms in Verbal Phrases

I. GENERAL

a) na dharmaphalam āpnoti yo dharmaṃ dogdhum icchati 3.32.5. (paryāyokta)

He does not get the fruit of virtuous acts who wants to exploit *dharma*.

b) juhvānaṃ samare prāṇān 6.94.4. (paryāyokta)

(Bhīṣma) offering his life as an oblation to battle . . .

c) bhūmiḥ pāsyati śoṇitam 3.13.5. (paryāyokta)

The earth will drink the blood (of Duryodhana and others).

d) paśumāram amārayat 1.142.38. (paryāyokta)

Bhīma caused Hiḍimba to die an animal's death (cf. 3.12.63).

e) nai 'ṣa kaścin mayi sthite 1.140.7.

He is nothing, while I am here (Bhīmasena assures Hiḍimbā that Hiḍimba is too weak to face the former's strength).

II. PERIPHRASES EXPRESSIVE OF DEATH

1. Euphemistic

a) śete sā bhuvi tanvaṅgī mama śokavivardhinī 1.9.3.

(Ruru lamenting his wife's death): She (Pramadvarā) of delicate limbs is sleeping on the ground, increasing my grief.

b) pañcatvam agamad rājā 1.3.18.

King Parīkṣit went to the state of five (i.e., his body was dissolved into the five elements).

c) tato diṣṭāntam āpannaḥ sarpeṇā 'nativartitam 1.45.15.

Then King Parīkṣit was brought to the unavoidable fated end by the snake (cf. jagāma kāle dharmātmā diṣṭāntam 1.53.24, with reference to Āstīka).

d) tenā 'cireṇa kālena jagāmā 'stam ivā 'ṃśumān 1.112.17.

Therefore King Vyuṣitāśva set like the sun in a short time (cf. 1.96.58).

2. General

When one kills someone, he sends him to Yama's home (anayad yamasādanam 6.50.73; 60.28,31,32; 75.11; 79.15; 92.45; cf. 1.37.12,19; 38.32; 56.10; 141.7: 3.15.12; 40.32; 126.20: 6.50.69,70,74; 51.34; 75.57; 79.45; 83.36; 96.3; 100.1).

Similarly one who dies goes to Yama's home (gataś cā 'si yamasya sadanaṃ prati 3.12.66; cf. 1.48.23; 49.7; 56.58: 3.120.5).

III. EXPRESSIONS FOR GOODBYE

a) āpṛṣṭo me 'si kaunteya svasti prāpnuhi pāṇḍava 3.38.27.

(Draupadī to Arjuna leaving for Indrakīla): Goodbye, O Arjuna. May you attain well-being (cf. Megha. 1.6).

b) śivās te santu panthānaḥ 3.292.11.

(Kuntī's farewell to her newly born child Karṇa): May your journey be auspicious!

10. FIGURES OF SOUND (ŚABDĀLAMKĀRA)

I. REPETITION OF CONSONANTS (ANUPRĀSA)

Like the similes among the figures of meaning, *anuprāsa* (repetition of consonants) among the figures of sound deserves special treatment.

Hemacandra defines *anuprāsa* as a repetition of consonants (vyañjanasyā 'vṛttir anuprāsaḥ, Kāvyānuśāsana 5.104.1). This includes alliteration, rhyme, and consonance in broader terms. The definition, however, excludes the possibility of assonance being an independent figure; assonance may occur only as a part of rhyme.[1]

Hopkins cites examples of alliteration from our corpus:[2] (*a*) jagrāhā 'jagaro grāhaḥ 3.60.20; (*b*) kā 'si kasyā 'si kalyāṇi 3.61.113; (*c*) phalapuṣpopaśobhitaḥ 3.61.94. The following examples are, however, based on the classification of *anuprāsa* as proposed by Hemacandra in his Kāvyānuśāsana, viz., (1) repetition of a consonant more than once, $C_1 \ldots C_1 \ldots C_1 \ldots$; (2) repetition of more than one consonant once, $C_1 \ldots C_1 \ldots C_2 \ldots C_2 \ldots$; (3) repetition of more than one consonant more than once, $C_1 \ldots C_1 \ldots C_2 \ldots C_1 \ldots C_2 \ldots$; (4) *lāṭānuprāsa*, or repetition of a word or words having the same meaning but differing in relation to their immediate constituents (śabdārthayor abhede 'pi anvayamātrabhedino 5.105.2); e.g., in *vasudhāṃ vasudhādhipaḥ* 3.54.38, *vasudhā-* has been repeated, though the immediate constituent of *vasudhā-*$_1$ is *-m* (the accusative suffix), while that of *vasudhā-*$_2$ is the zero allomorph of the genitive suffix as related to *adhipa-*. Rhyme (antyānuprāsa) may be added to Hemacandra's list.

The above classification is not exhaustive: it leaves out many other possibilities of consonantal repetition; e.g., a single repetition of a consonant does not constitute *anuprāsa* according to Hemacandra. The following examples, however, are cited in keeping with his classification.

1. Repetition of a Consonant More Than Once ($C_1 \ldots C_1 \ldots C_1 \ldots$)

(*a*) tasmin garbhe saṃbhṛte 'tha pulomāyāṃ bhṛgūdvaha 1.1.12. (*b*) śaśāsa śiṣyam āsīnam 1.54.21. (*c*) sarvapāpapraṇāśinīm 1.81.9. (*d*) alaṃkṛtām ābharaṇair arajombaradhāriṇīm 1.94.30. (*e*) kā tvaṃ tāmramukhī śyāmā sumṛṣṭamaṇikuṇḍalā 1.73.17; cf. 3.54.4. (*f*) taṃ vane vijane garbhaṃ siṃhavyāghrasamākule 1.66.10. (*g*) puṣpaprakaraśobhitam 1.213.31. (*h*) śālatālaśilāyudham 3.264.30. (*i*) vānīrava-

[1] Cf. SD 10.639; Cleanth Brooks, J. T. Purser, and R. P. Warren, *An Approach to Literature* (New York, 1946), pp. 627–628.

[2] E. W. Hopkins, *The Great Epic of India* (New York, 1901), p. 203.

namālinī 3.87.2. (*j*) dadarśa dāvaṃ dahyantam 3.63.1. (*k*) bhūr bhāti bharataśreṣṭha 6.74.34. (*l*) saveṇuvīṇāpaṇavānunādinam 1.178.14. (*m*) bhūtabhāvodbhavakaro 6.30.3. (*n*) na babhūva bhayaṃ kiṃcid devebhyo 'pi kathaṃcana 1.191.1. (*o*) manonayananandanaḥ 3.107.1. (*p*) velādolānilācalam 1.19.9.

2. Repetition of More Than One Consonant Once ($C_1 \ldots C_2 \ldots C_1 \ldots C_2 \ldots$)

(*a*) harṣas tadā varṣati vāsava 1.22.5. (*b*) pibantyo madhumādhavīm 1.76.3. (*c*) daivādhīnā naṣṭaceṣṭādhikārāḥ 1.84.6. (*d*) śantanor api santānam 1.97.24. (*e*) so 'py atrā 'trir bhagavān ājagāma 1.114.41. (*f*) raṅgāṅgaṇagato 1.125.6. (*g*) lābhāl lobho vyavardhata 1.196.21. (*h*) veṇuvīṇāmṛdaṅgānām 1.214.25. (*i*) sāṭṭāṭṭālakagopurā 3.16.6. (*j*) kṣaṇena kṣīṇabāṇo 'tha 3.40.35. (*k*) manye manyusamudbhūtaḥ 3.46.31. (*l*) varavarṇinī 3.50.27; cf. 3.54.26, etc., etc. (*m*) analo 'nilasārathiḥ 3.80.77. (*n*) sadā tadbhāvabhāvitaḥ 6.30.6. (*o*) divyamālyāmbara dharam 6.33.11. (*p*) bhūribhārāvapīḍitā 1.89.24.

3. Repetition of More Than One Consonant More Than Once ($C_1 \ldots C_1 \ldots C_2 \ldots C_2 \ldots C_1 \ldots C_2 \ldots$)

(*a*) manīṣiṇo mānasamānabhaktam 1.85.27. (*b*) janayām āsa sa munir menakāyāṃ śakuntalām / prasthe himavato ramye mālinīm abhito nadīm // 1.66.8. (*c*) kuntyāḥ prasravasaṃmiśrair asraiḥ klinnam uro 'bhavat 1.125.13. (*d*) sainyasugrīvayuktena kiṅkiṇījālamālinā 1.212.3; cf. 1.213.41. (*e*) abhirāmanadīkuñjanirjharodārakandaram / apsaronūpuraravaiḥ pranṛttabahubarhiṇam // 3.146.26. (*f*) mṛdaṅgabherīpaṭahapraṇādā nemisvanā dundubhinisvanāś ca / sasiṃhanādāś ca babhūvur ugrāḥ 6.55.104. (*g*) neminirhrādasaṃnādo mahāstrodayapāvakaḥ // 6.114.5. (*h*) tam eva cā 'dyam puruṣaṃ prapadye yataḥ pravṛttiḥ prasṛtā purāṇī 6.37.4. (*i*) mahānty anīkāni mahāsamucchraye samāgame pāṇḍavadhārtarāṣṭrayoḥ / cakampire śaṅkhamṛdaṅganisvanaiḥ prakampitānī 'va vanāni vāyunā // 6.42.6. (*j*) hayair api hayārohāś cāmarāpīḍadhāribhiḥ / haṃsair iva mahāvegair anyonyam abhidudruvuḥ // 6.44.20. (*k*) ghoraṃ jalacarārāvaraudraṃ bhairavanisvanam / gambhīrāvartakalilaṃ sarvabhūtabhayaṃkaram // 1.19.8.

4. Repetition of Words and Meanings Differing Only in Relation to Their Immediate Constituents (Lāṭānuprāsa)

(*a*) vasudhāṃ vasudhādhipaḥ 3.54.38. (*b*) abhijagmus tadā bhīmaṃ rājāno bhīmaśāsanāt 3.51.9. (*c*) bhīmo bhīmaparākramaḥ 1.141.18; 114.9; 142.32; 150.3: 3.50.5,9; cf. 1.127.10; 192.4. (*d*) ugro bhīmaratho bhīmo bhīmabāhur alopanaḥ 6.60.25. (*e*) nīlo nīlāyudhaiḥ saha 6.52.12. (*f*) tāṃ vānarapatiḥ patiḥ 3.264.18. (*g*) bhāskaraṃ bhāskaradyutiḥ 3.213.26. (*h*) priyaṃ bhārata bhāratam 6.10.8; cf. 6.10.5. (*i*) tam ugram ugrakarmāṇam ugrāṃ buddhiṃ samāsthitam 6.63.12. (*j*) lokaṃ lokavidāṃ varaḥ 6.94.3. (*k*) yamau yamasutāv iva 1.197.18. (*l*) śaktinā vīryaśaktinā 1.166.10. (*m*) tato navatyā navatir mukhānām 1.28.24. (*n*) tān dīnān dīnarūpo 'bhyabhāṣata 1.41.5. (*o*) vasur vasupradaḥ 1.57.35. (*p*) śaktyā śaktimatāṃ varaḥ 1.63.17. (*q*) satāṃ vṛttam cā 'dadītā 'ryavṛttaḥ 1.82.10. (*r*) yogakṣemaṃ pārthiva pārthivaḥ san 1.87.16. (*s*) tārāṃ tārādhipānanām 3.264.18. (*t*) anāyudhā sāyudhāyā 1.73.11. (*u*) apragalbhāṃ pragalbhaḥ sa 1.160.33. (*v*) sasenāḥ sasenena 1.105.14. (*w*) guṇā guṇeṣu vartante 6.25.28. (*x*) aśastraṃ śastrapāṇayaḥ 6.23.46. (*y*) mahābāho bahubāhūrupādam 6.33.29; cf. 2. (*z*) durbalair balavān api 3.34.68. (*aa*) hayair api hayārohāś 6.44.20. (*bb*) rajasvalāṃ nāthavatīm anāthavat 1.1.106. (*cc*) saṃbabhūva tataḥ kāmī tayā sārdham akāmayā 1.98.12. (*dd*) amānuṣo mānuṣānām 1.109.1. *Vide* section II.

5. Rhyme (antyānuprāsa)

(*a*) dharmakāmārthaśāstrāṇi śastrāṇi vividhāni ca 1.1.47. (*b*) śakropamam amitraghnaṃ paravāraṇavāraṇam 1.63.6. (*c*) pṛthivyāṃ yāni ratnāni guṇavanti guṇānvite / tāny āpnuhi tvaṃ kalyāṇi sukhinī śaradāṃ śatam // 1.191.11. (*d*) puṃnāgair nāgapuṣpaiś ca lakucaiḥ panaśais tathā / śālatālakadambaiś ca bakulaiś ca saketakaiḥ // manoharaiḥ puṣpitaiś ca phalabhārāvanāmitaiḥ / prācīnāmalakair lodhrair aṅkolaiś ca supuṣpitaiḥ // 1.199.40–1. (*e*) divyābharaṇabhūṣitām / sūkṣmambaradharām ekām padmodarasamaprabhām // 1.92.27. (*f*) rūpaudāryaguṇopetāṃ maṇḍanārhām amaṇḍitām / candralekhām iva navāṃ vyomni nīlābhrasaṃvṛtām // 3.65.16. (*g*) sindhuvārān atho 'dārān manmathasye 'va tomarān 3.155.57; cf. chapter 1,I,11. (*h*) athā 'paśyan kurabakān vanarājiṣu puṣpitān / kāmavaśyotsukakarān kāmasye 'va śarotkarān // 3.155.58. (*i*) tathā 'naṅgaśarākārān sahakārān manoramān / apaśyan bhramarārāvān mañjarībhir virājitān // 3.155.60. (*j*) hemamālī tato vālī 3.264.18. (*k*) buddhimantaṃ hanūmantaṃ himavantam iva sthitam 3.284.10. (*l*) āyuṣmaṃs tvaṃ mayā nityaṃ rakṣitavyas tvayā 'py aham / rakṣitavyo rathī nityaṃ iti kṛtvā 'payāmy aham // . . . raṇam matvā 'payāmy aham 3.19.9–10. (*m*) paśyañ śṛṇvan spṛśañ jighrann aśnan gacchan svapañ śvasan // pralapan visṛjan gṛhṇann unmiṣan nimiṣann api / 6.27.8–9. (*n*) daṃṣṭrākarālāni ca te mukhāni dṛṣṭvai 'va kālānalasaṃnibhāni 6.33.24. (*o*) vāsāṃsi jīrṇāni yathā vihāya navāni gṛhṇāti naro 'parāṇi / tathā śarīrāṇi vihāya jīrṇāny anyāni saṃyāti navāni dehī // 6.24.22. (*p*) bhagnadantān bhagnakaṭān bhagnasakthāṃś ca vāraṇān / bhagnapṛṣṭhān bhagnakumbhān nihatān parvatopamān // 6.58.47. (*q*) anekavaktranayanam anekādbhutadarśanam / anekadivyābharaṇaṃ divyānekodyatāyudham // 6.33.10. (*r*) divyamālyāmbaradharaṃ divyagandhānulepanam / sarvāścaryamayaṃ devam anantaṃ viśvatomukham // 6.33.11.

Cf. 1.3.185; 4.2; 17.20–30; 23.1–5; 26.45; 40.11; 46.22, 28; 47.9; 49.13; 52.13; 54.16; 55.15; 57.5,7,77; 63.17; 64.32; 65.12; 66.5; 68.52,55; 72.12; 82.13; 84.1,16; 85.25; 88.7; 92.7; 92.44; 93.40; 94.19; 99.6; 126.3,8; 173.7; 183.2; 190.5; 199.12,20,33,200,19; 201.30; 202.23; 209.4,11,17; 210.1; 211.4; 214.21,25; 215.9; 218.30; 219.17,33; 220.22,23; 223.4; 224.11: 3.1.13; 2.27,54,57; 3.25,27,28; 4.9,12,57; 13.24,38,42,48–9,89,92, 93,95,116; 15.8,11; 16.6,19; 17.5–6,15,18,19; 18.18; 19.18–9; 23.16,49,50; 24.2; 25.18; 31.33; 39.13; 42.17; 44.1; 45.27; 52.11; 54.4,26; 59.10; 60.13; 61.1,90,102; 69.12; 77.15; 81.89; 87.23; 123.7; 124.23; 133.1; 134.34; 145.28; 146.3,17,47,54; 147.4; 153.2,10,12; 155.51–52,66; 161.16; 172.18; 175.18; 181.34; 186.10; 213.26; 221.63; 226.14; 233.19; 261.15; 264.30; 272.9,10; 281.47,52: 6.20.18; 23.10; 24.19,20; 25.17,28; 26.25; 29.21; 55.82,96,114; 91.72; 97.10; 104.7.

II. CHIME (YAMAKA).

The chime (*yamaka*) is the consecutive repetition of a group of sounds in the same order (i.e., $C_1V_1C_2\ [V_2C_3] + C_1V_1C_2\ [V_2C_3]$), provided that the repeated units are not similar in meaning.[3]

The *yamakas* are not well developed in the Mahābhārata. Such passages as (*a*) paravāraṇavāraṇam 1.63.6, (*b*) saṃkhye 'saṃkhyeyavikramaḥ 1.96.40, (*c*) khecaraḥ khe carann iva 3.70.11, (*d*) vihitān hi tān[4] 6.29.22, and (*e*) vaikuṇṭho 'kuṇṭhasāyakaḥ 6.21.15, are very rare.

The difference between the *lāṭānuprāsa* and *yamaka* lies in the fact that in the former the repeated word units have the same meaning, differing only in relation to their immediate constituents and do not necessarily occur in consecutive order, while in the latter, the repeated units must occur in consecutive order and must not have the same meaning, preferably with at least one of the pairs having no meaning at all (e.g., in *saṃkhye*$_1$ / *saṃkhye*$_2$ / *yavikramaḥ*, *saṃkhye*$_2$ does not have any meaning; in *vi* / *hitān*$_1$ / *hi tān*$_2$ /, *hitān*$_1$ and *hi tān*$_2$ have two altogether different meanings, viz., 'done' and '. . . them' respectively.

[3] Cf. SD 10.642. *Vide* Ragh. 9.1–54; Magha, Śiśupālavadha 4.1–66.
[4] The MSS $S_1K_{0.3}$Ck.n.śp. up read *hitān* for *hi tān*.

III. PARONOMASIA (ŚLEṢA)

Vide chapter 1,III (1.127.7), XXII (1.199.30,49; 3.54.5), XXVI (3.34.57), chapter 6, Virodha, and chapter 8,IX, Samāsokti, for examples of paronomasia (śleṣa). We do not, however, find in the Mahābhārata any examples of the complex type of śleṣa like the one in *pṛthukārtasvarapātram* (to be construed as (1) *pṛthu* + *kārtasvara* + *pātram*, 'a place having gold utensils,' (2) *pṛthuka* + *ārtasvara* + *pātram*, 'an abode of the distressed cries of hungry children'), found in the passage quoted by Viśvanātha (SD 7.587).

IV. INDIRECT MODE OF EXPRESSION (VAKROKTI)

The indirect mode of expression may be intonational or paronomastic (kākuvakrokti or śleṣavakrokti). We do not yet have any examples of paronomastic indirect mode of expression (śleṣavakrokti) in this corpus. One example of intonational indirect mode of expression (kākuvakrokti) has already been noted in chapter 1,XXXVIII,13 (tayor apatyaṃ kasmāt tvaṃ puṃścalī 'vā 'bhidhāsyasi 1.68.75).

V. REPETITION OF PHRASES OR WORDS IN A SET OF VERSES

Such repetitions as are not covered by the rules of *anuprāsa* or *yamaka*, (as above) may be placed here. These are mainly of three types, viz., (1) linkage or concatenation, (2) repetition of similar or identical words within verses, and (3) chiasmus.

1. Linkage or Concatenation

Sometimes an introduction and refrain may continue without change throughout a series of verses. Compare the introduction yadā 'śrauṣam and refrain tadā nā 'śaṃse vijayāya saṃjaya continuing in 1.1.102–129, 131–155; verse 156 breaks off by not using the refrain and is followed by two more verses in the same meter; verse 130 has the refrain, but only *yadā* of the introduction.

Compare verses 6.114.55–60 where just the refrain ne 'me bāṇāḥ śikhaṇḍinaḥ continues throughout. Similar is the refrain na saṃjvaren nā 'pi hṛṣyet kadācit in 1.84.7,8.

Sometimes, the refrains show slight variations. Thus the refrain yo madbhaktaḥ sa me priyaḥ (6.34.14,16) occurs as mukto yaḥ sa ca me priyaḥ; bhaktimān yaḥ sa me priyaḥ; bhaktimān me priyo naraḥ; and bhaktās te 'tī 'va me priyāḥ in verses 6.34.15,17,19, and 20 respectively Verses 6.24.19–21 have nā 'yaṃ hanti na hanyate, na hanyate hanyamāne śarīre, and kaṃ ghātayati hanti kim as refrains respectively.

An example of what we may call discontinuous refrain is dadṛśāte tadā tatra samudraṃ nidhim ambhasām 1.19.3ab, which is repeated as dadṛśāte mahārṇavam in 15d and as vistīrṇam dadṛśatur ambaraprakāśam in 16c. Similarly, the refrain prasīda deveśa jagannivāsa 6.33.25 is repeated in 6.33.45.

Verse 6.24.28 is an example of complete substitution of synonymous forms where the refrains nā 'nuśocitum arhasi, nai 'naṃ śocitum arhasi, and na tvaṃ śocitum arhasi of the preceding verses (6.24.24–27) have been replaced by tatra kā paridevanā. Similarly, the refrains sthitaprajñas tado 'cyate 6.24.55 and sthitadhīr munir ucyate 6.24.56 are replaced by tasya prajñā pratiṣṭhitā in 6.24.57,58,61,68 and buddhiḥ paryavatiṣṭhate in 6.24.65.

Sometimes, the nuclear terms of the preceding verse are repeated in the succeeding verse in somewhat altered form; e.g., acchedyo 'yam adāhyo 'yam akedyo 'śoṣya eva ca (6.24.24) is just a repetition of the preceding verse, nai 'naṃ chindanti śastrāṇi nai 'naṃ dahati pāvakaḥ / na cai 'naṃ kledayanty āpo na śoṣayati mārutah. Cf. 6.24.43d bhogaiśvaryagatiṃ prati and 6.24.44a bhogaiśvaryaprasaktānām; 6.38.19cd kṣipāmy ajasram aśubhān āsurīṣv eva yoniṣu and 6.38.20ab āsurīṃ yonim āpannā mūḍhā janmani janmani; 6.23.43cd utsādyante jātidharmāḥ kuladharmāś ca śāśvatāḥ and 6.23.44ab utsannakuladharmāṇāṃ manuṣyāṇāṃ janārdana; 6.40.47cd svabhāvaniyataṃ karma kurvan nā 'pnoti kilbiṣam and 6.40.48ab sahajaṃ karma kaunteya sadoṣam api na tyajet; 6.40.49cd naiṣkarmyasiddhiṃ paramāṃ saṃnyāsenā 'dhigacchati and 6.40.50ab siddhiṃ prāpto yathā brahma tathā 'pnoti nibodha me; 6.40.53d brahmabhūyāya kalpate and 6.40.54a brahmabhūtaḥ prasannātma; 6.40.57d maccittaḥ satataṃ bhava and 6.40.58a maccittaḥ sarvadurgāṇi . . .; 6.40.58cd atha cet tvam ahaṃkārān na śroṣyasi vinañkṣyasi and 6.40.59ab yad ahaṃkāram āśritya na yotsya iti manyase; 6.40.72cd kaccid ajñānasaṃmohaḥ pranaṣṭas te dhanaṃjaya and 6.40.73a naṣṭo mohaḥ smṛtir labdhā; 6.46.25d śokopahatacetanaḥ and 6.46.26a śokārtaṃ pāṇḍavaṃ jñātvā; 6.48.25d rājan vivyādha pāṇḍavam and 6.48.26a sa tair viddho maheṣvāsaḥ; 6.48.39cd parivārya raṇe bhīṣmaṃ sthitā yuddhāya māriṣa and 6.48.40 tathai 'va pāṇḍavāḥ sarve parivārya dhanaṃjayam / sthitā yuddhāya mahate . . . .

2. Repetition of Similar or Identical Words Within Verses

A type of repetition of identical or similar words within verses (viz., *lāṭānuprāsa*) has already been noted. The repeated units of the *lāṭānuprāsa* have different grammatical correlations, while the type of repetition we are discussing here does not show any difference on the grammatical level. This repetition may occur in two ways: (A) repetition at the beginning of each *pāda* or of alternate *pādas*, and (B) repetition throughout several *pādas* of a verse.

A. Repetition at the beginning of each pāda or of alternate pādas.—(*a*) tataḥ śuklāmbaradharaḥ śuklayajñopavītavān / śuklakeśaḥ sitaśmaśruḥ śuklamālyānulepanaḥ // 1.124.17. (*b*) varaṃ kūpaśatād vāpī varaṃ vāpīśatāt kratuḥ / varaṃ kratuśatāt putraḥ satyaṃ putraśatād varam // 1.69.21. (*c*) puṇyaṃ prāṇān dhārayati puṇyaṃ prāṇadam ucyate 1.143.15. (*d*) vikrameṇa mahī prāptā bharatena mahātmanā / vikrameṇa ca lokāṃs trīn jitavān pākaśāsaniḥ // 1.194.17; cf. 1.194.18. (*e*) kruddhaḥ pāpaṃ naraḥ kuryāt kruddho hanyād gurūn api / kruddhaḥ paruṣayā vācā śreyaso 'py avamanyate // 3.30.4. (*f*) diṣṭyā dharanti te vīrā diṣṭyā jīvati sā prajā / diṣṭyā purocanaḥ pāpo 1.195.13. (*g*) lohitāmbarasaṃvīto lohitasragvibhūṣaṇaḥ / lohitāsyo mahābāhur 3.221.63. (*h*) sa dadarśa nagān naikān naikāś ca saritas tathā / naikāṃś ca parvatān ramyān naikāṃś ca mṛgapakṣiṇah // 3.61.104. (*i*) kva cid añjanavarṇābhāḥ kva cit kāñcanasaṃnibhāḥ / dhātavo haritālasya kva cid dhiṅgulikasya ca // 3.155.80. (*j*) santo hi satyena nayanti sūryaṃ santo bhūmiṃ tapasā dhārayanti / santo gatir bhūtabhavyasya rājan 3.281.47. (*k*) bhūmau hi jāyate sarvaṃ bhūmau sarvaṃ praṇaśyati 6.5.20. (*l*) āścaryavat paśyati kaś cid enam āścaryavad vadati tathai 'va cā 'nyaḥ / āścaryavac cai 'nam anyaḥ sṛṇoti . . . 6.24.29. (*m*) sarvataḥ pāṇipādaṃ tat sarvato 'kṣiśiromukham / sarvataḥ śrutimal loke sarvam āvṛtya tiṣṭhati // 6.35.13. (*n*) yatra yogeśvaraḥ kṛṣṇo yatra pārtho dhanurdharaḥ 6.40.78.

Cf. 1.1.188–190: 3.186,66–7: 6.24.23; 25.17; 33.10,11; 40.67.

B. Repetition throughout several pādas of a verse.—(*a*) moghāśā moghakarmāṇo moghajñānā vicetasaḥ 6.31.12. (*b*) yat karoṣi yad aśnāsi yaj juhoṣi dadāsi yat / yat tapasyasi kaunteya tat kuruṣva madarpaṇam // 6.31.27. (*c*) brahmāgnāv apare yajñaṃ yajñenai 'vo 'pajuhvati // śrotrādīnī 'ndriyāṇy anye saṃyamāgniṣu juhvati / śabdādīn viṣayān anya indriyāgniṣu juhvati . . . // . . . ātmasaṃyamayogāgnau juhvati jñānadīpite // 6.26.25–27. (*d*) matkarmakṛn matparamo madbhaktaḥ saṃgavarjitaḥ 6.33.55. (*e*) manmanā bhava madbhakto madyājī māṃ namaskuru 6.40.65. (*f*) brahmā 'rpaṇaṃ brahma havir brahmāgnau brahmaṇā hutam / brahmai 'va tena gantavyaṃ brahmakarmasamādhinā // 6.26.24. (*g*) tadbuddhayas tadātmānas tanniṣṭhās tatparāyaṇāḥ 6.27.17. (*h*) yo 'ntaḥsukho 'ntarārāmas tathā 'ntarjyotir eva yaḥ 6.27.24 (note the chiasmus yo . . . yah). (*i*) dharme cā 'rthe ca kāme ca mokṣe ca bharatarṣabha / yad ihā 'sti tad anyatra yan ne 'hā 'sti na tat kvacit // 1.56.33. (*j*) agne tvam eva jvalanas tvaṃ dhātā tvaṃ bṛhaspatiḥ / tvam aśvinau yamau mitraḥ somas tvam asi cā 'nilaḥ // 1.220.29.

3. Chiasmus

The following are some examples of chiasmic repetition. It will be observed that this is of two types, one in which both members of the chiastic pairs are the same (*c*, *e*, *k*); the other in which only one member is found in both pairs and the other member differs in one way or another (*d*), etc. Sometimes, the two halves of a passage as a whole are involved in chiastic repetition (*g* and *m* are examples of double chiasmus).

(*a*) yācatas tvaṃ hi duhitā stuvataḥ pratigṛhṇataḥ / sutā 'haṃ stūyamānasya dadato 'pratigṛhṇataḥ // 1.73.10; cf. 1.73.32. (*b*) vividhās tvaṃ śrutīr vettha vettha vedāṃś ca sarvaśaḥ 1.97.5. (*c*) nā 'sato vidyate bhāvo nā 'bhāvo vidyate sataḥ 6.24.16. (*d*) nā 'sti buddhir ayuktasya na cā 'yuktasya bhāvanā 6.24.66. (*e*) vāsāṃsi jīrṇāni yathā vihāya navāni gṛhṇāti naro 'parāṇi / tathā śarīrāṇī vihāya jīrṇāny anyāni saṃyāti navāni dehī // 6.24.22. (*f*) jātasya hi dhruvo mṛtyur dhruvaṃ janma mṛtasya ca 6.24.27. (*g*) yā niśā sarvabhūtānāṃ tasyāṃ jāgarti saṃyamī / yasyāṃ jāgrati bhūtāni sā niśā paśyato muneḥ // 6.24.69. (*h*) saktāḥ karmaṇy avidvāṃso yathā kurvanti bhārata / kuryād vidvāṃs tathā 'saktaś cikīrṣur lokasaṃgraham // 6.24.25. (*i*) yadā yadā hi dharmasya glānir bhavati bhārata / abhyutthānam adharmasya tadā 'tmānaṃ sṛjāmy aham // 6.26.7. (*j*) yad akṣaraṃ vedavido vadanti viśanti yad yatayo vītarāgāḥ 6.30.11. (*k*) yathā pradīptaṃ jvalanaṃ pataṃgā viśanti nāśāya samṛddhavegāḥ / tathai 'va nāśāya viśanti lokās tavā 'pi vaktrāṇi samṛddhavegāḥ // 6.33.29. (*l*) uddhared ātmanā 'tmānaṃ nā 'tmānam avasādayet / ātmai 'va hy atamano bandhur ātmai 'va ripur ātmanaḥ // 6.28.5–6. (*m*) karmaṇo hy api boddhavyaṃ boddhavyaṃ ca vikarmaṇaḥ / akarmaṇaś ca boddhavyam . . . 6.26.17. (*n*) yathai 'dhāṃsi samiddho 'gnir bhasmasāt kurute 'rjuna / jñānāgniḥ sarvakarmāṇi bhasmasāt kurute tathā // 6.26.37. (*o*) mānāvamānayos tulyas tulyo mitrāripakṣayoḥ 6.36.25. (*p*) namo namas te 'stu sahasrakṛtvaḥ punaś ca bhūyo 'pi namo namas te 6.33.39.

11. TECHNIQUE OF ORAL POETRY

C. M. Bowra, in his *Heroic Poetry*,[1] has discussed at length the distinctive features of heoric poetry. As his analytical study of such poetry in Homeric Greek, Mesopotamian and Hittite, Old Germanic and Old Romance, South Slav, East European, Uzbek, Yakut, Ainu, etc., shows, heroic poetry is primarily oral; it is basically recited for the audience rather than written for general readers, until it "reaches a kind of finality," its texts are fixed, and it passes into a national heritage "when it may be written down and circulated and become widely known." For this recitation, the poet or rhapsodist first of all has to acquaint himself with the main outlines of the story or stories concerned and then learn a large number of formulae, both short and long, suited to the meter in which he composes. The larger the number of formulae he has mastered, the quicker the successive flow of recitation.

The formulae are in the main traditional and are of two kinds: noun-adjective combinations, e.g., 'blue sea,' 'dark death,' 'stone-built Moscow,' 'broad highway,' 'silver-breasted lark,' and 'black mother night'; and "repeated phrases which may be parts of lines, or single whole lines or sets of whole lines"; e.g., in Homer when dawn comes, it is usually put: "Now when the early born rosey fingered Dawn had arisen."

He has further observed that when a poet recites the same lay on several occasions, his versions are not always the same. The poet in fact each time composes afresh his poem (i.e., improvises) as he recites. But thanks to the traditional poetic formulae he has already mastered, "it is not a wild flood of words which flows from his lips but an orderly stream which his hearers find familiar in vocabulary and in meter." The formulaic nature of poetry not only helps the poet in his oral composition but also adds to the hearing patience of the audience, who feel more or less relaxed on account of their familiarity with such expressions—old friends as it were.

Coming to early Indian literature in general, Emeneau[2] rightly remarks:

> "Old as is writing in the history of the culture of India in its classical form, there is literature there that is even older than writing. The Vedas, the oldest religious texts of Hinduism, contain in their earliest layers hymns and other ritual utterances, the beginning of which can be conservatively placed in the second millennium B.C. These texts present clear evidence that they are oral compositions. Perhaps the most striking kind of evidence is the extensive repeated use, in the verses, of traditional

[1] C. M. Bowra, *Heroic Poetry* (London, 1952), pp. 215–253.

[2] M. B. Emeneau, "Oral Poets of South India: The Todas," *Journal of American Folklore*, LXXI (1958), 313–314.

poetic units. Maurice Bloomfield in his intensive study of the phenomenon in the two volumes called *Riga Veda Repetitions* found that in the Rigvedic collection of over a thousand hymns, approximately a fifth of the lines are involved in this repetitive use. . . . The marks of oral composition and of a very early synthesis of numerous oral recitations into one unified text are clearly evident in both these epics [the *Rāmāyaṇa* and the *Mahābhārata*] (as they are in Homer). The tradition of the transmittal of the *Mahābhārata* (and of the *Rāmāyaṇa* too) even illustrates the postulate that in a living oral tradition and barring special conditions, no two oral recitations of what purports to be the same work are identical, but each recitation is a fresh composition. For we are told in the *Mahābhārata* itself that its length is not always the same (Book 1, adhyāya 1) and that the text as we have it is the third recitation in a succession of famous recitations of different lengths. This oral characteristic . . . did not come to an end even after the *Mahābhārata* was written down, perhaps in the fourth century A.D., perhaps somewhat earlier. The copyists have never ceased to add more good, bad, or indifferent passages or stories to their versions when they could do so. It is only recognition of the oral technique of composition and its implications that makes it possible to deal with the Sanskrit epic in any but the most fumbling way."

An attempt is accordingly made here to show how the tradition of oral composition is reflected in the repetitions of various types that are found in the corpus.

We have already noted in chapter 10,V the occurrence of repetitive phrases or words in a set of verses as (1) linkage or concatenation, (2) repetition of similar or identical words within verses, and (3) chiasmus.

As Hopkins,[3] Sukthankar,[4] Kane,[5] Belvalkar,[6] and Renou[7] have elsewhere shown, quite a large number of the Mahābhārata passages are constituents of the traditional stock. That is to say, many versified formulae had perhaps already been fixed for expressing certain concepts; they are found repeated in the Mahābhārata as elsewhere, so much so that it is often very difficult to trace their original source. The following passages dealing with (*a*) the superiority of learning to old age and (*b*) the description of the husband as the best ornament of a woman may be cited as examples:

(*a*) na tena sthaviro bhavati yenā 'sya palitaṃ śiraḥ / bālo 'pi yaḥ prajānāti taṃ devāḥ sthaviraṃ viduḥ // na hāyanair na palitair na

[3] E. W. Hopkins, *The Great Epic of India* (New York, 1901), pp. 403–444.

[4] V. S. Sukthankar, "The Nala Episode and the Rāmāyaṇa," *Sukthankar Memorial Edition*, vol. I, *Critical Studies in the Mahābhārata* (Bombay, 1944–1945), pp. 406 ff.

[5] P. V. Kane, "Mahābhārata Verses and Very Ancient Dharmasūtras and Other Works," in S. M. Katre and P. K. Gode, eds., *A Volume of Eastern and Indian Studies Presented to Professor F. W. Thomas . . . on his 72nd Birthday . . .*, New Indian Antiquary, extra series I (Bombay, 1939), pp. 128–133.

[6] S. K. Belvalkar, "The Cosmographical Episode in the Mahābhārata and Padmapurāṇa," *ibid.*, pp. 19 ff.

[7] Louis Renou, "L'Hymne aux Aśvin de l'Ādiparvan," *ibid.*, pp. 177 ff.

vittena na bandhubhiḥ / ṛṣayaś cakrire dharmaṃ yo 'nūcānaḥ sa no mahān // 3.133.11–12; cf. Manu 2.154, 156.

(*b*) bhartā nāma paraṃ nāryā bhūṣaṇaṃ bhūṣaṇair vinā / eṣā virahitā tena śobhanā 'pi na śobhate // 3.65.18, cf. Rām. 5.16.26.

Likewise, the expression 'climbing the palace of wisdom' (prajñaprāsādam āruhya 3.198.93) occurs sound for sound in the Dhammapada 11.8 (paññāpāsādam āruyha). Similarly, the indication of Sītā's insulting rebuff to Rāvaṇa by placing straw between them (tṛṇam antarataḥ kṛtvā 3.265.17), occurring in the Rāmāyaṇa 3.56.1, 5.21.3 and Adhy. Ram. 5.2.31, continues down to the sixteenth century (cf. Tulasī, Rāmacaritamānasa 5.9.3).

The following passages may be cited as examples of repetition of one full verse as a poetic unit within the text, with only inconsequential variants.

yadā yadā ca (var. hi) dharmasya
glānir bhavati sattama (var. bhārata) /
abhyutthānam adharmasya
tadā 'tānaṃ sṛjāmy aham //

Whenever moral law is on the decline and vice prevails, I (i.e., Lord Viṣṇu) create Myself (i.e., become incarnate) 3.187.26: 6.26.7.

anantavijayaṃ rājā
kuntīputro yudhiṣṭhiraḥ /
nakulaḥ sahadevaś ca
sughoṣamaṇi puṣpakau //
kāśirājaś ca śaibyaś ca
śikhaṇḍī ca mahārathaḥ /
dhṛṣṭadyumno virāṭaś ca
sātyakiś ca mahāyaśāḥ //

Yudhiṣṭhira, the son of Kuntī, blew the conch shell Anantavijaya; Nakula and Sahadeva (blew) Sughoṣa and Manipuṣpaka respectively. The King of Kāśī, Śaibya, Śikhaṇḍin, the great charioteer, Dhṛṣṭadyumna, Virāṭa, and the illustrious Sātyaki (all blew their respective conch shells) 6.47.26–7; cf. 6.23.16–17.

The examples of repetition of a full *pāda* as a poetic unit are: (*a*) tasthau girir ivā 'calah (a warrior stands [against his opponents' attacks] like an immovable mountain) 1.179.14; 181.4: 3.11.23; 40.27; 157.39; 230.25; 255.19: 6.49.11; 88.12; 90.12. (*b*) yato dharmas tato jayaḥ (where there is virtue, there is victory) 6.2.14; 21.11; 61.16; 62.34; 117.33; cf. 1.197.25: 3.81.142 (yatra yogeśvaraḥ sthāṇuḥ svayam eva vṛṣadhvajaḥ); 88.25 (yatra nārāyano devaḥ); 6.21.12,13; 40.78 (yatra yogeśvaraḥ kṛṣṇo);

TABLE 1

Occurrence of Objects of Comparison

Item	Primary *tertia comparationis*	Frequency of occurrence	Section of chapter 1 referred to
1. Indra	Brilliance, prominence, etc.	247	I,2
2. Sun (Sūrya)	Splendor	164	V
3. Cloud (Megha)	Grace, blackness, deep sound	158	XII
4. Fire (Agni)	Splendor, destruction	155	IV
5. Mountain (Parvata)	Hugeness, endurance	110	XIX
6. Yama	Destruction, terror	104	I,12
7. Elephant (Gaja)	Might, vitality	92	XXII
8. Gods (Deva)	Brilliance	81	I,1
9. Moon (Candra)	Grace, charm	74	VI
10. Lotus (Kamala)	Charm	74	XXXI
11. Snake (Sarpa)	Terror, shape of arrows	69	XXV
12. Lion (Siṃha)	Might, dignity, pride	65	XXIII
13. Wind (Vāyu)	Speed, force, noise	63	XIV
14. Ocean (Samudra)	Expanse, deepness, wealth	62	XV
15. Cattle (Go)	Strength, weakness, bewilderment	38	XX
16. Gold (Svarṇa)	Brightness	24	XXXII,1
17. Tree (Vṛkṣa)	Subordination, death, coöperation	19	XXX,1
18. Cotton (Tūla)	Softness, destruction	19	XXX,20
19. Planets (Graha)	War	18	VII
20. Father (Pitṛ)	Affection	17	XXXIV
21. Birds (Pakṣin)	Freedom, speed	17	XXXIV,1
22. Śiva	Invincibility, terror	14	I,3
23. Sacrificial objects (Yajña)	Grace, purity	14	III
24. Śrī	Feminine beauty	13	II,3
25. Brahmā	Prominence, honor	12	I,5
26. Viṣṇu	Conquest, protection	12	I,4
27. Stars (Tārā)	Grace, innumerability	12	IX
28. Weapon (Astra)	Speed	12	XL,6
29. Moth (Śalabha)	Multitude, destruction	12	XXVIII,1
30. Tiger (Vyāghra)	Might, supremacy, pride	11	XXIV
31. Garuḍa	Speed, strength	10	XXVII,2
32. Lightning (Vidyut)	Charm, speed	9	XIII
33. Sal (Śāla)	Height, might	9	XXX,4
34. Swan (Haṃsa)	Whiteness	9	XXVII,3
35. Yayāti	Performance of sacrifice	9	XXXVI,1
36. Palmyra palm (Tāla)	Height, fall	8	XXX,3
37. *Butea frondosa* (Kiṃśuka)	Bloodshed, ineffectiveness	8	XXX,2
38. River (Nadī)	Motion, vastness of army	8	XVII
39. Frantic person (Unmatta)	Bewilderment	8	XXXVIII,8
40. Kubera	Wealth	8	I,9

and 41.55 (yato dharmas tataḥ kṛṣṇo yataḥ kṛṣṇas tato jayaḥ). (*c*) atrā 'py udāharantī 'mam (itihāsaṃ purātanam) (here also they refer to this ancient history) 3.29.1; 30.35; 31.20; 136.3; 207.6; 246.34. (*d*) tad adbhutam ivā 'bhavat (it was wonderful indeed) 1.1.77; 201.9: 3.20.11; 126.26; 166.5,17; 169.19; 234.2: 6.1.21; 43.56,72; 49.29; 50.74; 51.9; 53.15; 58.27; 69.32; 74.25; 78.29,46; 79.16; 91.62; 106.40; 112.61; 114.65; cf. tatrā 'dbhutam apaśyāma 6.70.21; 77.40; 78.38; 92.30; 98.16; 106.26; 107.26; 110.19; 112.89. (*e*) śataśo 'tha sahasraśaḥ ([warriors, etc.] by hundreds and thousands) 3.167.17; 274.6: 6.82.44; 96.46; 99.2; 101.22; 102.19,23; 112.134. (*f*) tataḥ pravavṛte yuddham (then the war broke out) 6.49.40; 52.19; 65.21; 89.18; 92.18; 99.44; 100.37; 104.17; 107.22; 109.48; cf. 6.79.12; 88.25; 91.24; 107.31. (*g*) śaraiḥ saṃnataparvabhiḥ (with arrows bent down) 6.75.24; 78.44; 79.13,48; 97.28; 98.8; 99.18; 100.14,23; 101.18,20; 105.5; 106.32; 107.8,18; 108.26; 109.39; 110.1,25; 112.30,43,67; 116.42. (*h*) bhīmo bhīmaparākramaḥ (Bhīma of terrible might) 1.2.184; 114.9; 141.18; 142.32; 150.3: 3.50.5,9; 66.1; 78.2; 146.13,72; 276.6; cf. 3.50.9; 71.19; 145.2,9; 151.11: 6.15.16; 46.4; 48.7; 93.41; 104.50. (*i*) eṣa dharmaḥ sanātanaḥ (this is eternal law) 1.113.13; 3.136; 30.50; 152.9; 281.20; cf. 1.113.7; 158.20; 195.2: 3.32.28; 87.21; 147.10; 204.27; 281.34; also Rāmāyaṇa 2.19.26; 21.49; 24.13.

Particularly interesting from the point of view of a study of the elements of poetry in the corpus is repetition of similes, i.e., poetic formulae of comparison. Apart from their value as representative of contemporaneous artistic taste, imaginative trend, and popular belief, these similes serve as the best tools in the composition of the oral poetic material.

The analysis of similes presented in chapter 1 involves in all 232 objects of comparison (upamāna) occurring in at least 2,299 passages. Some of the most productive objects of comparison are listed in order of frequency in the accompanying table.

Repetitions under each head may be seen in the respective sections referred to in the table. In terms of Bowra's noun-adjective combinations, a few may, however, be noted here. (By definition, nouns and adjectives include subjects and objects of comparisons respectively.)

Thus a warrior is brilliant like Indra, Śiva, the gods, the sun, the fire, or gold (devarājasamadyutiḥ; bhūtapatiprakāśaḥ; amarapratimaḥ; tejasā bhāskaropamaḥ; vibhāvasusamadyutiḥ; kanakaprabhaḥ); he is terrific like Śiva at the time of the destruction of the age (yugāntakāle saṃkruddhaḥ pinākī 'va mahābalaḥ) or Yama (kālāntakayamopamaḥ); he is a bull or lion or tiger among men (puruṣarṣabha; narasiṃha; puruṣavyāghra); he is like an elephant in must or an elephant with his temple exuding must fluid or an elephant sixty years old or a Himālayan elephant in must (mattavāraṇavikramaḥ; prabhinna iva vāraṇaḥ; vāraṇau ṣaṣṭihāyanau; mattā yathā haimavatā gajendrāḥ); his might is like that of ten or ten thousand elephants (daśanāgabalānvitaḥ; nāgāyutasamaprāṇaḥ). Wars between warriors or armies are terrific like those between (i) the gods and demons (devadānavayor iva); (ii) Indra and Vṛta (vṛtravāsavayor iva), or Maya (mayaśakrau yathā purā), or Prahlāda (śakraprahlādayor iva), or Śambara (śakraśambarayor iva), or Bali (balivāsavayor iva); or (iii) Vāli and Sugrīva (vālisugrīvayor bhrātror yathā . . .); or (iv) two oceans (adhara and uttara samudra) agitated at the time of the destruction of the age (dvayoḥ sāgarayor iva); or (v) planets (samīyatuḥ susaṃkruddhāv aṅgārakabudhāv iva; śukrāṅgārakayor iva; yathā budhaś ca śukraś ca; yathā tivi mahāghorau rājan budha-śanaiścarau). The attack of one enemy or more is symbolized by (i) the planets attacking the sun or the moon (rākṣasaṃ dudruvuḥ sarve grahāḥ pañca yathā ravim; yathā yugakṣaye ghore candramāḥ pañcabhir grahaiḥ; rāhuḥ khe śaśinaṃ yathā), or (ii) the demons attacking Indra or the gods (vajrapāṇim ivā 'surāḥ; balo vajradharaṃ yathā; vṛtro devacamūṃ yathā), or (iii) Yama with his mouth open (vyāditāsyam / vyāttānanam ivā 'ntakam), or (iv) the wind shaking or breaking a tree (vāyuś caṇḍa iva drumam), or (v) one elephant or more attacking another elephant or a group of elephants (matto mattam iva dvipam; yuddhārthī vāśitāhetor gajaḥ pratigajaṃ yathā), or (vi) a lion attacking small animals (siṃhaḥ kṣudramṛgaṃ yathā), or (vii) Garuḍa attacking a snake (garutmān iva pannagam). The bewilderment of an army compares with that of cattle or camels sunk in mire (gāvaḥ paṅkārditā iva; pravivyathuḥ paṅkagatā ivo 'ṣṭrāḥ), or cattle troubled by cold (trātāraṃ nā 'dhyagacchanta gāvaḥ śītārditā iva), or cattle without a cowherd (agopam iva co 'dbhrāntaṃ gokulaṃ tad balaṃ mama), or small animals at the sight of a lion (siṃhaṃ kṣudramṛgā iva). A warrior's resistence to his opponents' attacks compares with the firm endurance of a mountain (tasthau girir ivā 'calaḥ; bhidyamāna ivā 'calaḥ). Weapons are terrific like Indra's vajra (indrāśanisamasparśa-; vajrāśanisamasparśa-), or Yama's rod (kāladaṇḍopama-; yamadaṇḍāśaniprabha), or snakes (sarāṃś cā 'śīviṣopamān). Dispersal of the enemy compares with the fire burning a heap of cotton (tūlarāśim ivā 'nalaḥ), or the wind blowing away the clouds (divī 'vā 'bhrāṇi mārutaḥ). A huge army is ocean-like (sāgarapratimaṃ). Fast-moving chariots, etc., compare with the wind or mind or both (vātaraṃhasaḥ; manojava; manomārutaraṃhasaḥ) or arrows (tariṣyanta ivā 'śugāḥ), or Garuḍa (garutmān iva vegavān). The herd of elephants is like the massive clouds and vice versa (gajānīkaṃ meghavṛndam ivo 'dyatam; [meghāḥ] gajakulaprakhyāḥ). Similarly a huge body compares with a mountain (mahīdharapratimam).

Whiteness is symbolized by cow's milk, the jasmine flower, the moon, the fibers of the lotus stalk, silver, or all of them taken together (śaṅkhāṃś ca gokṣīranibhān; śaśisaṃnibham; aśvaiś ca rajataprakhyaiḥ; tato gokṣīrakundendumṛṇālarajataprabham), or a swan (haṃsācchavarṇair bahubhiḥ; haṃsacandrapratīkāśam), or snow (tato bhasma kṣatād rājan nirgataṃ himasaṃnibham); Bhīṣma with his white steed and white bow compares with the rising planet Venus (śvetagraham ivo 'ditam).

One with delightful appearance is likened to the moon (somavat priyadarśanaḥ), or the Aśvins (sa cā 'śvirūpasadṛśo), or Kāma (kandarpa iva rūpeṇa). A beautiful woman is described as of charming complexion (varavarṇinī), or of a complexion like that of the gods (amaravarṇinī), or charming like Lakṣmī or Rati or Kiṃnarī or Apsaras or an intoxicated person (śrīr iva rūpiṇī; ratīm iva; kiṃnarīm iva; striyaś cā 'psarasopamāḥ; mattakāśinī); her slim waist is compared with the hourglass-shaped sacrificial altar (vedīvilagnamadhye 'va); her thighs compare in shape with the plaintain stem (rambhoru) or an elephant's trunk (ūrū gajakaropamau); she is fair-hipped (varārohā). Candra (moon) and Rohiṇī, Vasiṣṭha and Arundhatī, Agastya and Lopāmudrā, Nala and Damayantī, Indra and Śacī, Mudgala and Indrasenā are, generally speaking, the standards of conjugal love; cf. 3.113.22–4.

Innumerability (of gifts) is symbolized by stars and clouds (yathā vā divi tārakāḥ; yathā vā varṣato dhārā). Depth is compared with that of the ocean (samudra iva gāmbhīrye). Self-destruction is symbolized by the moth (yathā 'nalaṃ prajvalitaṃ pataṅgāḥ samabhidrutāḥ), or the female crab (ādāsyase karkaṭakī 'va garbham), or the bamboo or reed (yathā ca veṇuḥ kadalī nalo vā phalaty abhāvāya na bhūtaye 'tmanaḥ). Growth is symbolized by the moon (śuklapakṣe yathā śaśī), or the ocean (vardhate . . . kulaṃ sāgaravad yathā), or the lotus (sarve vavṛdhur alpena kālenā 'psv iva nīrajāḥ). Height is symbolized by sal and Palmyra palm trees (mahāśāla ivo 'dgataḥ; prāṃśuḥ kanakatālābhaḥ). Honor and prominence are symbolized by Brahmā, Viṣṇu, Śiva, and Bṛhaspati (devānām iva deveśaṃ prajāpatim upāsatām; prajāpatisamo vipro; ādityānāṃ yathā viṣṇuḥ; divaukasa ive 'śvaram; yathā śakro bṛhaspateḥ). Affection is compared with that of a father (pite 'va putrān). Inattentiveness and detachment are symbolized by the lotus (yathā parṇe puṣkarasye 'va siktaṃ jalaṃ na tiṣṭhet pathyam uktam tathā 'smin; na teṣu sajjate snehaḥ padmapatreṣv ivo 'dakam; padmapatram ivā 'mbhasā).

The examples cited above show that the oral poets of the Mahābhārata were well equipped with a large number of poetic formulae, which they very often used in proper contexts. It may be noted, however, in this connection, that sometimes they were so overpowered by these formulae that the usual semantic propriety of the words used in the formulae was perhaps lost sight of. The context of 1.113.7,13, (sa hi) eṣa dharmaḥ sanātanaḥ, may be cited as an example. Here the eternal law (dharmaḥ sanātanaḥ) refers to the freedom of women in matters relating to their conjugal life, in earlier times; the women of all castes were of old not shut up; as do cattle so did mankind in all their various castes (anāvṛtā hi sarveṣāṃ varṇānām aṅganā bhuvi / yathā gāvaḥ sthitās tāta sve sve varṇe tathā prajāḥ 1.113.14). This *sanātana dharma* is, however, found obsolete and is accordingly remodeled by Śvetaketu in order to avoid the resultant social disorderliness, though Pāṇḍu still persuades Kuntī to follow it in action. If the peculiarities of the oral poetic technique of repetition are not taken into account, the usual dependence on syntactical sequence is bound to mar the values of the interpretation of the ethical ideal of the Mahābhārata. Similarly, when the poetic formulae describing the plight of Sītā in Rāvaṇa's *aśoka* garden in the Rāmāyaṇa are found repeated *mutatis mutandis* in Sudeva's soliloquy describing Damayantī in the Mahābhārata, they appear as borrowed plumes that do not quite fit in the context.[8] Again, when we find Ghaṭotkaca, a demon, being addressed as godlike (amarasaṃkāśa) we feel somewhat confused. But all this can be better explained if we recognize the fact that the oral poets were sometimes overpowered by their tools, i.e., their poetic formulae. Are we not accustomed to use the formula 'you see' as a syntactical ornamentation even though there is nothing specific to see in the usual sense?

As Bowra has rightly shown, when an oral poet recites the same lay on several occasions, his versions are not always the same; in fact, he each time composes afresh the poems that he recites. This very often leads to syntactical or grammatical incongruity that is baffling to commentators and textual critics alike. Thus māghamāse gavām iva occurring in 6.114.60 and 12.137.85 being improvised over yathā hi śaiśiraḥ kālo gavāṃ marmāṇi kṛntati (6.113.7) has given rise to all sorts of speculations on the part of commentators and textual critics. A detailed discussion on this point may be seen in chapter 1,XX. This anomaly can be brought to a harmonious conclusion only when we recognize the technique of oral poetic composition involved.

As we know, a spoken language differs from a written language in the sense that the former is perhaps less refined than the latter. This dif-

[8] V. S. Sukthankar, "The Nala Episode . . .."

ference reflects itself in the sphere of literature also. The oral literature is devoid of that artificial refinement in syntax or embellishments which may be said to be the property of a written literature. That is why to a student of Naiṣadhīyacarita, Śiśupālavadha, Kirātārjunīya, or even Raghuvaṃśa, the style of Mahābhārata appears to be somewhat naive, illogical, or full of syntactical irregularities. But if he realizes that the Mahābhārata was orally transmitted to the audience rather than written down for general readers, he will find it all a natural phenomenon of oral poetry, whose chief interest lies in rhythmical stories leading to a philosophical, ethical, or emotional effect on the audience. That is what we learn also from Bāṇa's Kādambarī,[9] who used to listen to the *music* of the Mahābhārata with the accompaniment of bamboo flutes.

[9] Bāṇabhaṭṭa, Kādambarī, ed. by Peter Peterson (Bombay, 1889), p. 209.

INDEX